Advanced Introduction to Employee Engagement

Elgar Advanced Introductions are stimulating and thoughtful introductions to major fields in the social sciences and law, expertly written by the world's leading scholars. Designed to be accessible yet rigorous, they offer concise and lucid surveys of the substantive and policy issues associated with discrete subject areas.

The aims of the series are twofold: to pinpoint essential principles of a particular field, and to offer insights that stimulate critical thinking. By distilling the vast and often technical corpus of information on the subject into a concise and meaningful form, the books serve as accessible introductions for undergraduate and graduate students coming to the subject for the first time. Importantly, they also develop well-informed, nuanced critiques of the field that will challenge and extend the understanding of advanced students, scholars and policy-makers.

For a full list of titles in the series please see the back of the book. Recent titles in the series include:

Technology Policy
Albert N. Link and James A. Cunningham

Urban Transport Planning
Kevin J. Krizek and David A. King

Legal Reasoning
Larry Alexander and Emily Sherwin

Sustainable Competitive Advantage in Sales
Lawrence B. Chonko

Law and Development
Second Edition
Mariana Mota Prado and Michael J. Trebilcock

Law and Renewable Energy
Joel B. Eisen

Experience Economy
Jon Sundbo

Marxism and Human Geography
Kevin R. Cox

Maritime Law
Paul Todd

American Foreign Policy
Loch K. Johnson

Water Politics
Ken Conca

Business Ethics
John Hooker

Employee Engagement
Alan M. Saks and Jamie A. Gruman

Advanced Introduction to

Employee Engagement

ALAN M. SAKS

Professor of Human Resources Management and Organizational Behavior, Centre for Industrial Relations and Human Resources, University of Toronto, Canada

JAMIE A. GRUMAN

Professor of Organizational Behavior, Gordon S. Lang School of Business and Economics, University of Guelph, Canada

Elgar Advanced Introductions

 **Edward Elgar**
PUBLISHING

Cheltenham, UK • Northampton, MA, USA

Published by
Edward Elgar Publishing Limited
The Lypiatts
15 Lansdown Road
Cheltenham
Glos GL50 2JA
UK

Edward Elgar Publishing, Inc.
William Pratt House
9 Dewey Court
Northampton
Massachusetts 01060
USA

A catalogue record for this book
is available from the British Library

Library of Congress Control Number: 2021939226

Printed on elemental chlorine free (ECF)
recycled paper containing 30% Post-Consumer Waste

ISBN 978 1 80037 224 5 (cased)
ISBN 978 1 80037 225 2 (eBook)
ISBN 978 1 80037 226 9 (paperback)

Printed and bound in the USA

For Kelly, Justin, and Brooke – Alan Saks
To Michi, Tommi and Solly, as always – Jamie Gruman

Contents

Figures

Tables

Preface

Employee engagement has a unique and interesting place in research and practice in the fields of organizational behavior, organizational psychology, and management. For starters, it is a relatively new construct and area of research that really only began to gather steam around ten years ago. What makes this somewhat surprising is that the first actual study on employee engagement was conducted 30 years ago by William Kahn. In other words, Kahn's (1990) study and model of personal engagement received relatively little attention until around 2010 and, even then, the number of citations remained relatively low. While few academics were studying employee engagement at that time, practitioners and consultants had already realized its importance and potential value to organizations. When the academics finally began to study employee engagement they emphasized the job or what has become known as job or work engagement while the practitioners and consultants focused more on the organization with respect to the definition and measurement of employee engagement. This divide continues to this day although organization engagement has been receiving more attention in the academic literature in recent years.

Today, employee engagement is a popular topic among academics, employees, practitioners, consultants, managers, and organizations. There has been and continues to be a large number of research publications on employee engagement each year and to date there have been numerous review articles and meta-analyses, a handful of books on employee engagement including several edited volumes, and a number of special topic journal issues devoted to employee engagement. Thus, research and practice on employee engagement continue to be subjects of great interest to both academics and practitioners. A Google search today on employee engagement will provide you with 500,000,000 hits!

We have been studying and writing about employee engagement for about 15 years. During this time, we have published numerous articles and book chapters that have to do with various aspects of employee engagement such as its antecedents and consequences, its measurement, how to translate engagement research into practice, and its relevance for performance management and newcomers. When the opportunity to write a book on employee engagement presented itself it seemed like the right thing to do as everything we had been writing about for the last decade and a half was in effect preparation for just that – a book on employee engagement. In addition, given the large number of papers that have been published in the last decade, we thought that an introductory book on employee engagement could serve as an important resource for researchers, practitioners, and managers.

In writing this book, we have tried to be thorough in our coverage of the research on employee engagement. At the same time, we also wanted to produce a book that would provide those who are new to the topic with a strong and complete understanding of what is known about employee engagement. Thus, this book will be of value to those who are not familiar with employee engagement research as well as those who are knowledgeable about the topic and do their own research on employee engagement. The book has also been written to provide guidance and directions for practitioners and managers who are most interested in the application and practice of employee engagement.

Therefore, in this book you will find information about how employee engagement has been defined and how it differs from other more popular constructs such as job satisfaction and organizational commitment; the theories that have been developed and used to explain and study employee engagement; the different instruments that have been developed and used to measure employee engagement; the results of research that has studied the antecedents and consequences of employee engagement; the engagement of newcomers to organizations; research on employee engagement in different countries and cultures; how to translate employee engagement research into practice; and some issues that require more research attention.

In addition to covering the main issues and research on employee engagement, we have also included material on topics that are more novel and less likely to be found in other books on employee engagement, such as the difference between employee engagement targets and referents and how to develop measures for different targets and referents of engagement; the process variables that link antecedents to employee engagement; the engagement of newcomers; an employee engagement practice model for developing an employee engagement program in organizations; the use of a balance framework for the study of employee engagement; what it means for employee engagement to be strategic; the relevance and importance of organization caring for employee engagement; and the difference between job engagement and organization engagement.

In total, we believe that readers of this book will find it full of useful information that will not only help them to better understand what is known about employee engagement but will also help them to identify future research topics as well as how to translate academic research and knowledge of employee engagement into organizational practices that generate more engaged employees. Of course, this will not be the last word on employee engagement. However, we do hope that this book will contribute to future employee engagement research and practice.

Alan M. Saks
Jamie A. Gruman
January, 2021
Toronto, Canada

1 Introduction to employee engagement

There are very few variables that have received so much attention from so many stakeholders in such a short period of time as employee engagement. So many have sung the praises of employee engagement that it has taken on a kind of super-variable status as something that can bring greatness to employees and organizations. However, at the same time many consider employee engagement to be nothing more than "old wine" in a new bottle. As noted by Macey and Schneider (2008), an important question is "whether engagement is a unique construct or merely a repackaging of other constructs" (p.4) or what is known as the "Jangle Fallacy."

Unlike many other workplace topics, the academic community became interested in employee engagement after the practitioner and consulting world grabbed hold of it (Macey & Schneider, 2008). Despite the common interest, there remains a very large gap between employee engagement research and practice when it comes to the meaning and measurement of employee engagement. Nonetheless, much of the emphasis and research on employee engagement has been driven by practitioners and consultants.

Given all of the interest in employee engagement today, one might ask, *If employee engagement is so important for employees and organizations than why have we only recently learned about it and why all this sudden attention? Is it really something new and different from other variables that have been studied in the workplace for decades?* In this book, we try to answer these questions and learn more about what employee engagement is and where it fits into the existing research on employee job attitudes and behavior.

Unlike most concepts, constructs, and theories related to work behavior, for many years employee engagement received more attention from practitioners and consultants than academics even though the first study in the academic literature was conducted 30 years ago (Kahn, 1990). Thus, employee engagement is an anomaly in that the impetus for it came from the world of practice and academics have been playing catch-up (Judge et al., 2012). But why is employee engagement so important and why should we care about it?

1.1   Why is employee engagement important?

Given all the attention that employee engagement has received in the last two decades by so many stakeholders, it is natural to ask why has it become so popular and why is it so important. There are several answers to this question and most of them revolve around one simple answer: *Employee engagement matters.*

As you will see in Chapter 5 on the antecedents and consequences of employee engagement, research has found that employee engagement is related to individual, group, and organizational outcomes that are important for employees and organizations. For example, employee engagement has been found to be strongly related to employee job attitudes (e.g., job satisfaction, organizational commitment), job behaviors (e.g., organizational citizenship behavior), turnover intentions, job performance, and employee health, stress, burnout, and well-being (Bailey et al., 2017; Crawford et al., 2010; Halbesleben, 2010; Saks, 2006). In addition, employee engagement has also been found to be positively related to organization outcomes such as firm performance as well as financial and customer service outcomes (Barrick et al., 2015; Schneider et al., 2018) and it is generally believed that engaged employees can provide organizations with a competitive advantage (Macey & Schneider, 2008; Rich et al., 2010).

A second reason for the continued attention and importance of employee engagement is that it is a new and unique organizational variable that has been shown to be distinct from many other better-known and well-studied variables such as job satisfaction and organizational commitment. Furthermore, when compared to other variables several studies have shown that employee engagement is a better predictor of work outcomes. For example, Rich et al. (2010) found that employee engagement was a stronger predictor of task performance and organizational citizenship behavior (OCB) than job involvement, job satisfaction, and intrinsic motivation. Dalal et al. (2012) found that employee engagement explained more variance in multivariate job performance (task performance, OCB, and counterproductive work behavior) than job satisfaction, job involvement, and organizational commitment, and it was the most important predictor of OCB. In addition, a meta-analysis of employee engagement found that engagement explained incremental variability in task and contextual performance over job satisfaction, organizational commitment, and job involvement (Christian et al., 2011). Thus, if organizations are concerned about improving employee attitudes, behaviors, and job performance, not to mention organizational performance and gaining a competitive advantage, then employee engagement appears to be one of the most important variables to focus on for improvement.

A final reason for the importance and continued interest in employee engagement is that many surveys of employee engagement have shown that only a small percentage of employees around the globe are "actively engaged" and in fact most employees are disengaged (Albrecht et al., 2015; Kowalski, 2003). According to one report, only 21 percent of employees around the globe are engaged and employee engagement is on the decline (Klie, 2009; Silliker, 2010). Another report indicates that engagement levels in North America have hit a four-year low (Zinger, 2010). Thus, many organizations suffer from low levels of employee engagement or an engagement gap, and this not only means that they are missing out on the many benefits of a highly engaged workforce, but it also means that they are incurring considerable costs given that it has been estimated that disengaged employees cost businesses billions of dollars a year in lost productivity and revenue (Harter et al., 2002; Johnson, 2004).

In summary, employee engagement is an important variable that has implications for employees and organizations. When employees are highly engaged, they will have more positive job attitudes, behaviors, performance, and well-being. Furthermore, organizations with highly engaged employees will outperform their competitors and benefit from a competitive advantage. Macey and Schneider (2008) have noted that one way to think about highly engaged employees is that they "exemplify behavior both qualitatively and quantitively different from those less engaged" (p.15). Thus, when it comes to improving employee performance, health, and well-being as well as organization performance, it makes sense to focus on improving employee engagement because *employee engagement matters*.

1.2   A model of employee engagement

To begin thinking about employee engagement, we start with a basic model of the relationship between the antecedents and consequences of employee engagement. A model of employee engagement serves several purposes. First, it indicates the nomological network of relationships between engagement and other important variables. Second, it helps us to understand the process through which employee engagement influences important employee and organization outcomes. And third, it helps us to distinguish between different variables that are associated with employee engagement. This is important because there has often been confusion about employee engagement and the variables that are associated with it. For example, it has at times been confused with variables that predict it (e.g., challenging work) as well as variables that are consequences of it (e.g., organizational citizenship behavior).

Figure 1.1 presents a model of employee engagement that will form the basis of this book and subsequent chapters. The model makes a distinction between the following variables: antecedents of employee engagement (also known as predictors or drivers); process variables associated with employee engagement (also known as mechanisms or intervening variables); employee engagement; employee outcomes of engagement (also known as employee consequences or work outcomes); and organization outcomes of engagement (also known as organization consequences).

The model shows that the employee engagement process unfolds in the following manner. First, various antecedents or drivers of engagement lead to process variables that are important for employee engagement. For example, providing employees with job autonomy or control in terms of how they perform their job is an antecedent variable that will provide employees with a greater sense of meaningfulness in their work. Thus, autonomy and control are the antecedents and meaningfulness is an example of a process variable. Second, the process variables will lead to a higher level of employee engagement. Thus, meaningfulness functions as a process or intervening variable for explaining the relationship between autonomy and control and employee engagement. Third, employee engagement will have a positive effect on employee work outcomes such as job attitudes (e.g., job satisfaction), behavior (e.g., organizational citizenship behavior), and job performance. Fourth, employee engagement will also have a positive effect on organization outcomes (e.g., firm performance) through its effect on employee attitudes, behaviors, and performance.

Figure 1.1   Model of employee engagement

There are several other points worth noting about the model of employee engagement. First, as you will see later in this book, antecedents include many things that can have a positive or negative effect on employee engagement. Positive factors are generally referred to as job resources and negative factors tend to be job demands. In addition, while most antecedents come from the work environment and the work itself, some antecedents such as personal resources and personality traits originate within individuals.

Second, there are many different process variables that help to explain the relationship between the antecedents and employee engagement. Furthermore, different antecedents will operate through different process variables and some process variables (e.g., meaningfulness) will be more strongly related to employee engagement than others.

Third, although the term "employee engagement" is generally used to refer to the engagement construct, it is important to realize that engagement is a role-specific variable which means that when we refer to employee engagement it is necessary to indicate the role or target that we are concerned about. In most cases, when we think about employee engagement we are thinking about the "work" or "job" that an employee performs or what is generally known as work or job engagement. However, as you will learn in Chapter 2, there are different targets of engagement that correspond to the different roles that employees can occupy in an organization.

Thus, employees can be engaged to various degrees in their job as well as specific tasks, activities, and behaviors that are associated with their team, department, or organization. Furthermore, the relationship between employee engagement and employee work outcomes will depend on the target of engagement.

Fourth, employee engagement has been found to be related to many work outcomes. Therefore, it is important to distinguish these outcomes in a meaningful and understandable way. In general, employee engagement has been found to be related to job attitudes (e.g., job satisfaction), intentions (e.g., intention to remain or quit), work behaviors (e.g., organizational citizenship behaviors), job performance (e.g., task performance, contextual performance), and health and well-being outcomes (e.g., stress, burnout, life satisfaction).

Fifth, employee engagement has been found to be related to organization and business unit outcomes. These outcomes have included various financial indicators of firm performance such as return on assets (ROA) as well as customer metrics (The American Customer Satisfaction Index) (see Barrick et al., 2015; Schneider et al., 2018).

Finally, it is also important to recognize the mediating processes involved in getting from the antecedents to the organization outcomes. That is, the antecedents of employee engagement should result in positive organization outcomes because of the process variables, employee engagement, and employee work outcomes. Along the way, the antecedents should lead to higher employee engagement because of the effect they have on the process variables; the antecedents should lead to higher employee work outcomes because of the process variables and employee engagement; and employee engagement should result in more positive organization outcomes because of the effect it has on employee work outcomes.

In the remainder of this book, you will learn much more about each of the variables in the model of employee engagement. For now, it is important that you are aware of the variables in the model and how they are related to employee engagement and to each other.

1.3   The employee engagement journey

After reading this book, you will know a great deal about employee engagement as we cover the most important issues pertaining to employee engagement research and what is known about the meaning, measurement, antecedents, and consequences of employee engagement, as well as how to translate the science of employee engagement into practice.

In Chapter 2 we discuss the meaning of employee engagement and compare it to other constructs that are related to but distinct from employee engagement. This chapter explains how employee engagement has been defined in the academic literature and how it is different from other better-known constructs such as job satisfaction and organizational commitment.

Chapter 3 describes the different theories that have been used to explain the employee engagement process. This includes theories that have been developed specifically for employee engagement as well as more established theories that have been used to explain and understand the employee engagement process.

One of the most misunderstood and contentious topics in employee engagement research is the measurement of employee engagement. In Chapter 4, we discuss how to measure employee engagement along with the measures that have been developed in the academic literature and the main problems with most measures of employee engagement. We also discuss how to measure employee engagement for different targets and referents.

Chapter 5 deals with the most-often studied area of employee engagement – its antecedents and consequences. First, we discuss research on the antecedents of employee engagement and try to make sense of all the variables that have been found to predict employee engagement. Second, we discuss research on the consequences of employee engagement and try to understand the extent to which employee engagement predicts various employee and organization outcomes.

Chapter 6 deals with a special topic when it comes to employee engagement: How to get newcomers engaged. Newcomers are a special group of employees when it comes to employee engagement. Newcomers enter organizations ready and willing to be engaged and they are more malleable than employees who have been in an organization for many years. This means that organizations have a window of opportunity to get newcomers engaged before they settle in and potentially become disengaged. Thus, organizations should devote special attention to getting newcomers highly engaged as soon as they enter the organization and throughout the organizational entry and socialization process. Chapter 6 describes how to get newcomers engaged by providing them with various socialization resources throughout their first year of employment.

Although a great deal of research has been conducted on employee engagement, most of this research has been conducted in North America and Europe. As a result, much less is known about employee engagement in other parts of the world. Therefore, in Chapter 7 we focus on cross-cultural issues associated with employee engagement and consider the manifestation, measurement, and promotion of employee engagement around the globe.

One of the most challenging tasks for organizations and Human Resource professionals is translating employee engagement research into practice. Given the many definitions, measures, and drivers of employee engagement that can be found in the literature, it can be a daunting task to figure out how to translate engagement research into practice. Chapter 8 is devoted to this topic and describes an Employee Engagement Practice Model which consists of seven steps for developing an employee engagement survey and for developing and implementing an employee engagement strategy. This chapter also describes how to develop a strategic employee engagement HRM system that focuses on the development of an employee engagement climate, and how to use the Employee Engagement Management Process to improve and maintain high levels of employee engagement on an ongoing basis.

Although we have learned a great deal about employee engagement, there remain many problems and unresolved issues in the literature. Therefore, Chapter 9 describes various limitations and opportunities in the research on employee engagement and some of the main issues and questions that should be the focus of future research to move the area forward.

The employee engagement journey ends in Chapter 10, in which we make some final conclusions and comments about employee engagement. We will provide a revised model of employee engagement and describe what it means for employee engagement to be strategic or what we refer to as strategic employee engagement. We also discuss the role that caring plays in the employee engagement process, and consider some of the differences between job engagement and organization engagement.

By the end of this journey, you will have a very complete and thorough understanding of the research and science of employee engagement, and you will also know how to translate employee engagement research into practice. We hope you enjoy this journey as much as we have!

1.4 Conclusion

Employee engagement has become a topic of great interest to both academics and practitioners. This is due in large part to the fact that employee engagement is strongly related to employee and organization outcomes, and reports that many employees around the globe today are disengaged. Thus, employee engagement matters to employees and organizations. The employee engagement model describes employee engagement as a process in which antecedents lead to process variables that are positively related to employee engagement, employee engagement is related to employee work outcomes, and employee work outcomes are related to organization outcomes. In the next chapter, we define employee engagement and explain how it is different from other better-known and more established work-related constructs.

2   The meaning of employee engagement

It should be easy to define something that has been so extensively studied in the last two decades. However, when it comes to employee engagement, what it means depends on who you ask. As noted by Saks (2017), when translating employee engagement research into practice, the first major barrier is understanding what employee engagement means and how to define it. This stems in large part from the many ways it has been defined and the fact that it has often been defined as organizational commitment or as discretionary effort (Macey & Schneider, 2008). Furthermore, not only are there differences between the academic and practitioner literatures, but even within each group there is a lack of consensus on what employee engagement means. As noted by Macey and Schneider (2008), human resource (HR) consulting firms and academic researchers are "saddled with competing and inconsistent interpretations of the meaning of the construct" (p.3).

One of the main issues in defining employee engagement is the need to differentiate it from other better-known and -studied constructs. In the practitioner literature, employee engagement has often been defined in terms that overlap with more established constructs such as job satisfaction, organizational commitment, and discretionary effort or what is more generally known as organizational citizenship behavior. When employee engagement is defined in ways that overlap with these other constructs, it not only fails to acknowledge that it is a distinct and unique construct, but it also leads to the belief that employee engagement is just "old wine in a new bottle" or a repackaging of similar constructs (Christian et al., 2011).

The definition and meaning of employee engagement is an important first step towards being able to measure, study, and improve employee engagement in organizations. If employee engagement is defined using terms that overlap with other constructs, then it is very likely that it will not be properly measured. Thus, it will be difficult to adequately monitor and change employee engagement if it is defined and measured as job satisfaction, organizational commitment, or some other construct that is being used to represent it.

In this chapter, we will first describe and define related constructs that have most often been confused with employee engagement. We will then discuss the main definitions of employee engagement that have been developed in the academic literature.

2.1   Related constructs

It is important to first understand the meaning of constructs that are similar or related to employee engagement so that they are not confused with engagement, and to ensure that the meaning and definition of engagement is distinct and unique. Making these distinctions explicit is important to avoid the notion that employee engagement is simply "old wine in a new bottle" and to avoid what is generally known as construct redundancy. It is also important to recognize that when defining employee engagement, one must avoid using words and jargon that overlap with these and other constructs (e.g., words such as *involvement, commitment, discretionary effort*, and so on). This is also important when designing measures of employee engagement which will be described in more detail in Chapter 4.

Definitions of employee engagement have often been based on the following better-known and -studied constructs: job satisfaction, organizational commitment, job involvement, organizational identification, intrinsic motivation, and organizational citizenship behavior.

Job satisfaction. Job satisfaction is an attitude towards one's job and is one of the most important attitudes that employees hold. It represents psychological responses to one's job and internal evaluations of the favorability of one's job (Judge et al., 2012). Thus, it is an evaluative judgment (positive or negative) that one makes about their job or job conditions and characteristics (Christian et al., 2011).

Job satisfaction can be understood as a general or overall attitude towards one's job (*"In general, I am very satisfied with my job"*) as well as satisfaction with specific aspects or facets of one's job (e.g., satisfaction with one's pay, co-workers, working conditions, supervisor, etc.). Research on job satisfaction has found that it is positively related to a variety of job behaviors (e.g., organizational citizenship behaviors, attendance at work, turnover), job performance, as well as overall life satisfaction. Employee job satisfaction is determined by factors in the work environment (e.g., job characteristics) as well as dispositional and personality factors (e.g., Big Five personality factors, core self-evaluations) (Judge & Bono, 2001; Judge et al., 2000; Judge et al., 2002; Judge et al., 2012).

Organizational commitment. Organizational commitment is an attitude that employees have towards their organization. It represents the extent to which there is a bond, linkage, or attachment between an individual and their organization (Mathieu & Zajac, 1990). Allen and Meyer (1990) developed a three-component model of organizational commitment that consists of three dimensions or components of organizational commitment: affective commitment, continuance commitment, and normative commitment. *Affective commitment* involves an emotional attachment, identification, and involvement to one's organization. *Continuance commitment* is a form of commitment that involves a consideration of the perceived costs of leaving an organization. *Normative commitment* is based on a perceived obligation to remain in an organization (Meyer et al., 2002).

Affective commitment is the best-known and most studied type of organizational commitment and the most often confused with employee engagement. It is measured by items such as *"I feel a strong sense of belonging to my organization"* and *"I feel personally attached to my work organization"* (Rhoades et al., 2001).

A meta-analysis of the antecedents and consequences of organizational commitment found that the three types of organizational commitment are differentially related to work experiences and work outcomes. With respect to antecedents, work experience variables such as perceived organizational support (POS), organizational justice, and transformational leadership are positively related to affective commitment while role ambiguity and role conflict are negatively related. Role conflict is also negatively related to continuance commitment and POS is positively related to normative commitment. The availability of alternatives and the transferability of skills and education is negatively related to continuance commitment (Meyer et al., 2002).

As for consequences, affective commitment is most strongly and positively related to job performance and organizational citizenship behavior, and most negatively related to turnover, absenteeism, stress, and work-family conflict, followed by normative and then continuance commitment. Continuance commitment is unrelated to some work outcomes, negatively related to job performance, and positively related to stress and work-family conflict (Meyer et al., 2002).

Job involvement. Job involvement has to do with the "extent to which a person identifies psychologically with his or her work or the importance of work in the total self-image" (Brown, 1996, p.236). Thus, job involvement is a cognitive belief or state that has to do with psychological identification with one's job and the extent to which an individual's job is central to their identity (Brown, 1996). It reflects the centrality of job performance to the individual and the extent to which someone's job performance will affect their self-esteem and the job will satisfy their needs (Christian et al., 2011). Job involvement scales include items such as, *"The most important things that happen to me involve my present job"* and *"I consider my job to be very central to my existence"* (Kanungo, 1982).

In his meta-analysis of job involvement, Brown (1996) found that both individual differences and situational factors predict job involvement. Job challenge, enriched jobs, and participative decision making were found to be especially strong predictors of job involvement. With respect to the consequences, Brown (1996) found that job involvement is strongly and positively related to job satisfaction and organizational commitment, and negatively related to turnover intentions. However, it is only weakly related to work behaviors and job performance.

Organizational identification. Organizational identification is a cognitive construct that has to do with the congruence between the values of an individual and their organization. Definitions of organizational identification indicate that it represents the extent to which an individual has linked their self-concept to that of their organization (Riketta, 2005). Measures of organizational identification include items such as, *"When I talk about this organization, I usually say 'we' rather than 'they'"* and

"*When someone praises this organization, it feels like a personal compliment*" (Mael & Tetrick, 1992).

A meta-analysis of research on organizational identification found that demographic variables such as organizational tenure, age, and job level as well as context variables such as job scope/challenge and organizational prestige are positively related to organizational identification. Further, organizational identification is positively related to work attitudes such as job satisfaction and organizational commitment, negatively related to intentions to leave, and positively related to in-role and extra-role performance (Riketta, 2005).

Intrinsic motivation. Intrinsic motivation is a form of motivation that stems directly from the task itself such that the motivation derives from feelings of achievement, accomplishment, or just the enjoyment experienced from performing the task rather than from any potential outcome or incentive that can be obtained as a result of task performance (Cerasoli et al., 2014). Intrinsic motivation is often contrasted with extrinsic motivation which is motivation that is based on the expectation that one will receive an incentive or reward for performing a task. Intrinsic motivation is measured by items such as, "*When I do work well, it gives me a feeling of accomplishment*" and "*I feel a great sense of personal satisfaction when I do my job well*" (Cummings & Bigelow, 1976).

A meta-analysis of intrinsic and extrinsic motivation found that intrinsic motivation is a medium to strong predictor of performance even when incentives are provided. In fact, the authors found that incentives boosted the relationship between intrinsic motivation and performance. Furthermore, intrinsic motivation has been found to be a better predictor of the quality of performance while incentives were a better predictor of the quantity of performance, although intrinsic motivation was a moderately strong predictor of performance quantity (Cerasoli et al., 2014). There is also evidence that intrinsic motivation is especially beneficial for performance of complex tasks while extrinsic motivation is more important for performance of mundane tasks (Kanfer et al., 2017).

Organizational citizenship behavior. Organizational citizenship behavior (OCB) (also known as extra-role behavior) refers to behaviors that employees perform to improve organization functioning and effectiveness but that are not part of or critical to their tasks or job. This usually

Table 2.1   Constructs related to employee engagement

Construct	Definition
Job satisfaction	An attitude towards one's job that represents internal evaluations of the favorability of one's job as well as job conditions and characteristics.
Organizational commitment	An attitude that employees have towards their organization that represents the extent to which there is a bond, linkage, or attachment between an individual and their organization.
Job involvement	A cognitive belief or state that has to do with psychological identification with one's job and the extent to which an individual's job is central to their identity.
Organizational identification	A cognitive construct that has to do with the congruence between the values of an individual and their organization and the extent to which an individual has linked their self-concept to that of their organization.
Intrinsic motivation	A form of motivation that stems directly from the task itself such that the motivation derives from feelings of achievement, accomplishment, or just the enjoyment experienced from performing the task rather than from any potential outcome or incentive that can be obtained as a result of task performance.
Organizational citizenship behavior	Discretionary behaviors that employees perform to improve organization functioning and effectiveness but are not part of or critical to their tasks or job.

involves discretionary behaviors such as helping co-workers, volunteering for extra-job activities, and attending functions that are not required (Lee & Allen, 2002; Organ & Ryan, 1995). Thus, OCB involves the tendency for employees to be cooperative and helpful (LePine et al., 2002). OCB can be directed at individuals or the organization. OCB directed towards individuals is measured by items such as, "*Willingly give your time to help others who have work-related problems*" and "*Adjust your work schedule to accommodate other employees' requests for time off.*" OCB directed towards the organization is measured by items such as, "*Attend functions that are not required but that help the organizational image*" and "*Take action to protect the organization from potential problems*" (Lee & Allen, 2002).

The results of several meta-analysis of the predictors of OCB found that job attitudes such as job satisfaction, in addition to perceived fairness, organizational commitment, and leader support, are strong predictors of OCB. The results also indicate that the relationship between job satisfaction and OCB is stronger than the relationship between job satisfaction and job performance (Lepine et al., 2002; Organ & Ryan, 1995).

2.1.1   Summary

Table 2.1 summarizes constructs that have been shown to overlap with employee engagement. These constructs are well known and developed and have been the subject of extensive research for decades. Unfortunately, they have at times been used to describe employee engagement and some measures of employee engagement include items that are used to measure these constructs. Some of these constructs are more likely to be predictors of employee engagement (e.g., job involvement) while others such as job satisfaction, organizational commitment, and OCB have been found to be outcomes or consequences of employee engagement. Therefore, when defining employee engagement, it is important to avoid using terms that overlap with these constructs and to define it in a way that represents a new, unique, and distinct construct that does not overlap with other constructs.

2.2   The meaning of employee engagement

As indicated earlier, various definitions of employee engagement can be found in both the practitioner and academic literature. Although the academic literature has focused more on job or work engagement than organization engagement, the practitioner literature has been more concerned with the organization than the job when defining and measuring employee engagement. The definitions of engagement provided by consulting firms explicitly focus on the organization (e.g., speaking positively about the organization) rather than one's job (e.g., working with intensity on one's job; Schneider et al., 2017).

In the academic literature, most attention has been given to Kahn's (1990) definition of personal engagement and Schaufeli et al.'s (2002) definition of work engagement. In addition, Saks (2006) extended the definition and meaning of employee engagement by linking engagement to a particular target.

2.2.1   Kahn's (1990) definition of personal engagement

The first and one of the most-cited definitions of employee engagement was provided by Kahn (1990) in his ethnographic study of personal engagement and disengagement at work. According to Kahn (1990), personal engagement involves "the harnessing of organization members' selves to their work roles; in engagement, people employ and express themselves physically, cognitively, and emotionally during role performances" (p.694). Self-employment involves devoting personal energies into role behaviors. Self-expression involves displaying one's true self in the performance of a role. Thus, there are two main components to Kahn's (1990) definition of personal engagement: Self-employment and self-expression.

According to Kahn (1990), personal engagement involves the investment of an individual's full and complete self into a work role in terms of three dimensions: physical, cognitive, and emotional. He further notes that engagement is the "simultaneous employment and expression of a person's 'preferred self' in task behaviors that promote connections to work and to others, personal presence (physical, cognitive, and emotional), and active, full role performance" (Kahn, 1990, p.700). When engaged, people "keep their selves within a role" and display their "real identity, thoughts, and feelings" (Kahn, 1990, p.700). Thus, the essence of Kahn's (1990) definition of engagement is that personal engagement involves the simultaneous investment of all aspects of oneself (cognitive, emotional, and physical) in the performance of a work role.

In contrast, personal disengagement "is the simultaneous withdrawal and defense of a person's preferred self in behaviors that promote a lack of connections, physical, cognitive, and emotional absence, and passive, incomplete role performance" (Kahn, 1990, p.701). It involves "the uncoupling of selves from work roles; in disengagement, people withdraw and defend themselves physically, cognitively, or emotionally during role performances" (Kahn, 1990, p.694). When people defend themselves they hide their "true identity, thoughts, and feelings during role performance" (Kahn, 1990, p.701). When people are disengaged they are "physically uninvolved in tasks, cognitively unvigilant, and emotionally disconnected from others in ways that hide what they think and feel, their creativity, their beliefs and values, and their personal connections to others" (Kahn, 1990, p.702).

Another important component to Kahn's (1990) definition of engagement is that when people are engaged, they display their full and complete selves within the roles they are performing which captures the notion of self-expression. In other words, people vary in the extent to which they bring their true selves into the performance of their roles. Kahn (1990) refers to this as "self-in-role." When people are fully engaged in the performance of a role, they keep and maintain their true selves within the role they are performing. When individuals are disengaged, they decouple or remove their true selves when they are performing a role (Kahn, 1990). Thus, key to Kahn's (1990) definition of personal engagement is the relationship between the person and the role they are performing.

Kahn (1990) also refers to the notion of psychological presence in his definition of engagement, noting that employees who are engaged are psychologically present (Kahn, 1990, 1992). Psychological presence involves four dimensions: attentive, connected, integrated, and focused (Kahn, 1992). Being *attentive* means being open to oneself and to others. It involves being aware of one's own feelings, experiences, and actions as well as those of others. Being *connected* refers to having formed a connection with others and being able to identify with them and to relate to one's situation and others within it. *Integration* involves integrating all aspects of oneself when performing a task and interacting with others rather than being split off or fragmented. As stated by Kahn (1992), "Integration involves having different dimensions of one's self tapping into a given situation" (p.326). When integrated, people "use their physical experiences, thoughts, and feelings to guide how they respond to others and approach their tasks" (Kahn, 1992, p.326). Thus, integration involves the experience of a sense of wholeness and feeling complete such that all aspects of oneself are brought together simultaneously when interacting with others or when performing a task. Finally, *focus* involves staying within the boundaries of one's role and being able to fully attend to the situation at hand. In other words, focus involves staying completely in one's work role and the situation as opposed to absenting some part of oneself from the role or situation. Thus, when people are fully present they "focus on the present, on the here-and-now of their experience" (Kahn, 1992, p.328).

Kahn's (1990) definition of personal engagement has been elaborated and further developed by several others. For example, Rothbard (2001) described engagement as a role-specific construct or what she calls *role engagement*. According to Rothbard (2001), role engagement refers to "one's psychological presence in or focus on role activities and may be an important ingredient for effective role performance" (p.656). Rothbard (2001) noted that "within the context of the organization, people often must engage in multiple roles to fulfill job expectations" (p.65). She further noted that role engagement has two critical components: attention and absorption. *Attention* "refers to cognitive availability and the amount of time one spends thinking about a role" while *absorption* "means being engrossed in a role and refers to the intensity of one's focus on a role" (Rothbard, 2001, p.656). Rothbard (2001) also noted that while attention and absorption are distinct, they are also related because they both represent motivational constructs or the motivation to act.

Rich et al. (2010) noted that Kahn's (1990) definition suggests that engagement is a "holistic investment of the self into one's role" and as such engagement "represents something that is distinct and fundamental" (p.617). In elaborating on Kahn's (1990) definition they state: "People exhibit engagement when they become physically involved in tasks, whether alone or with others; are cognitively vigilant, focused, and attentive; and are emotionally connected to their work and to others in the service of their work" (p.619). Thus, engagement as defined by Kahn (1990) involves "the degree to which people choose to invest their full selves into role-related activities" (Rich et al., 2010, p.629).

According to Rich et al. (2010), engagement is a more complete representation of the self (given that it involves the simultaneous investment of cognitive, affective, and physical energies into role performance) than other constructs such as job involvement, job satisfaction, and intrinsic motivation, which represent much narrower aspects of the self (e.g., cognitive or affective). As such, engagement "provides a more comprehensive explanation for job performance than do concepts that depict the self more narrowly" (p.618). Furthermore, engagement is motivational because it involves the allocation of one's resources to the performance of a role as well as the intensity and persistence with which one applies one's resources. Thus, based on Kahn (1990) they conclude that engagement is a "multidimensional motivational concept reflecting the simultaneous investment of an individual's physical, cognitive, and emotional energy in active, full work performance" (p.619).

Christian et al. (2011) reviewed the engagement literature for commonalities in how engagement has been defined and they used Kahn's (1990) work as a starting point. They noted that engagement involves "high levels of personal investment in the work tasks performed on a job" (p.89) and that it is a broad construct that "involves a holistic investment of the entire self in terms of cognitive, emotional, and physical energies" (p.97). Based on Kahn (1990), they stated that "work engagement is fundamentally a motivational concept that represents the active allocation of personal resources toward the tasks associated with a work role" (p.91). They argued that engagement is distinguishable from job satisfaction, organizational commitment, and job involvement because it is broader, involves a holistic investment of the entire self, focuses on work performed at a job, and involves a willingness to dedicate physical, cognitive, and emotional resources to one's job. Thus, work engagement is a unique higher-order motivational construct.

Christian et al. (2011) identified two characteristics of Kahn's (1990) definition of engagement as noteworthy. First, work engagement involves a psychological connection with the performance of work tasks rather than an attitude towards one's job or organization. Second, work engagement involves the self-investment of personal resources in work. In other words, "engagement represents a commonality among physical, emotional, and cognitive energies that individuals bring to their work role" (p.91). Thus, engagement involves the investment of multiple dimensions of oneself (physical, emotional, and cognitive) rather than the investment of a single aspect of oneself, and this investment is simultaneous, holistic, and involves a connection with work on multiple levels.

Another important factor noted by Christian et al. (2011) in defining engagement is that engagement is a "state" rather than a "trait." This follows from research which indicates that "engagement is subject to moderate day-level fluctuations around an average level" (Christian et al., 2011, p.94). Thus, they refer to engagement as a "state of mind that is relatively enduring but may fluctuate over time" (p.94).

Based on their review of the engagement literature, Christian et al. (2011) defined work engagement as a "relatively enduring state of mind referring to the simultaneous investment of personal energies in the experience or performance of work" (p.95).

2.2.2   Summary

In summary, Kahn's (1990) definition of personal engagement considers engagement to be a multidimensional motivational construct that involves the simultaneous investment of an individual's full and complete self into the performance of a role (Rich et al., 2010). Thus, it has to do with the extent to which employees are willing to use and apply their physical, cognitive, and emotional resources when they are performing their job or any work-related task or role (Christian et al., 2011). There are, however, a number of key features that are unique to Kahn's (1990) definition of engagement.

First, although Kahn's (1990) study focused on workers performing their jobs, his definition views engagement as a role-specific construct that involves person-role relationships. In fact, the first sentence of his paper reads, "People occupy roles at work; they are the occupants of the houses that roles provide" (Kahn, 1990, p.692). Kahn (1990) was interested in "how people occupy roles to varying degrees ... how fully they are psychologically present during particular moments of role performances" (p.692). In other words, engagement can refer to any role, target, activity, or behavior. Thus, employees can be engaged to various degrees with respect to different targets or tasks.

Second, it is important to recognize that unlike other constructs such as organizational commitment which are generalized states or attitudes for which individuals maintain certain levels over a period of time, Kahn's (1990) engagement is a dynamic state that fluctuates over time such that individuals will experience ebbs and flows and moments of engagement over time and across situations (Rich et al., 2010). In other words, employees' level of engagement might vary throughout a day and from day to day or what Kahn (1990) refers to as moments of personal engagement and disengagement and fluctuations of self-in-role.

And third, an important aspect of Kahn's (1990) definition of engagement is that it pertains to authenticity with regard to how individuals conduct themselves or what he calls self-expression. Thus, when individuals are engaged they express and act on their true feelings, beliefs, opinions, and values. Those who are disengaged will not act on or reveal their true selves but will withdraw and absent their true selves from a situation.

2.2.3   Schaufeli, Salanova, Gonzalez-Roma, and Bakker's (2002) definition of work engagement

Another definition of engagement that has been frequently used in the academic literature comes from the literature on job burnout. According to the job burnout perspective of engagement, job engagement is the opposite or positive antithesis of burnout (Maslach et al., 2001). Burnout involves a "prolonged response to chronic emotional and interpersonal stressors on the job" and the erosion of engagement with one's job (Maslach et al., 2001, p.397). The experience of burnout is associated with three core dimensions: overwhelming exhaustion, feelings of cynicism and detachment from one's job, and inefficacy or sense of ineffectiveness and lack of accomplishment (Maslach et al., 2001). Research on burnout has concluded that it "is an unpleasant and stressful condition that can pose problems for both the individual and the organization" (Maslach & Leiter, 2008, p.501).

As the positive antithesis of burnout, engagement is characterized by energy, involvement, and efficacy which are the direct opposites of the burnout dimensions of exhaustion, cynicism, and inefficacy (Maslach et al., 2001). Thus, engagement involves "an energetic state of involvement with personally fulfilling activities that enhance one's sense of professional efficacy" (Maslach & Leiter, 2008, p.498).

This definition of engagement conceptualizes people's psychological relationship to their jobs as a continuum between burnout at one end (a negative experience) and engagement (a positive experience) at the opposite end which are associated with the three interrelated dimensions of exhaustion-energy, cynicism-involvement, and inefficacy-efficacy (Maslach & Leiter, 2008). According to Maslach and Leiter (2008), this "multi-dimensional concept of engagement provides a more complete and thorough perspective of people's relationships with their work, over and above such single concepts as organizational commitment, job satisfaction, or job involvement" (p.499).

Adopting a somewhat different perspective, Schaufeli et al. (2002) argued that burnout and engagement are independent states that should be defined and measured in distinct ways. Although they maintained that engagement is the opposite of burnout, they defined work engagement "as a positive, fulfilling, work-related state of mind that is characterized by vigor, dedication, and absorption" (Schaufeli et al., 2002, p.74). *Vigor* involves high levels of energy and mental resilience while working and a willingness to invest effort in one's work and persistence in the face of difficulties. *Dedication* refers to being strongly involved in one's work and a sense of significance, enthusiasm, inspiration, pride, and challenge. *Absorption* refers to being fully concentrated and deeply engrossed and immersed in one's work such that the time passes quicky and it is difficult to detach oneself from work.

According to Schaufeli et al. (2002), vigor and exhaustion, and dedication and cynicism are direct opposites while inefficacy and absorption are not direct opposites and are conceptually distinct. Thus, "engaged employees have high levels of energy and are enthusiastic about their work" and "they are often fully immersed in their work so that time flies" (Bakker & Demerouti, 2008). However, engagement is not a momentary and specific state, but rather, it is "a more persistent and pervasive affective-cognitive state that is not focused on any particular object, event, individual, or behavior" (Schaufeli et al., p.74).

Finally, this definition of engagement is associated with positive organizational behavior (POB) which is defined as "the study and application of positively oriented human resource strengths and psychological capacities that can be measured, developed, and effectively managed for performance improvement in today's workplace" (Luthans, 2002, p.59). Thus, this definition of engagement considers engagement to be a POB construct and an indicator of occupational well-being for employees and organizations (Bakker & Demerouti, 2008).

2.2.4 Summary

The burnout perspective of employee engagement is more aligned with the positive psychology movement and a focus on human strengths, optimal functioning, and employee well-being (Schaufeli et al., 2002). As with Kahn's (1990) definition, Schaufeli et al. (2002) also consider engagement to be a multidimensional construct that consists of three dimensions. However, this definition of engagement considers it to be a more persistent state rather than a dynamic state that fluctuates over time.

2.2.5   Saks' (2006) multidimensional definition of employee engagement

Given the role-related nature of employee engagement, Saks (2006) suggested that employee engagement should be defined in terms of a specific role or target. He conducted one of the first studies on multiple targets of employee engagement and developed separate measures of job engagement and organization engagement. This recognizes that employees can be engaged to different degrees in both their job and the organization.

Saks (2006) tested a model in which he predicted that both types of employee engagement will be related to various antecedents and consequences. He found that the two targets of engagement were significantly correlated (r=.62, p<.001) but there was also a significant difference between them as job engagement (M=3.06) was higher than organization engagement (M=2.88). In addition, there were differences in both the antecedents and consequences of job and organization engagement. For example, perceived organizational support (POS) was a significant predictor of job and organization engagement, while job characteristics only predicted job engagement, and procedural justice only predicted organization engagement. In addition, both job and organization engagement predicted job satisfaction, organizational commitment, intention to quit, and organizational citizenship behavior towards the organization; however, only organization engagement predicted organizational citizenship behavior towards individuals. In a study that used single item measures of overall job and organization engagement, Saks (2019) found that job engagement was a stronger predictor of job-related consequences (i.e., job satisfaction and intention to quit one's job), and organization engagement was a stronger predictor of organization-related consequences (i.e., organizational commitment and organizational citizenship behaviors).

Saks and Gruman (2014) extended the multidimensional definition of employee engagement by noting that in addition to performing work and organizational roles, many employees also perform group or team roles as well as specific tasks and assignments. Thus, employee engagement can vary within and across employees with respect to various targets. In organizations, employees might vary in how engaged they are when they perform a specific task, their job, team-related tasks and behaviors, tasks and activities that are associated with being a member of a business unit or department, and tasks, activities, and initiatives that an employee performs as a member of an organization.

A multidimensional definition of employee engagement is important because it recognizes that employees have multiple roles in the workplace, and they will bring different degrees of themselves into the performance of each role. Thus, the extent or degree to which employees choose to employ and express themselves physically, cognitively, and emotionally will vary across the different roles they occupy. This means that an employee who has very low job engagement might be highly engaged in other roles or even in specific work tasks. In addition, it is also possible that engagement in one role will be related to and influenced by engagement in other roles. Thus, attempts to make changes in employee engagement in one role might have a positive or negative effect on engagement in other roles. In fact, there is some evidence that engagement in one task can influence engagement in other tasks, a concept that has been referred to as *residual engagement* (Newton et al., 2020). Engagement in one role can result in higher or lower levels of engagement in other roles.

There are also likely to be differences in the antecedents or drivers of engagement which will depend on the target. Thus, careful attention is required when trying to change employee engagement because some antecedents will be related to some targets of engagement but not others. The consequences of employee engagement are also likely to depend on the target of engagement. For example, while job engagement is important for work outcomes such as job satisfaction and job performance it might not be as strong a predictor of outcomes associated with other roles (e.g., team outcomes). As already indicated, Saks (2019) found that job engagement was a stronger predictor of job-related consequences (i.e., job satisfaction and intention to quit one's job) while organization engagement was a stronger predictor of organization-related consequences (i.e., organizational commitment and organizational citizenship behavior). This means that attempts to improve work outcomes (e.g., organizational citizenship behavior) through employee engagement might not be successful if the wrong target of engagement is the focus of the intervention.

2.2.6   Summary

The multidimensional approach to employee engagement does not change the definition or meaning of employee engagement but rather refers to engagement in relation to different roles and targets in terms of the extent to which an employee is psychologically present in a particular organizational role. In fact, using Kahn's (1990) definition of engagement we can refer to the extent to which an employee employs and expresses him-/herself physically, cognitively, and emotionally when performing their job, a particular task, team-related tasks, department or business unit activities and responsibilities, as well as organization-related tasks and duties. Given that individuals might be limited in how engaged they can be when performing various roles, it is possible that being highly engaged in one role might come at the expense of and therefore limit how engaged employees can be in other roles (Macey & Schneider, 2008).

2.3   Reconciling employee engagement definitions

There are two definitions of employee engagement that have received the most attention in the academic literature: Kahn's (1990) and Schaufeli et al.'s (2002). There are several important differences between them. First, Kahn (1990) considers engagement to be more of a role-related construct while Schaufeli et al. (2002) refer specifically to work engagement. Second, Kahn (1990) views engagement as a dynamic construct that can ebb and flow during a day and from day to day whereas Schaufeli et al. (2002) consider engagement to be a more persistent and pervasive state. Third, Kahn (1990) also considers engagement to include a certain degree of authenticity in that when a person is fully engaged, they bring their true and complete self into the performance of a role. In other words, what they say and do is representative of their true values, thoughts, beliefs, and feelings.

However, both definitions suggest that employee engagement is a multidimensional motivational construct that consists of three dimensions. While the three dimensions are specific to each definition, there is some agreement that Schaufeli et al.'s (2002) three dimensions of vigor, dedication, and absorption correspond to Kahn's (1990) physical, emotional, and cognitive dimensions (Bakker & Demerouti, 2008). Furthermore, compared to the constructs described earlier, employee engagement involves a more complete and holistic investment of the entire self in the performance of a job or a particular role.

Finally, when we factor in Saks' (2006) multidimensional definition of employee engagement, we can extend the definition of employee engagement to other targets and roles besides one's job. As shown in Table 2.2,

THE MEANING OF EMPLOYEE ENGAGEMENT   27

Table 2.2   Employee engagement targets

Target	Definition
Employee task engagement	The extent to which an employee is engaged in specific work tasks, projects, activities, or assignments.
Employee job/work engagement	The extent to which an employee is engaged when performing his/her job.
Employee team engagement	The extent to which an employee is engaged in team- or group-related activities and projects.
Employee business unit or department engagement	The extent to which an employee is engaged in tasks, events, and activities in his/her business unit or department.
Employee organization engagement	The extent to which an employee is engaged in events, activities, initiatives, and programs within the organization.

when it comes to employee engagement, we can refer to the following targets of engagement with regard to the roles that employees occupy as members of an organization: employee task engagement, employee job/work engagement, employee team engagement, employee business unit or department engagement, and employee organization engagement. Thus, it is important to be clear about the target when referring to employee engagement.

2.4   Conclusion

Although employee engagement has been defined using terms that overlap with and relate to other known constructs such as job satisfaction and organizational commitment, it is a different and unique construct that should be defined in a manner that clearly distinguishes it from these and other, better-known constructs. Employee engagement is a multidimensional motivational construct that includes cognitive, affective, and physical components. It is a more complete and holistic view of an individual than other constructs as it pertains to an individual's investment of cognitive, physical, and emotional resources and their full and complete self in the performance of their job or a specific task or work-related role.

Although engagement is considered by some to be a relatively enduring state, there is evidence that it is dynamic and fluctuates over time.

3 Theories of employee engagement

Theories are important for understanding how a construct such as employee engagement operates and why it might have certain effects on employees and organizations. If we understand the theories associated with employee engagement, then we will have a better idea of what antecedents will influence employee engagement as well as when and under what circumstances this is most likely to happen. In addition, we will also have a better idea of when, where, and why employee engagement will have an impact on various consequences or work outcomes.

There is no one main theory of employee engagement. Rather, there are a number of established theories that have been used to explain employee engagement, and there are several theories and models that have been developed about employee engagement. In this chapter, we will describe several theories that have been used to explain the employee engagement process as well as theories and models that have been specifically developed to explain the antecedents and consequences of employee engagement.

3.1 Theories used to explain employee engagement

Several well-known and established theories in the management and psychology literature have been used to explain the employee engagement process. These theories have been used to explain how, when, and why employees will be engaged and the consequences of engagement. They include job characteristics theory, social exchange theory, self-determination theory, conservation of resources (COR) theory, broaden-and-build theory of positive emotions, and the triangle model of responsibility.

3.1.1   Job characteristics theory

Job characteristics theory is a theory of job design that explains how to design jobs so that they will promote high levels of intrinsic motivation. The theory is based on the idea that there are five core job characteristics (skill variety, task identity, task significance, autonomy, and feedback from the job) that will have a psychological effect on workers and lead to positive work outcomes. The basic idea is that when you design a job that is high on these five core job characteristics it will lead to three critical psychological states (experienced meaningfulness of the work, experienced responsibility for outcomes of the work, and knowledge of the results of work activities), and the three psychological states will then lead to higher intrinsic work motivation and other positive work outcomes (Hackman & Oldham, 1980).

Research on job characteristics theory has found that the five core job characteristics are positively related to a variety of work outcomes such as intrinsic motivation, job satisfaction, and organizational commitment. In addition, some of the core job characteristics are also positively related to behaviors such as absenteeism and performance. Among the critical psychological states, experienced meaningfulness has been found to be the most important in terms of its relationship with work outcomes (Humphrey et al., 2007).

Job design and the job characteristics have often been used in research on employee engagement. In fact, Kahn (1990) based his theory in part on job characteristics theory in that his theory of personal engagement also includes three psychological conditions that are influenced by various antecedents and lead to engagement. Kahn (1990) noted that the extent to which people are engaged is based on their psychological experiences of self-in-role similar to the way critical psychological states influence intrinsic motivation. As you will see in Chapter 5, research on employee engagement has found that all of the core job characteristics are positively related to employee engagement.

Thus, according to job characteristics theory, employees will be more highly engaged when their jobs are designed with the core job characteristics. Furthermore, like job characteristics theory, Kahn (1990) also suggested that there are psychological states (meaningfulness, safety, and availability) that are influenced by job characteristics and will in turn be related to personal engagement.

3.1.2   Social exchange theory

Social exchange theory has been used in many studies to explain various types of employee attitudes and behaviors (Cropanzano & Mitchell, 2005). The basic idea is that when two parties such as employees and organizations are in a state of reciprocal interdependence, they develop obligations towards each other. As the relationship develops over time, it will result in mutual commitments as long as each party abides by certain rules of exchange. These rules of exchange are governed by the norm of reciprocity in which the actions of one party result in actions by the other party. Thus, when employees receive economic and socioemotional resources from their organization they will feel an obligation to repay their organization (Cropanzano & Mitchell, 2005).

For example, perceived organizational support (employee beliefs about how much the organization values their contributions and cares about their well-being), which has been found to be an antecedent of job and organization engagement (Saks, 2006), is believed to create a feeling of obligation to care about the organization's welfare and help the organization reach its objectives. Employees fulfill this felt obligation through greater organizational commitment and increased efforts to help the organization (Rhoades et al., 2001).

Social exchange theory has often been used to explain the employee engagement process (Bailey et al., 2017). The basic idea is that the extent to which employees are engaged in their jobs will depend on the resources they receive from their organization. When employees receive resources from their organization that are important to them such as rewards and recognition, they will feel a sense of obligation to repay their organization, and one way to repay the organization is with high levels of engagement. Thus, employees will reciprocate and repay their organization by being more engaged in their jobs. If they do not receive desired resources from their organization, they will withdraw their engagement and become disengaged (Saks, 2006).

Therefore, according to social exchange theory, employees will be more highly engaged when they receive resources that they value and are important for them. In other words, employees will feel obliged to reciprocate by being more engaged in their job when their organization has provided them with sufficient resources. Thus, "the amount of cognitive, emotional, and physical resources that an individual is prepared to devote in the performance of one's work roles is contingent on the economic and socioemotional resources received from the organization" (Saks, 2006, p.603). Employees will exchange their engagement for resources they receive from their organization.

3.1.3   Self-determination theory

Self-determination theory (SDT) is a theory of motivation that focuses on the satisfaction of three basic psychological needs for competence, autonomy, and relatedness. Competence refers to feeling a sense of mastery and being effective in one's environment. Relatedness refers to feeling connected to others. Autonomy refers to having choice and feeling volitional in one's behavior. According to SDT, these three needs are considered to be universal and the extent to which they are satisfied will determine an individual's motivation (Gagné & Deci, 2005).

According to SDT, there are two types of motivation. *Autonomous motivation* is a form of self-motivation and is similar to intrinsic motivation. When an individual's motivation is autonomous, it means that they are in control of their motivation and they will perform a task because they want to and find it interesting. *Controlled motivation* is a form of motivation that is based on obtaining extrinsic rewards and is similar to extrinsic motivation. When an individual's motivation is controlled, it means that they perform a task to obtain extrinsic rewards (Gagné & Deci, 2005).

Whether or not motivation is autonomous or controlled depends on the satisfaction of the three basic psychological needs. The satisfaction of the three basic psychological needs for competence, autonomy, and relatedness will result in autonomous motivation and positive work outcomes. When the three basic psychological needs are not satisfied, motivation will be controlled, performance will be poorer, and physical and psychological well-being will suffer (Meyer & Gagné, 2008). Furthermore, autonomous motivation is positively related to job attitudes, job performance, and psychological well-being while controlled motivation is related to negative outcomes such as psychological distress and turnover intentions (Gillet et al., 2013).

With respect to employee engagement, SDT provides an important theoretical basis for understanding how, when, and why employees will be more or less engaged because it provides an explanation and the underlying psychological mechanisms required for employee engagement (Meyer & Gagné, 2008). The satisfaction of the three basic psychological needs will lead to higher levels of employee engagement just like it results in autonomous motivation. Thus, the satisfaction of the basic psychological needs will serve as a mediating or psychological mechanism for explaining the relationship between various antecedents (e.g., job characteristics) and employee engagement (Meyer & Gagné, 2008). There is in fact some research evidence that the satisfaction of the three psychological needs is positively related to employee engagement and well-being (Van den Broeck et al., 2010).

Thus, according to SDT, employees will be more highly engaged when their three basic psychological needs of competence, relatedness, and autonomy are satisfied. Therefore, what is required for employee engagement is the implementation of antecedents that will satisfy each of the basic psychological needs.

3.1.4   Conservation of resources (COR) theory

Conservation of resources (COR) theory is a theory about the importance of resources for individuals' well-being. It is a motivational theory that is based on the need for individuals to acquire and conserve resources for survival. COR argues that individuals are motivated to obtain, retain, foster, and protect resources (Hobfoll et al., 2018).

According to Hobfoll (2002), "Resources are those entities that either are centrally valued in their own right (e.g., self-esteem, close attachments, health, and inner peace) or act as a means to obtain centrally valued ends (e.g., money, social support, and credit)" (p.307). Resources can be object resources, condition resources, personal resources, and energy resources (Hobfoll et al., 2018, p.106). In general, resources refer to things that people value and can be anything that an individual believes will help to attain one's goals (Halbesleben et al., 2014). Individuals experience stress when they are confronted with the potential or actual loss of resources (Hobfoll, 2002). Thus, individuals will invest their resources, protect against the loss of resources, and seek to acquire new resources. The loss of resources has been shown to be related to burnout and stress and can have a negative effect on employee well-being (Halbesleben et al., 2014).

One of the principles of COR theory is that "resource gain increases in salience in the context of resource loss. That is, when resource loss circumstances are high, resource gains become more important – they gain value" (Hobfoll et al., 2018). With respect to employee engagement, COR theory suggests that resources are important for employee engagement especially when there is a potential loss of resources. In other words, job resources are most likely to influence employee engagement when job demands are high. According to Bakker and Demerouti (2008), "job resources become more salient and gain their motivational potential when employees are confronted with high job demands (e.g., workload, emotional demands, and mental demands) because they can help goal accomplishment" (p.213).

In a study on teachers working in elementary, secondary, and vocational schools, Bakker et al. (2007) found that job resources (supervisor support, climate, innovativeness, and appreciation) were most strongly related to work engagement when there were high levels of pupil misbehavior. Pupil misbehavior was not determinantal for the work engagement of teachers who received support and appreciation from their supervisor and co-workers, and when they worked in a school that had a supportive climate and was innovative. Thus, job resources were most important for work engagement when job demands were high or the working conditions particularly stressful. Job resources helped teachers cope with difficult interactions with students and they acted as buffers and reduced the negative relationship between pupil misconduct and work engagement (Bakker & Demerouti, 2008).

Thus, according to COR theory the acquisition and conservation of resources is important for employee engagement, especially when faced with high job demands and stressful conditions. It is therefore important that employees be provided with sufficient resources to enable them to be engaged and to protect them against the loss of resources. Employees with sufficient resources will not only have higher levels of engagement but they will also be able to stay engaged even when confronted with job demands and stressful working conditions. Furthermore, the more resources that an individual has the more likely they will be able to invest resources. Because engaged employees tend to have more resources, they are likely to invest resources which can lead to positive outcomes (Halbesleben, 2011).

3.1.5   Broaden-and-build theory of positive emotions

The broaden-and-build theory of positive emotions is a theory about the development and effects of positive emotions. According to Fredrickson (2001), "certain discrete positive emotions – including joy, interest, contentment, pride, and love – although phenomenologically distinct, all share the ability to broaden people's momentary thought-action repertoires and build their enduring personal resources, ranging from physical and intellectual resources to social and psychological resources" (p.219). Positive emotions are also functional because they build personal resources and psychological resilience, and they trigger upward spirals that enhance emotional well-being.

The broaden-and-build theory of positive emotions highlights the importance of positive emotions for employee engagement. Positive emotions are likely to increase employee engagement for a number of reasons. First, positive emotions broaden people's momentary thought-action repertoires which means that individuals can draw on a wider range of behavioral responses and are more likely to be engaged (Bailey et al., 2017). Second, positive emotions help to build and increase resources which can stimulate engagement and lead to more resources and a positive gain spiral. This is because engaged employees tend to experience positive emotions which means that they can create their own job and personal resources and transfer their engagement to others (Bakker & Demerouti, 2008).

Thus, according to the broaden-and-build theory, employee engagement stems from positive emotions. Therefore, the main implication is to provide employees with resources that facilitate positive emotions which will lead to the development of more resources and higher levels of engagement. This can result in an upward spiral of work engagement, resources, and positive emotions (Bakker & Demerouti, 2008).

3.1.6   Triangle model of responsibility

Britt (1999) used the triangle model of responsibility to explain when soldiers will be engaged (Schlenker, 1997). The main premise of the triangle model of responsibility is that "responsibility is a necessary component of the process of holding people accountable for their conduct" (Schlenker et al., 1994, p.634). The model consists of three elements or linkages that determine how responsible an individual is in a particular situation.

According to the model, people are held responsible for an action or event "to the extent that a clear, well-defined set of prescriptions is applicable to the event (prescription-event link), the actor is perceived to be bound by the prescriptions by virtue of his or her identity (prescription-identity link); and the actor seems to have (or to have had) personal control over the event, such as by intentionally producing the consequences (identity–event link)" (Schlenker et al., 1994, p.649). The combined strength of these three elements determines the extent to which an individual is responsible for an action or event. The main premise of the model is that "responsibility serves as an adhesive that connects an individual to an event and to its outcomes" (Britt, 1999, p.698).

In his study of U.S. soldiers' self-engagement, Britt (1999) argued that the more responsible and committed an individual feels for a given event the more engaged the individual will be in the event. Britt (1999) found that soldiers were most engaged when the rules for their performance were clear (event-prescription link), performance was relevant to their training (identity-prescription link), and they had personal control for their performance (identity-event link). Each of the three elements was found to make an independent contribution in the prediction of engagement. In addition, unit differences in engagement were also explained by the three linkages of the responsibility model.

Therefore, the triangle model of responsibility suggests that employees will be more engaged to the extent that each of the three elements or linkages of the model are strong. In other words, individuals and groups will be more engaged in a job when there are clear guidelines for what they are doing, when what they are doing is relevant to their identity, and when they have control over what they are doing. Thus, one way to improve employee engagement is through interventions that are designed to strengthen each of the linkages in the model (Britt, 1999).

3.2   Employee engagement theories

While many studies on employee engagement have used one or more of the theories described in the previous section to explain how, when, and why employees will be more or less engaged, there are two theories that have been developed specifically to explain the employee engagement process and that have dominated the research and literature on employee engagement: Kahn's (1990, 1992) theory of personal engagement and psychological presence, and the job demands-resource (JD-R) model.

3.2.1   Kahn's (1990, 1992) theory of personal engagement and psychological presence

Kahn (1990, 1992) developed the first theory of employee engagement based on a qualitative ethnographic study of summer camp counselors and members of an architecture firm. He interviewed and observed employees at both organizations to investigate their moments of engagement and disengagement. At the camp, Kahn (1990) was both a participant and an observer as he was the head tennis counselor.

Based on the initial theory developed at the camp, Kahn (1990) conducted in-depth interviews at the architecture firm. Sixteen members of the organization were asked "to recall four different situations in which they had felt: (1) attentive, absorbed, or involved in their work, (2) uninvolved, detached, or distracted from their work, (3) differences between how they responded to a work situation and how they would have responded if they had not been at work, and (4) no differences from nonwork behavior in how they reacted to a work-related situation" (p.698). Participants were asked to describe and detail each situation noting their behaviors and experiences.

Kahn (1990) was interested in generating a theoretical framework about "the moments in which people bring themselves into or remove themselves from particular task behaviors" (p.692). More specifically, he "focused on delineating the psychological conditions in which people personally engage and disengage at work" (p.695). This involved identifying participants' personal engagement and disengagement experiences and the contextual factors associated with them.

As indicated in Chapter 2, Kahn (1990) defined personal engagement as "the simultaneous employment and expression of a person's 'preferred self' in task behaviors that promote connections to work and to others, personal presence (physical, cognitive, and emotional), and active full role performance" (p.700). Personal disengagement "is the simultaneous withdrawal and defense of a person's preferred self in behaviors that promote a lack of connections, physical, cognitive, and emotional absence, and passive, incomplete role performances" (p.701).

Kahn's (1990) main premise was that "people employ and express or withdraw and defend their preferred selves on the basis of their psychological experiences of self-in-role" (p.702). This is similar to the job characteristics model which states that critical psychological states are important for intrinsic work motivation. However, Kahn (1990) was interested in momentary rather than static situations that influence people's engagement.

Based on an analysis of the data, Kahn (1990) identified three psychological conditions that influenced the extent to which people experienced moments of engagement: psychological meaningfulness, psychological safety, and psychological availability. In fact, Kahn (1990) suggested that individuals unconsciously asked themselves three questions about their situation to determine the extent to which they would be personally engaged or disengaged: "(1) How meaningful is it for me to bring myself into this performance? (2) How safe is it to do so? and (3) How available am I to do so?" (p.703).

Psychological meaningfulness refers to the extent to which people derive meaning from their work and feel that they are receiving a return on their investments for their performance. According to Kahn (1990), psychological meaningfulness involves "a feeling that one is receiving a return on investments of one's self in a currency of physical, cognitive, or emotional energy. People experienced such meaningfulness when they felt worthwhile, useful, and valuable – as though they made a difference and were not taken for granted. They felt able to give to others and to the work itself in their roles and also able to receive" (pp.703–704).

Based on descriptive statistics that were calculated from ratings of 186 experiences from the two studies, Kahn (1990) found that people were more engaged in those situations in which they experienced more psychological meaningfulness. Three contextual factors were found to be associated with the experience of psychological meaningfulness: task characteristics, role characteristics, and work interactions.

Task characteristics are similar to the job characteristics of the job characteristics model. Participants were most likely to experience meaningfulness when the tasks they were doing had some variety and were "challenging, clearly delineated, varied, creative, and somewhat autonomous" (p.704). Two components of work roles influenced psychological meaningfulness: identity and status. People experienced more meaningfulness when the identity associated with their role was attractive and fit with their preferred self-image, and when their role carried a certain degree of status or influence that made them feel valued, valuable, important, and needed. Psychological meaningfulness was also experienced when participants had rewarding interpersonal work interactions with co-workers and clients as part of their task performances. In both settings, Kahn (1990) found that "meaningful interactions promoted dignity, self-appreciation, and a sense of worthwhileness" (p.707).

Participants experienced *psychological safety* when they were "able to show and employ [themselves] without fear of negative consequences to self-image, status, or career" (Kahn, 1990, p.708). People tended to feel most safe in situations that promote trust and are secure, predictable, consistent, clear, and nonthreatening.

Based on the descriptive statistics that were calculated from ratings of 186 experiences from the two studies, Kahn (1990) found that people were more engaged in situations in which there was more psychological safety. Kahn (1990) found four contextual factors influenced the experience of psychological safety: interpersonal relationships, group and intergroup dynamics, management style and process, and organizational norms.

Interpersonal relationships that were open, supportive, trusting, and flexible were associated with psychological safety. The dynamics within and between groups and the informal roles that people held also influenced psychological safety and the extent to which they could safely express their selves. In other words, people vary in the extent to which they can safely bring themselves into a role performance as a function of the role they occupy. Those in more powerful roles tend to feel more safe to personally engage as a result of the authority and respect accorded to their role. Similar dynamics occur between groups or organizational subgroups that differ in power, authority, prestige, and status.

Management style and processes also influence psychological safety. Participants felt safer in supportive managerial environments that allowed them to try things and to fail without fearing the consequences.

Participants also felt safe when management behaviors demonstrated support, resilience, consistency, trust, and competence, and when participants were provided with some control over their work.

Working within the organizational norms was also associated with psychological safety. According to Kahn (1990), "people that stayed within generally appropriate ways of working and behaving felt safer than those who strayed outside those protective boundaries. In this regard, safety meant not calling into question habitual patterns of thought and behavior that ensured predictability; questioning such patterns meant being treated as a deviant" (p.712). Thus, participants felt safe when they stayed within the boundaries of organizational norms and expectations.

Psychological availability is the belief that one has the physical, emotional, and psychological resources to invest oneself in a role performance and be engaged in a particular moment. Kahn (1990) found that "people were more or less available to place their selves fully into role performances depending on how they coped with the various demands of both work and nonwork aspects of their lives" (p.714). To be engaged, people need to be able to use their physical, intellectual, and emotional energies in the performance of a role.

The descriptive statistics from the ratings of 186 experiences indicated that people were more engaged in situations in which they were more psychologically available. Kahn (1990) found that four types of distractions influenced the experience of psychological availability: depletion of physical energy, depletion of emotional energy, individual insecurity, and outside lives.

Physical energy has to do with the amount of physical resources that one has available to invest oneself and engage in a role. When participants felt physically drained or depleted, they were unable or unavailable to engage themselves in role performances. Emotional energy has to do with the amount of emotional resources one has available to invest and engage oneself in the performance of a role. When participants were emotionally drained, they were psychologically unavailable to engage in role performances. As stated by Kahn (1990), people need "emotional resources to meet the demands of personal engagement" (p.715).

Kahn (1990) also found that security about one's work and status was important for people to feel psychologically available. Feeling insecure causes anxiety which takes away energy that might otherwise be used for engagement. An especially important dimension of insecurity was a lack of confidence. In order to be available, one has to feel confident about one's abilities and status and be able to focus on one's work rather than be concerned about security. Self-consciousness was also a distraction that interfered with a person's ability to be engaged. Insecurity was also influenced by people's ambivalence about their fit with the organization. Being concerned about one's fit with the organization can distract people from feeling psychologically available. As described by Kahn (1990), "It is difficult for people to engage personally in fulfilling work processes when organizational ends do not fit their own values ..." (p.716).

The fourth distraction that can influence people's psychological availability is outside lives. Kahn (1990) found that when people were preoccupied by issues and events in their lives outside of work they had less energy and resources to devote to their role performances at work, and they were less available to engage in role performances. However, Kahn (1990) also found that in some cases events in people's outside lives actually generated energies that made them more available at work.

Although Kahn (1990) refers to psychological presence in his definition of engagement, noting that employees who are engaged are psychologically present (Kahn, 1990), and states that he is interested in "moving toward a theory of people's psychological presence and absence at work" (p.717), it is only in a subsequent paper that he fully explains the concept of psychological presence and how it fits into his theory.

According to Kahn (1992), the concept of psychological presence is about "what it means to be fully present as a person occupying a particular organizational role such that one's thoughts, feelings, and beliefs are accessible within the context of role performances" (p.322). It is about what Kahn (1992) refers to as "depth" in terms of "how much of who people are becomes accessible to their work" (p.344). He further states that psychological presence "is the experiential state accompanying the behaviors of personally engaged role performances" (p.339).

Psychological presence consists of four dimensions: being attentive, connected, integrated, and focused (Kahn, 1992). As described in Chapter

2, being *attentive* has to do with being open to oneself and to others, aware of one's own feelings, experiences, and actions as well as those of others. Being *connected* means being connected to work and to others. *Integration* refers to the integration of all aspects of oneself when performing a task and interacting with others and a sense of wholeness and feeling complete. *Focus* means staying within the boundaries of one's role, the situation, and the relationship with others.

Psychological presence is manifested as personal engagement. In other words, psychological presence precedes and leads to personal engagement. Psychological presence is also manifested in terms of the authenticity which people interact with others in task performances. According to Kahn (1992), authenticity has to do with "working with one's real emotions within the context of one's role and task situation" (p.330). Thus, one must be fully present to be able to fully engage in task and role performances. Psychological presence leads to personal engagement, and personal engagement leads to various outcomes such as performance quality and the growth and productivity of organizations (Kahn, 1992).

3.2.2   Summary

In summary, Kahn's (1990, 1992) theory of personal engagement asserts that to be fully engaged in a task, job, or role, one must experience the three psychological conditions of meaningfulness, safety, and availability. Furthermore, the three psychological conditions "drive the extent to which people are psychologically present and thus personally engaging in task situations" (Kahn, 1992, p.340). Thus, the three psychological states lead to psychological presence (attentive, connected, integrated, and focused), which in turn leads to personal engagement which leads to positive work outcomes.

In the only empirical study to test Kahn's (1990) theory, May et al. (2004) found that meaningfulness, safety, and availability were significantly positively related to employee engagement. Job enrichment and role fit were positively related to meaningfulness; rewarding co-worker and supportive supervisor relations were positively related to safety while adherence to co-worker norms and self-consciousness were negatively related; and the availability of resources was positively related to psychological availability while participation in outside activities was negatively related.

From a practical perspective, the key factor for employee engagement according to Kahn's (1990, 1992) theory is to create the conditions and situations for employees to experience psychological meaningfulness, safety, and availability and to feel attentive, connected, integrated, and focused in work situations and in their role. This will require various antecedents of the psychological conditions (e.g., job characteristics help to develop psychological meaningfulness).

3.2.3   The job demands-resources (JD-R) model

The job demands-resources or JD-R model is the most studied theory or model of employee engagement (Bakker & Demerouti, 2007). The JD-R model began as a model of burnout (Demerouti et al., 2001) to demonstrate that burnout results from high job demands. High job demands can lead to exhaustion, and a lack of job resources can result in withdrawal behavior or disengagement from work. The JD-R model was then used to explain how job resources and job demands can also influence work engagement which was considered to be the opposite of burnout.

The JD-R model divides working conditions into two broad categories: job demands and job resources. Job demands are physical, psychological, social, or organizational features of a job that require sustained physical, mental, and/or psychological effort from an employee that can result in physiological and/or psychological costs. Job demands include work overload, job insecurity, role ambiguity, time pressure, and role conflict.

Job resources are physical, psychological, social, or organizational features of a job that are functional in that they help achieve work goals, reduce job demands, and stimulate personal growth, learning, and development. Job resources include job control or autonomy, participation in decision making, task variety, feedback, and social support from supervisors and co-workers. Job resources can come from the organization (e.g., pay, career opportunities, job security), interpersonal and social relations (supervisor and co-worker support, team climate), the organization of work (e.g., role clarity, participation in decision making), and from the task itself (e.g., skill variety, task identity, task significance, autonomy, performance feedback) (Bakker & Demerouti, 2007).

Job resources and job demands operate through several processes to influence work engagement and burnout. Job resources activate motivational

Table 3.1   Employee engagement theories

Theory	Description
Job characteristics theory	Five core job characteristics (skill variety, task identity, task significance, autonomy, and feedback from the job) have a psychological effect on workers and lead to positive work outcomes. The core job characteristics will also influence employee engagement through their effect on psychological conditions such as meaningfulness.
Social exchange theory	When employees receive economic and socioemotional resources from their organization they will feel an obligation to repay their organization (norm of reciprocity) and they will do this with high levels of engagement.
Self-determination theory	The satisfaction of three basic psychological needs for competence, autonomy, and relatedness will result in autonomous motivation and employee engagement.
Conservation of resources (COR) theory	Individuals are motivated to obtain, retain, foster, and protect resources. Employees with sufficient resources will have higher levels of engagement and will be able to stay engaged and cope better when confronted with job demands and stressful working conditions.
Broaden-and-build theory of positive emotions	Positive emotions broaden people's thought-action repertoires and build personal resources that will result in higher levels of employee engagement and will lead to more resources and an upward spiral of work engagement, resources, and positive emotions.

Theory	Description
Triangle model of responsibility	Individuals and groups will be more engaged in a job when they feel responsible for what they are doing which is most likely when there are clear guidelines for what they are doing, when what they are doing is relevant to their identity, and when they have control over what they are doing.
Kahn's (1990) theory of personal engagement and psychological presence	Three psychological conditions (meaningfulness, safety, and availability) lead to psychological presence (attentive, connected, integrated, and focused) which in turn leads to personal engagement.
Job demands-resources model	Job resources activate motivational processes that lead to higher levels of engagement while job demands exhaust employees' physical and mental resources and result in a depletion of energy and disengagement.

processes that lead to higher levels of work engagement, positive job attitudes, and well-being, and lower burnout (Bakker & Demerouti, 2007; Crawford et al., 2010). These motivational processes involve an intrinsic and extrinsic motivational process.

First, job resources can function through an intrinsic motivational process that satisfies basic psychological needs for autonomy, relatedness, and competence that will then facilitate growth, learning, and development. Second, job resources also function through extrinsic motivational processes because they are instrumental for the achievement of work goals (Bakker & Demerouti, 2007, 2008). In addition, job resources enable individuals to cope with job demands and they buffer or mitigate the negative effect of job demands on job strain, stress, and burnout (Bakker & Demerouti, 2007).

While job resources are motivational, job demands exhaust employees' physical and mental resources and result in a depletion of energy and increased stress that can result in burnout, disengagement, and health problems (Bakker & Demerouti, 2007, 2008). Thus, as noted earlier, job resources are most important for engagement when job demands are high (Bakker & Demerouti, 2007, 2008).

Research on the effects of job demands on burnout and work engagement has found that the effect of job demands depends on the type of job demand. Crawford et al. (2010) found that job demands that are hindrances or hindrance demands (stressful demands that can thwart personal growth, learning, and goal attainment such as role conflict, role ambiguity, role overload) are negatively related to work engagement. Job demands that are challenges or challenge demands (stressful demands that can promote mastery, personal growth, or future plans such as high workload, time pressure, high levels of job responsibility) are positively related to work engagement.

In addition to job resources, the JD-R model also includes personal resources. Personal resources are "aspects of the self that are generally linked to resiliency and refer to individuals' sense of their ability to control and impact upon their environment successfully" (Xanthopoulou et al., 2007, p.124). Personal resources are positive self-evaluations such as self-efficacy, optimism, resilience, and organizational-based self-esteem which have a positive effect on work engagement, can be changed and developed (Xanthopoulou et al., 2009a), and are also influenced by job resources (Bakker & Demerouti, 2007).

3.2.4   Summary

The JD-R model provides a good understanding of the factors that facilitate and hinder work engagement and the important role played by job resources and job demands. However, a major limitation is that it does not identify what job resources are most important for work engagement. Another limitation is that it does not include all possible factors that might be important for employee engagement. As noted by Crawford et al. (2010), a "limitation of the job demands-resources model is that it does not include all relevant predictors of employee engagement" and its "greatest use is to broadly categorize *working conditions* as either resources or demands in predicting engagement" (p.844).

In terms of practice, the JD-R model suggests that the key to employee engagement is the provision of resources to enable employees to be highly engaged. It also suggests that job demands should be removed or minimized and that job resources are most important for work engagement when job demands are high. In addition, the development of personal resources can also facilitate employee engagement given that individuals with more personal resources are more likely to be highly engaged.

3.3   Integration of employee engagement theories

Table 3.1 provides a brief description of the theories that have been used or developed to explain employee engagement. Given the different theories of employee engagement along with the theories that have been used to explain the employee engagement process, one might wonder which theory is most supported or valid, or if perhaps they should be combined in some way? Although there are differences between the theories, there are also similarities that lend themselves to integration.

All of the theories suggest that there are various antecedents that are important for employee engagement and that they operate through numerous process variables. If you recall the model of employee engagement in Chapter 1, it began with antecedents leading to process variables. Based on the theories described in this chapter, we can now elaborate on the antecedents and the process variables.

Both Kahn (1990) and the JD-R model consider multiple levels of influences and resources to be important for employee engagement, as do most of the theories that have been used to explain the employee engagement process. Kahn (1990) identified multiple levels of influences at the individual, interpersonal, group, intergroup, and organizational levels that influence people's personal engagement. Similarly, the JD-R model suggests that job resources can come from the organization, interpersonal and social relations, the organization of work, and from the task itself (Bakker & Demerouti, 2007). Thus, both theories are based on the notion that resources from multiple levels contribute to employee engagement. In effect, employees require resources from a variety of levels to be able to devote their own resources into the performance of a role. According to Kahn (1990), the extent to which people are engaged depends on the resources they perceive themselves to have or that are available. The JD-R model also suggests that job demands and personal resources will influence employee engagement.

Thus, Kahn's (1990) theory and the JD-R theory indicate that job resources, job demands, and personal resources are important antecedents of employee engagement. The job characteristics theory also suggests that the core job characteristics are important for employee engagement, and COR theory indicates that employees who have more resources and are able to acquire and protect their resources will be more engaged.

We have also seen that there are a number of process variables that have been implicated in generating employee engagement. Kahn's (1990) theory indicates the psychological factors that are important for employee engagement. That is, when employees experience psychological meaningfulness, safety, and availability they will be more engaged. We also know from SDT that the satisfaction of the three basic psychological needs is important for engagement. The broaden-and-build theory of positive emotions indicates that positive emotions are important for engagement, and the triangle model of responsibility indicates that responsibility is important for employee engagement. And according to social exchange theory, when employees receive resources that are important to them they will repay their organization with higher levels of engagement.

Figure 3.1 presents an integrative model of employee engagement based on the theories discussed in this chapter. The model shows that three categories of antecedent variables (job resources, job demands, and personal resources) will lead to five process variables (need satisfaction, positive emotions, psychological conditions, responsibility, social exchange). In effect what this means is that when employees receive sufficient resources from their organization, this will result in the satisfaction of their basic psychological needs, positive emotions, and the experience of psychological meaningfulness, availability, and safety. They are also more likely to feel responsible for what they do and feel obligated to repay the organization for the resources they have received. These process variables will then result in greater levels of employee engagement. Of course, this does not mean that all of these process variables will be activated or need to materialize for employees to be engaged, but in general they should result, to different degrees, from the provision of various resources by the organization. In addition, personal resources will have a positive effect on the process variables and job demands will have a negative effect.

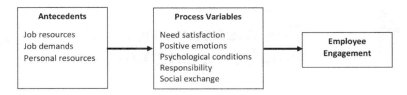

Figure 3.1   Integrative model of employee engagement

3.4   Conclusion

Several theories have been developed and used to explain the employee engagement process. While there are many differences between these theories, they all suggest that employees are most likely to be engaged when they are provided with the resources that they require to perform their job and work roles effectively. The theories also help us to understand why various resources will be more or less likely to result in high levels of employee engagement. Resources are functional for employee engagement because they can satisfy employees' basic psychological needs; elicit positive emotions; enable employees to experience the psychological conditions of meaningfulness, safety, and availability; and make employees feel responsible for what they are doing. When there are strong norms of reciprocity in an organization, employees can be expected to repay their organization for the resources they have received with high levels of engagement.

4   The measurement of employee engagement

The measurement of employee engagement is one of the most important and confusing topics in the engagement literature. Unlike many constructs in organizational behavior, there is no one accepted measure of employee engagement. To make matters even more complicated, the measurement of employee engagement by practitioners and consulting firms differs from how academics have conceptualized and measured employee engagement. In this chapter, we will review the measures of employee engagement that have been developed in the academic literature and research that has compared engagement measures. We will then discuss some important issues when measuring employee engagement, namely the target of engagement and the referent of engagement. We begin with a brief overview of what to look for when considering the usefulness and validity of employee engagement measures.

4.1   Key considerations for measuring employee engagement

The measurement of employee engagement is a difficult but critical issue when it comes to the study and practice of employee engagement. If one does not get the measurement right, then everything else that follows will be questionable and it will be difficult to know how to improve employee engagement and if one has made a difference following engagement interventions. As noted by Byrne et al. (2016): "Conclusions about engagement for both practice and science are useless if the measurement of the construct, and consequently the construct itself, is considered indistinguishable from other construct measures" (p.1201).

Measures of employee engagement have been plagued by several problems. As a result, many measures of engagement are contaminated and therefore not valid measures of employee engagement. There are basically three main problems that can contaminate employee engagement measures. First, some measures of employee engagement contain items that measure other constructs such as organizational commitment. In fact, measures that are very similar to organizational commitment have often been used to measure employee engagement (Byrne et al., 2016). In effect, measures of organizational commitment have been labeled as measures of employee engagement when in fact what is being measured is organizational commitment. Using items to measure employee engagement that are similar or even identical to items that are used to measure other constructs such as job satisfaction or organizational commitment is known as the "Jangle Fallacy," which amounts to putting "old wine in a new bottle" (Christian et al., 2011; Macey & Schneider, 2008).

Second, some employee engagement measures include items that are antecedents of engagement. For example, challenging or interesting work is a predictor or antecedent of engagement but it is not engagement and it should not be included in measures of engagement. Engagement measures should not include items that are predictors or antecedents of engagement. Third, some measures of engagement include items that are outcomes or consequences of engagement such as intention to remain in one's job or organization, and organizational citizenship behavior (Dalal et al., 2008; Dalal et al., 2012). Not only are measures that include such items not measuring employee engagement, but they are then used to predict similar outcomes. This will result in inflated relationships between employee engagement and work outcomes. As noted by Dalal et al. (2012), "the inclusion of citizenship-like behavioral items in measures of employee engagement is likely to inflate the relationship between employee engagement and OCB" (p.E314).

These three problems all stem from a lack of differentiation between employee engagement scale items and items used to measure its antecedents and consequences. Employee engagement measures that are contaminated by including items from its antecedents and consequences will result in a measure that lacks validity and will not measure employee engagement accurately. Furthermore, research that tests relationships between predictors and consequences of employee engagement will be inflated to the extent that the engagement measure includes items that overlap with antecedents being used to predict engagement or items that overlap with outcomes that engagement is predicting (predictor-criterion redundancy).

Measures of employee engagement have often consisted of items from other constructs. As noted by Macey and Schneider (2008), many measures of employee engagement have included a potpourri of items representing job satisfaction, organizational commitment, psychological empowerment, and job involvement. They also note that some practitioners have used direct assessments of satisfaction with the job, the company, and work environment characteristics to measure employee engagement, noting that the measurement of engagement in the world of practice is often similar to measures that are used to measure job satisfaction but with a new label. Other practitioner measures consist of descriptive conditions of the work environment which are then used to infer employees' engagement but do not directly measure engagement (Macey & Schneider, 2008). Thus, questions such as, *"How satisfied are you with your job"* or *"I feel a strong sense of belonging to my organization"* do not measure employee engagement.

With these problems in mind, let's take a closer look at the measures of employee engagement that have been developed in the academic literature.

4.2   Employee engagement measures

There are many measures of employee engagement in both the academic and practitioner literature. There are some important differences between academic and practitioner measures. For starters, the practitioner measures of employee engagement have tended to focus more on the organization while the academic measures focus more on work or one's job.

Second, many of the practitioner measures consist of items that are similar to those used to measure other variables such as job satisfaction and organizational commitment (Macey & Schneider, 2008). Often an engagement index is used that consists of items that measure one's overall satisfaction with one's company, recommending the company as a great place to work, thinking about looking for a new job with a new company, and being proud to work for one's company (Saks, 2017).

An increasing number of measures are being developed to measure employee engagement. Most of these measures are based on the burnout perspective or Kahn's (1990) research on personal engagement. In this section, we review the measures that have been published in referred journals in the academic literature. For each measure, we provide a brief description of its content and development.

4.2.1   Maslach Burnout Inventory (MBI) and the Oldenburg Burnout Inventory (OLBI)

Two measures of burnout have been used to measure employee engagement. The Maslach Burnout Inventory (MBI) is the primary measure for assessing the three core dimensions of burnout and the burnout-engagement continuum (Maslach et al., 2001; Maslach & Leiter, 2008). When engagement first emerged as the opposite or antithesis of burnout, it was measured using the MBI. The MBI measures the three dimensions of the burnout-engagement continuum (exhaustion-energy, cynicism-involvement, and inefficacy-efficacy). It consists of statements about job-related feelings (e.g., "*I feel confident that I am effective at getting things done*") using a 6-point frequency scale that ranges from never to daily (Maslach & Leiter, 2008). Burnout is indicated by higher scores on exhaustion and cynicism and a lower score on efficacy. The opposite pattern of scores represents the measurement of engagement (Maslach et al., 2001). In other words, low scores on exhaustion and cynicism, and high scores on efficacy represent engagement. Thus, burnout and engagement are operationalized as favorable and unfavorable scores on the MBI (Maslach et al., 2001).

The Oldenburg Burnout Inventory (OLBI) is also a measure of burnout that has been used to measure engagement. The OLBI was originally developed in Germany and measures two dimensions of burnout: exhaustion and disengagement from work. Each dimension consists of a continuum that ranges from disengagement to dedication (the identification continuum) and a continuum that ranges from exhaustion to vigor (the energy continuum) (Reis et al., 2015). The OLBI defines disengagement as "distancing oneself from one's work and experiencing negative attitudes toward the work object, work content, or one's work in general" (Demerouti et al., 2003, p.17).

A key difference between the MBI and the OLBI is that, unlike the MBI, the OLBI includes both positively and negatively worded items (Demerouti et al., 2003). In a study that compared the two scales, Demerouti et al. (2003) found that the scales exhibit high convergent validity but they are not identical. The exhaustion items of both scales loaded on one factor as did the cynicism items of the MBI and the disengagement items of the OLBI.

With the development of measures of employee engagement, measures of burnout have fallen out of favor for measuring employee engagement, especially as engagement is now considered to be an independent but related construct. Thus, research on employee engagement has used the other scales described in this section, especially the Utrecht Work Engagement Scale (UWES).

4.2.2   Britt (1999)

Britt (1999) developed one of the first measures of employee engagement for a study on responsibility and soldier engagement. He developed a five-item scale to measure soldiers' engagement in their job. The scale includes items such as, "*I feel responsible for my job performance*," "*I am committed to my job*," and "*How I do in my job matters a great deal to me*." The scale items are based on a definition of job engagement as "the extent to which the individual feels responsible for his or her job performance and whether job performance matters to the individual" (Britt, 2003, p.35). Thus, the items are meant to assess perceived responsibility and commitment and perceived influence of job performance on the individual (Britt & Bliese, 2003). Respondents use a 5-point Likert scale with anchors, 1=Strongly disagree to 5=Strongly agree. Similar scales have been used in several other studies by Britt (Britt, 2003; Britt et al., 2001; Britt & Bliese, 2003; Britt et al., 2005). Although the reliability of the scale has been high in all studies in which it was used (alpha=.84 to .91), the items are similar to those used to measure other constructs such as organizational commitment and job involvement and do not reflect engagement as it has been defined by Kahn (1990) or Schaufeli et al. (2002).

4.2.3   Rothbard (2001)

Rothbard (2001) developed a nine-item scale to measure work engagement based on the two critical components of role engagement from Kahn (1990): attention and absorption. As indicated in Chapter 2, attention "refers to cognitive availability and the amount of time one spends thinking about a role" and absorption "means being engrossed in a role and refers to the intensity of one's focus on a role" (Rothbard, 2001, p.656). Rothbard (2001) based her measure of engagement on the definition of engagement as attention devoted to and absorption in work.

Attention was "operationalized as time spent thinking about and concentrating on the role" (p.665) using four items such as, *"I spend a lot of time thinking about my work* and *I pay a lot of attention to my work."* Absorption was "operationalized as losing track of time and becoming engrossed in role performance" (p.665) and was measured by five items such as, *"When I am working, I often lose track of time"* and *"When I am working, I am totally absorbed by it."* Respondents use a 7-point Likert scale with anchors, 1=Strongly disagree to 7=Strongly agree. The reliability of the work attention and work absorption scales was .78.

Saks and Gruman (2011) used the Rothbard (2001) scale in a study on newcomer engagement. They averaged the nine attention and absorption items to form a newcomer engagement score (alpha=.87).

4.2.4   Schaufeli, Salanova, Gonzalez-Roma, and Bakker (2002)

Although Schaufeli et al. (2002) consider engagement to be the opposite of burnout, they argued that it should be measured independently rather than using the MBI. They state that "contrary to Maslach and Leiter (1997) we do *not* feel that engagement is adequately measured by the opposite profile of MBI scores. Although we concur that, conceptually speaking, engagement is the positive antithesis of burnout, we acknowledge that the measurement of both concepts, and hence its structure, differs. As a consequence, engagement is operationalized in its own right" (p.75).

With that, Schaufeli et al. (2002) designed the Utrecht Work Engagement Scale (UWES) to measure work engagement. It measures the three components of their definition of engagement (i.e., vigor, dedication, absorption). In effect, items from the MBI have been rephrased from a negative to a positive state (Byrne et al., 2016). The UWES has become the most popular and frequently used measure of employee engagement (Bailey et al., 2017; Rich et al., 2010).

The UWES consists of 17 items that measure vigor (six items; *"At my work, I feel bursting with energy"*), dedication (five items; *"I am enthusiastic about my job"*), and absorption (six items; *"I am immersed in my work"*). Participants respond to a 7-point frequency rating scale with anchors, 0=Never to 6=Always/Every day.

Schaufeli et al. (2002) found support for a three-factor model with vigor, dedication, and absorption as separate factors. However, the three scales were highly correlated with each other, especially vigor and absorption. The reliability of the three scales was reasonable (alpha=.79, .72, and 89 for vigor, absorption, and dedication). They concluded that the "three-factor model of engagement with VI, DE, and AB as separate but (highly) correlated factors fits quite well to the data of both samples" and [the scales] do not load on one underlying factor (p.83). They also found that the engagement scales were negatively related to burnout.

Two shorter versions of the UWES have also been developed. Schaufeli et al. (2006) developed a nine-item short form of the UWES or the UWES-9. They collected data from ten countries on the complete UWES scale and then used an iterative process to identify the most characteristic items for each scale. The result was a nine-item scale with three items each to measure vigor, absorption, and dedication. They found that a three-factor model provided a better fit to the data than a one-factor model although the one-factor model also provided a reasonable fit. In addition, the three dimensions were highly correlated. Across the ten countries the median reliability was .77, .85, and .78 for vigor, dedication, and absorption. The median alpha for the total nine-item scale was .92. In addition, each of the scales was highly correlated with the corresponding longer version of the scale and negatively related to burnout. The authors concluded that "practically speaking, rather than computing three different scores for VI, DE, and AB, researchers might consider using the total nine-item score as an indicator of work engagement" (p.712). Thus, they recommend that the total UWES-9 score be used as an overall measure of work engagement. According to Schaufeli et al. (2019), "the UWES-9 may be considered a parsimonious version of the UWES-17 that yields similar reliable and valid work engagement scores" (p.578).

Schaufeli et al. (2019) developed a three-item ultra-short version of the UWES (UWES-3) that consists of one item for each of the three dimensions. According to the authors, three items from the UWES-9 (one from each dimension) were selected based on face validity, theoretical reasoning, and feedback from respondents. The three items are: vigor: "*At my work, I feel bursting with energy*"; dedication: "*I am enthusiastic about my job*"; absorption: "*I am immersed in my work.*" In a study that involved five national samples, Schaufeli et al. (2019) found that the UWES-3 had similar reliability and validity as the UWES-9 although its correlations with measures of well-being, job demands, job resources, personal resources, and outcomes were slightly lower than for the UWES-9. They noted that the three items of the UWES-3 are highly representative of the nine items of the UWES-9. Based on these results, the authors concluded that the "UWES-9 can be shortened, without any significant loss of information, to an ultra-short version with only three items, each representing one particular aspect of work engagement: vigor, dedication, and absorption" (p.586). Thus, to measure work engagement, the UWES-3 can be used as an alternative to the longer versions of the UWES.

Although the UWES has been validated in several countries and there is some support for a three-factor structure (Bakker et al., 2011; Bakker & Demerouti, 2008), the three-factor structure of the long and short form of the scale has not always been supported (Sonnentag, 2003). As a result, the three dimensions are often combined into a total work engagement score (Saks & Gruman, 2014).

4.2.5   May, Gilson, and Harter (2004)

May et al. (2004) developed the first measure of employee engagement based on Kahn's (1990) definition of personal engagement and his three dimensions of personal engagement. The scale was developed for a study that tested Kahn's (1990) model of engagement. The May et al. (2004) scale which they refer to as "psychological engagement," consists of 13 items that measure the three components of Kahn's (1990) definition of engagement (cognitive, emotional, and physical engagement).

The results of a factor analysis based on an initial set of 24 items failed to result in three distinct factors so they used an overall scale with 13 items to measure engagement. Of the 13 items, four items measure cognitive engagement (*"Performing my job is so absorbing that I forget about everything else"*), four items measure emotional engagement (*"I really put my heart into my job"*), and five items measure physical engagement (*"I exert a lot of energy performing my job"*). Respondents use a 5-point Likert scale with anchors, 1=Strongly disagree to 5=Strongly agree and the authors report that the scale demonstrated good reliability.

4.2.6   Saks (2006)

Saks (2006) developed two six-item scales to measure job engagement (*"I really 'throw' myself into my job"*) and organization engagement (*"Being a member of this organization is very captivating"*). The items were written "to assess participant's psychological presence in their job and organization" (p.608). Participants respond using a 5-point Likert scale with anchors, 1=Strongly disagree to 5=Strongly agree. Saks (2006) conducted a factor analysis that provided support for two factors that correspond to job engagement (five items) and organization engagement (six items). The reliability of both scales was high (alpha=.82 and .90 for job engagement and organization engagement, respectively).

In a subsequent paper, Saks (2019) found that single items from the two scales that measure overall job engagement (*"I am highly engaged in this job"*) and overall organization engagement (*"I am highly engaged in this organization"*) operated similarly to the complete scales in terms of relationships between antecedents and consequences.

4.2.7   Rich, Lepine, and Crawford (2010)

Rich et al. (2010) developed an 18-item scale (the job engagement scale) based on Kahn's (1990) definition and conceptualization of engagement. Their goal was to measure Kahn's (1990) three dimensions of engagement (cognitive, physical, and emotional) "in such a way that the commonality of those dimensions would adequately reflect engagement" (p.623). They identified items from existing scales and supplemented them with items that they wrote to "fill out the content domain of each dimension" (p.623).

Rich et al. (2010) collected data from several samples to test the factor structure of the scale. The final scale consists of six items each that measure physical engagement (*"I work with intensity on my job"*), emotional engagement (*"I am enthusiastic in my job"*), and cognitive engagement (*"At work, my mind is focused on my job"*). Participants respond using a 5-point Likert scale with anchors, 1=Strongly disagree to 5=Strongly agree. The results of a confirmatory factor analysis (CFA) supported three first-order factors that in turn loaded on a second-order factor which provided a good fit with the data and high reliability (alpha=.95).

4.2.8   Soane, Truss, Alfes, Shantz, Rees, and Gatenby (2012)

Soane et al. (2012) developed a measure of employee engagement known as the Intellectual, Social, and Affective Engagement Scale (ISA Engagement Scale) to be used by human resource development (HRD) scholars and practitioners. Building on Kahn's (1990) theory, they suggested that engagement has three facets or dimensions which they refer to as intellectual engagement, affective engagement, and social engagement.

Intellectual engagement is defined as "the extent to which one is intellectually absorbed in work" (p.532). *Affective engagement* is defined as "the extent to which one experiences a state of positive affect relating to one's work role" (p.532). *Social engagement* is defined as "the extent to which one is socially connected with the working environment and shares common values with colleagues" (p.532).

Based on a factor analysis, scale reliabilities, and item content, Soane et al. (2012) chose the best nine items for the scale. The nine-item scale includes three items each to assess intellectual engagement (*"I focus hard on my work"*), social engagement (*"I share the same work values as my colleagues"*), and affective engagement (*"I feel positive about my work"*). Participants respond using a 7-point Likert scale with anchors), 1=Strongly disagree to 7=Strongly agree. A confirmatory factor analysis provided support for the three factors and the reliability was high for the overall scale (alpha=.91) as well as for each of the three dimensions (alpha=.90, .92, and .94 for intellectual, social, and affective engagement, respectively).

4.2.9   Stumpf, Tymon, and van Dam (2013)

Stumpf et al. (2013) developed a two-dimensional measure of employee engagement for work groups of professionals who perform technical work. They generated items based on the engagement literature and propositions from Macey and Schneider's (2008) paper on the meaning of employee engagement.

Stumpf et al. (2013) wanted to develop a measure of engagement that would measure "employee's personal, emotional connections with their work" as well as "the behaviors which demonstrate an investment of personal resources such as high levels of energy, activity beyond that which is expected, and observable actions that demonstrate work engagement" (p.256). With this in mind they developed a measure of felt engagement and behavioral engagement for work groups of professionals that do technical work that could be used for self-report as well as assessments by others.

A factor analysis provided support for a 14-item scale with two dimensions that consist of five items that measure felt engagement ("*I am enthusiastic about my work*") and nine items that measure behavioral engagement ("*I often take extra initiative to get things done*"). Participants respond using a 5-point Likert scale with anchors, 1=Little or no extent to 5=Great extent.

The authors used the scale as a self-report measure of engagement for work group members as well as assessments made by others (those familiar with the work group). For others' assessment, the wording of the items was changed from "I" to "They" (e.g., "*I am enthusiastic about my work*" becomes "*They are enthusiastic about their work*"). Thus, assessments by others are directed towards the entire work group rather than specific individuals within the group (a shift in reference to the work group). The reliability was high for both dimensions (alpha=.89 for felt engagement and .92 for behavioral engagement).

4.2.10 Shuck, Adelson, and Reio (2017)

Shuck et al. (2017) developed a 12-item three-dimensional measure of employee engagement they call the employee engagement scale (EES). The items for their scale are theoretically grounded in Kahn's (1990) conceptualization of personal engagement. However, unlike other scales which mostly focus on the job and work engagement, their scale is more generally a measure of employee engagement which focuses on the "fuller experience of employees' active roles within the experience of their work, including their work, job, team, and organization" (p.956).

In developing items for their scale, Shuck et al. (2017) defined employee engagement as "an active, work-related positive psychological state operationalized by the intensity and direction of cognitive, emotional, and behavioral energy" (p.959). Shuck et al. (2017) argue that employee engagement consists of three dimensions which are similar to Kahn's (1990): *cognitive engagement, emotional engagement,* and *behavioral engagement.*

Cognitive engagement is defined as "the intensity of mental energy expressed toward positive organizational outcomes" (p.956). They further note that a "cognitively engaged employee would be proportionately concentrated, focused, and attentive toward work-related experiences (i.e., his or her work, his or her job, or within the active role of working)" (p.957). *Emotional engagement* refers to "an employee's intensity and willingness to invest emotionally toward positive organizational outcomes" (p.957). Further, emotional engagement "demonstrates a deep, active, and emotional connection to the active working experience" (p.957). *Behavioral engagement* refers to "the psychological state of intention to behave in a manner that positively affects performance" (p.957). In addition, "behaviorally engaged employees see themselves as psychologically *willing* to give more and *often* going above and beyond in a way that characterizes their forward movement" (p.957).

A key difference between this scale and other measures of engagement is that it includes items that refer to the job (*"I concentrate on my job when I am at work"*), the organization (*"Working at [my current organization] has a great deal of personal meaning to me"*), and the team (*"I often go above what is expected of me to help my team be successful"*), as well as general items (*"I am willing to put in extra effort without being asked"*).

The 12-item EES consists of four items for each of the three dimensions (cognitive engagement: *"I am really focused when I am working"*; emotional engagement: *"Working at my current organization has a great deal of personal meaning to me"*; and behavioral engagement: *"I really push myself to work beyond what is expected of me"*). Participants respond using a 5-point Likert scale with anchors, 1=Strongly disagree to 5=Strongly agree. Reliability was high for all three scales (alpha=.88, .91, and .94 for emotional, behavioral, cognitive engagement scales, respectively). Shuck et al. (2017) note that their measure is the first to measure employee engagement rather than job, work, or organization engagement.

4.2.11 Summary

When considering the scales that have been developed to measure employee engagement, we can observe several similarities and differences. First, most of the scales are based on Kahn's (1990) conceptualization of personal engagement, except for Britt's scale (1999) which is based on Schlenker's (1997) triangle model of responsibility and the UWES which is based on the burnout literature. Second, most of the scales focus on the job or work as the target of engagement and therefore measure job or work engagement. The exceptions are the Saks (2006) organization engagement scale and the Shuck et al. (2017) employee engagement scale which includes items that refer to the job, organization, and team. Third, most of the scales consist of several dimensions except for the Britt (1999) and Saks (2006) scales which are unidimensional. Fourth, most of the measures use a 5- or 7-point Likert scale while the UWES uses a 7-point frequency rating scale. Fifth, the scales also differ in terms of the number of items, which vary from as few as 1 in the case of Saks (2019) to as many as 18 for the Rich et al. (2010) job engagement scale.

Sixth, there are similarities in the content of the scales. For example, most scales include items that have to do with being attentive, focused, and absorbed in one's job. Examples of this are Rothbard's (2001) attention and absorption scales, the absorption dimension of the UWES, the cognitive dimension of the May et al. (2004), Rich et al. (2010), and Shuck et al. (2017) measures, and the intellectual dimension of the Soane et al. (2012) measure. Most scales also have items that have to do with effort, energy, and intensity, such as the UWES vigor dimension, the May et al. (2004) and Rich et al. (2010) physical dimension, and the Shuck et al. (2017) behavioral dimension. And most scales have items that have to do with being enthusiastic, excited, and positive about one's job, such as the dedication dimension of the UWES, the emotional dimension of the May et al. (2004) and Rich et al. (2010) scales, the felt dimension of the Stumpf et al. (2013) scale, and the affective dimension of the Soane et al. (2012) scale.

There are also a number of differences in the items and dimensions of some of the engagement measures. For example, the social dimension of the Soane et al. (2012) ISA scale consists of items that have to do with sharing the same work values, goals, and attitudes as colleagues. They included this dimension to assess Kahn's (1990) notion of being socially connected to others. The emotional scale of Shuck et al.'s (2017) EES consists of items that have to do with caring about the future of the company and a strong sense of belonging which deviates somewhat from the emotional dimension of the May et al. (2004) and the Rich et al. (2010) scales. Also, the behavioral dimension of the Stumpf et al. (2013) scale includes items that have to do with behaviors that go beyond expected in-role behaviors such as work performance.

When reviewing the actual items of the employee engagement scales one can see that some of the scales include items that are similar to other constructs or appear to be antecedents or consequences of engagement. For example, the UWES has been criticized for containing items that overlap with job attitudes. In fact, Newman and Harrison (2008) have shown that for most of the items of the UWES there are nearly identical items that can be found on well-known measures of job satisfaction, job involvement, positive affect, or organizational commitment. Newman et al. (2016) refer to the UWES as a compound construct because it consists of items that come from job satisfaction, organizational commitment, job affect, and job involvement scales, a process that they refer to as construct mixology (building new psychological constructs by combining older constructs). Rich et al. (2010) have also pointed out that the UWES "includes items that confound engagement with the antecedent conditions suggested by Kahn. For instance, the UWES includes items that tap respondent perceptions of the level of meaningfulness and challenge of work" (p.623).

The other scales also include items that overlap with other measures. For example, Britt's (1999) scale includes an item that refers to commitment (e.g., "I am committed to my job"); Stumpf et al.'s (2013) scale includes the item, "The work I do is very satisfying to me" which overlaps with job satisfaction; Stumpf et al.'s (2013) scale also includes the items, "I often take extra initiative to get things done" and "My work performance goes beyond expectations" which are similar to measures of performance; the Soane et al. (2012) scale includes an item about work attitudes ("I share the same work attitudes as my colleagues"); and the Shuck et al. (2017) scale includes the item, "I care about the future of my company" which is similar to items that measure organizational identification. The May et al. (2004) scale has been noted for having a number of items that overlap with OCB ("I stay until the job is done") (Dalal et al., 2012).

Finally, all of the measures of employee engagement focus on Kahn's (1990) notion of self-employment. That is, the measurement of engagement involves the employment of various aspects of one's self – physical, cognitive, and emotional energies. The other component of Kahn's (1990) definition of personal engagement is the expression of a person's preferred self or what he also refers to as self-expression. This has to do with bringing one's true self with respect to one's thoughts, feelings, and real identity into the performance of a role. This component of his definition of engagement has not been included in any of the measures of employee engagement.

Measures of self-expression would involve asking about the extent to which an employee is able to present their true self and identity when they are at work performing their job. This is missing from all existing measures of employee engagement which have more or less focused on the employment aspects of engagement which also include the dimensions that are used in the UWES measure of work engagement (i.e., vigor, dedication, absorption). A measure of the self-expression component of engagement should include questions such as, *"When I am at work, I am able to be myself,"* or *"I can express my true feelings about things on my job."* None of the engagement scales includes items like this that assess the self-expression component of Kahn's (1990) definition of personal engagement.

In summary, while there are similarities between the different measures of employee engagement there are also a number of important differences. In general, the measures of employee engagement tend to be multidimensional (e.g., vigor, dedication, absorption) or unidimensional and they focus on a particular target (e.g., job engagement, work engagement, organization engagement) or several targets (e.g., job, organization, and team; Shuck et al., 2017, Employee Engagement Scale). Although many of the measures overlap in terms of the items and dimensions they measure, they are not interchangeable and are likely to produce different research results (Byrne et al., 2016; Viljevac et al., 2012).

4.3   Research on employee engagement measures

Several studies have investigated the validity of employee engagement scales. For example, Viljevac et al. (2012) investigated the psychometric properties and the validity of the UWES and the May et al. (2004) scale in a study of call center employees in two finance organizations. Because the physical, emotional, and cognitive dimensions of the May et al. (2004) scale correspond with the vigor, dedication, and absorption dimensions of the UWES, they expected to find higher correlations between the corresponding pairs. However, only the absorption and cognitive dimensions were more strongly related to each other than to the other dimensions.

In terms of the factor structure, although three dimensions provided the best fit for both scales, confirmatory factor analysis provided weak support for a three-dimensional scale for both measures. When comparing the scales to other variables, the UWES scale was distinguished from organizational commitment, job involvement, and intent to stay while the May et al. (2004) scale could only be distinguished from organizational commitment. Neither scale could be clearly distinguished from job satisfaction. Both person-job (PJ) and person-organization (PO) fit were related to the UWES and the May et al. (2004) scale; however, they were both more strongly related to the UWES.

Viljevac et al. (2012) found that the two scales are measuring overlapping but not identical constructs and that the May et al. (2004) measure performed less well than the UWES in terms of convergent and predictive validity. However, the dedication dimension of the UWES had the highest correlations with the four attitudinal measures which the authors noted raises concerns about its distinctiveness as a measure of engagement. Viljevac et al. (2012) concluded that "neither measure should be considered an adequate measure of work engagement" and "it is not clear whether engagement is a multi-dimensional or a unidimensional construct or how best to measure it" (p.3706). Of most concern was that neither measure showed discriminant validity with job satisfaction.

Wefald et al. (2012) examined the UWES-9 and the Britt, Thomas, and Dawson (2006) engagement scale in a sample of employees and managers in a financial institution. They did not find a good fit for the three-factor or the one-factor model of the UWES-9 although the three-factor model was a better fit to the data than the one-factor model. They did find a good fit for the single factor model for the Britt et al. (2006) engagement measure. However, neither scale added to the prediction of turnover intentions beyond that of job satisfaction and affective organizational commitment. According to the authors, the findings suggest that "the way engagement is typically measured may be inherently flawed, and that engagement, as measured by both Schaufeli and Britt, may be redundant with the more established constructs of job satisfaction and affective organizational commitment" (p.87).

Anthony-McMann et al. (2016) investigated relationships between the Rich et al. (2010) job engagement scale and the ISA engagement scale (Soane et al., 2012) in a sample of IT professionals in community hospitals. They found differences in the relationships between each measure of engagement and workplace stress and burnout. In general, the negative relationships between workplace stress and engagement, and between burnout and engagement were much stronger for the ISA scale than the job engagement scale. They also found that burnout explained more of the relationship between workplace stress and engagement when the ISA measure was used. These differences are due to the relationships between the dimensions of each scale and workplace stress and burnout. For example, the cognitive dimension of the job engagement scale had weak relationships with workplace stress and burnout and the physical dimension had nonsignificant relationships. However, the affective and social dimensions of the ISA had strong relationships with workplace stress and burnout.

Anthony-McMann et al. (2016) concluded that their study "confirms that although both measures of employee engagement employed in the proposed study are conceptually based on Kahn's (1990) needs-satisfaction framework, even they do not measure the same aspects of employee engagement" (p.188). They further note that "different employee engagement instruments (even those that are similarly conceptualized) will all have different predictive properties and thus different utility" (p.188).

Cole et al. (2012) conducted a meta-analysis of work engagement and burnout in an effort to determine if they are redundant constructs using the MBI to measure burnout and the UWES to measure work engagement. Their results indicate that the burnout and engagement dimensions are strongly correlated. With respect to relationships with antecedents (job resources and demands) and outcomes, they found that the engagement and burnout dimensions had similar although opposite and at times identical patterns of relationships which supports the view that engagement and burnout are empirically redundant and share a nomological network. In addition, with the burnout dimensions controlled, the engagement dimensions explained substantially less variance in work outcomes (i.e., job satisfaction, organizational commitment, health complaints) and declined by over 70 percent for all three outcomes.

According to Cole et al. (2012), their "overall findings suggest employee engagement, as gauged by the UWES, overlaps to such an extent with job burnout, as gauged by the MBI, that it effectively taps an existing construct under a new label" (p.1573). Based on their results, Cole et al. (2012, p.1576) concluded that:

> ...construct redundancy is a major problem in understanding and advancing burnout-engagement research. The most frequently used inventory of employee engagement (viz., UWES) is shown to be empirically redundant with a long-established, widely employed measure of job burnout (viz., MBI). Accordingly, researchers interested in advancing contemporary thinking on engagement should avoid using the UWES as if it were tapping a distinct, independent phenomenon.

Byrne et al. (2016) investigated the validity of the UWES and the Rich et al. (2010) job engagement scales in a series of studies that compared the relationships between the two scales with several antecedents and consequences. In terms of the structure of the scales, Byrne et al. (2016) found that the dimensions of the UWES and the JES are positively related and each scale consists of three factors. In addition, the UWES and the JES were found to be distinct from several other constructs such as commitment and burnout. Thus, they found that the construct of engagement is different from burnout and is not simply its opposite although they are negatively related.

However, the two scales related differently to many variables including stress, job performance, physical strains, psychological availability and meaning, job commitment, and burnout. Thus, they had dissimilar relationships with several variables that are part of the engagement nomological network. As a result, the authors concluded that "the two measures are not interchangeable, and are either assessing different but related constructs, or assessing different dimensions of engagement" (p.1214). When testing different models for the mediating effects of each measure of engagement, the authors concluded that the results "demonstrate the UWES and the JES do not relate similarly to variables within the engagement nomological network, providing additional confirmation the UWES and JES either assess different but related constructs (not both assessing engagement), or different aspects/dimensions of the same engagement construct" (p.1215). Based on the results, Byrne et al. (2016) concluded that although the UWES and JES are related they are not interchangeable and they "measure different aspects of engagement, as opposed to different but related constructs" (p.1215). Given that the UWES and JES are moderately correlated, they are assessing some aspect of the engagement construct.

So how do these two measures compare when it comes to measuring engagement? According to Byrne et al. (2016), the UWES assesses a broader domain than the JES given its higher correlations with most of the variables included in the study. The higher correlations between the UWES and the other variables, however, do not mean that the UWES is a superior measure of engagement than the JES. As noted by Byrne et al. (2016), "these higher correlations should not be interpreted to mean the UWES is necessarily a better measure or that it more accurately assesses engagement" (p.1216). The higher correlations between the UWES and the other variables might indicate greater overlap between the UWES and other variables in the nomological network. Thus, according to Byrne et al. (2016), "the UWES assesses a broader portion of the engagement nomological network than does the JES, wherein the UWES's assessment includes overlapping peripheral attitudes related to engagement" (p.1218). Thus, the UWES appears to be measuring some portion of job attitudes and therefore overlaps with attitudes more than the JES. They also suggest that there is a need to develop better measures of engagement.

Finally, Saks (2019) tested a model of the antecedents and consequences of employee engagement using his measures of job and organization engagement as well as the UWES. He found similar results regardless of which engagement measure was used. That is, the same antecedents were related to the UWES, and the UWES was related to the same consequences, and the UWES similarly mediated the relationships between the antecedents and the consequences. However, the UWES was more strongly related to the antecedents and some of the consequences. Saks (2019) concluded that these results are "consistent with those of Byrne et al. (2016) in that the UWES tends to be more highly correlated to antecedents and consequences than other measures of engagement" (p.31). He further notes that "like the JES, job and organization engagement appear to have less overlap with job attitudes than the UWES" (p.31).

4.3.1   Summary

The results of several studies that have compared and contrasted employee engagement measures suggest that different measures of employee engagement are related and seem to be measuring some aspects of the same construct. However, they are not the same and therefore they are not interchangeable. With respect to the UWES, which is the most used and studied measure of employee engagement, it appears to be especially highly correlated with job attitudes and burnout. This should not be surprising given that many of the items are similar to items used to measure various job attitudes as well as burnout (Byrne et al., 2016; Cole et al., 2012; Newman & Harrison, 2008). Thus, the results of research on employee engagement and the nature and strength of relationships between employee engagement and its antecedents and consequences are likely to be influenced in part by the scale used to measure employee engagement.

4.4   Employee engagement targets

As described in Chapter 2, the multidimensional model of employee engagement defines employee engagement as a role-specific construct that should be measured in terms of a specific role or target. Thus, employees can be engaged to different degrees to specific work tasks, their job, their team, their business unit or department, and their organization. In addition, we can also consider the engagement of employees with respect to specific events or activities such as learning and training initiatives, change programs, and voice engagement (Saks, 2017).

However, all of the measures of employee engagement except for three focus specifically on the job as the target of engagement. As previously noted, Saks (2006) designed a measure of organization engagement that was distinct from the items used to measure job engagement, and Rothbard (2001) measured job and family engagement with the same items by asking participants to indicate their engagement in their work and their family. Shuck et al. (2017) designed a general measure of employee engagement that includes three targets (the job, team, and organization).

The problem with the Shuck et al. (2017) EES measure, however, is that it confounds the target of engagement with the dimension of engagement. This is because all of the cognitive items are for the job; three of the emotional items are for the organization; and there is one item each for the job, organization, and team and one general item for the behavioral dimension. Furthermore, half of the 12 scale items refer to work and the job, four refer to the organization, and only one refers to the team. This makes it difficult to interpret the meaning of a score on the EES given that an employee's engagement score will be based on their engagement in all three roles or targets. For example, if an employee is highly engaged in their team but they have low engagement in their job and their organization, they will have a relatively low engagement score overall that will mask their high score on team engagement. In addition, two employees might have the same engagement score but it might be the result of different combinations of job, team, and organization engagement. Thus, the EES cannot provide a meaningful score on a particular target of engagement and it is not possible to know from an employee's EES score what they are and are not engaged in with respect to different targets and roles.

Therefore, measures of employee engagement should consider the role or target in question. Following the multidimensional model of employee engagement (Saks, 2006), research on different targets of employee engagement should ask employees about their engagement in a specific task (employee task engagement), their job (employee job engagement), team (employee team engagement), department or function (employee department/function engagement), or organization (employee organization engagement).

This is relatively easy to do by adapting and rewording scale items of existing measures of work and job engagement such as the job engagement scale (Rich et al., 2010). Items such as, "*I devote a lot of energy to my job*" and "*I am enthusiastic about my job*" can be used for any role or target by changing "job" to the desired target (task, team, business unit/ department, organization). Rothbard's (2001) scale can also be easily adapted to any target. She used the same two scales (attention and absorption) to measure work and family engagement by inserting "family" and "work" in each item (e.g., "*I spend a lot of time thinking about my work/ family*"). All of the items in her scale can be used to measure any target of engagement by inserting the desired target (e.g., "*I spend a lot of time thinking about my task/team/business unit/organization*").

Table 4.1   Measuring employee engagement targets

General measures based on Saks (2006, 2019)
I am highly engaged in my job.
I am highly engaged in my team.
I am highly engaged in my department.
I am highly engaged in my organization.

Inserting target into items from Rothbard (2001)
I spend a lot of time thinking about my job/team/department/organization.
I focus a great deal of attention on my job/team/department/organization.

Inserting target into items from Rich et al. (2010)
I exert my full effort to my job/team/department/organization.
I am interested in my job/team/department/organization.
At work, I devote a lot of attention to my job/team/department/organization.

Using an opening statement to indicate the target
Indicate the extent to which each item listed below describes you when you
are doing tasks and activities for your job/team/department/organization.
Intensity.
Effort.
Interested.
Excited.
Attention.
Absorption.

Using scale items specific to a target (e.g., department)
Indicate the extent to which you are fully and completely immersed and
engaged when performing each of the following tasks and activities for your
department.
Attend department meetings.
Participate in department special events.
Participate in department committees.
Working on department initiatives.
Attend department functions.

Another way to measure different targets of engagement is to take items
from work and job engagement scales and remove the word "job" or
"work" from them and then preface the scale with a statement that tells
respondents what they should be thinking about when they answer each
question (e.g., a certain task, their job, their work group/team, their
department, their organization). Thus, an opening statement might ask
participants to answer each question thinking about their team. They then
respond to items such as those from Rich et al. (2010) without the target
included (e.g., I exert my full effort, I devote a lot of energy, I feel positive,
My mind is focused, I am absorbed, etc.). Thus, employees can be asked
to respond to these items for any given target.

Besides adapting scales of work and job engagement, one might develop separate scales for each target of engagement. This is in fact what Saks (2006) did to develop scales to measure job engagement (e.g., "*This job is all consuming; I am totally into it*") and organization engagement (e.g., "*One of the most exciting things for me is getting involved with things happening in this organization*"). Scale items can be written to reflect the main components of Kahn's (1990) conceptualization of engagement (e.g., physical, emotional, and cognitive dimensions) with reference to a specific target.

A final way to measure employee engagement for a specific target is to identify the main activities, tasks, and behaviors associated with the performance of a specific role. If for example the target is the team, one would identify the main tasks and activities that all team members must perform in addition to their actual job. The measure would then list the team tasks and activities and employees would be asked to indicate the extent to which they fully and completely immerse and engage themselves in each task and activity (e.g., meet with my team to discuss problems). This would result in a target-specific engagement scale that could only be used to measure engagement for the target it was designed to measure.

4.4.1   Summary

In summary, measures of employee engagement can be adapted or designed for any target. This can involve simply inserting the desired target in a work or job engagement scale or designing a scale specifically for a target. Table 4.1 provides some examples of how to measure employee engagement for different targets.

4.5   Employee engagement referents

In addition to employee engagement targets, measures of employee engagement can also vary in terms of the referent used to measure employee engagement. Research on the referent of employee engagement has to do with whose engagement is being considered regardless of the target. The referent for most studies on job or work engagement has been oneself. However, there have been some interesting exceptions.

For example, Barrick et al. (2015) conducted a study on collective organizational engagement defined as a shared perception among organizational members about how engaged members of the organization are when they perform their job. While they were interested in job engagement, the referent was one's co-workers. They used items that correspond to Rich et al.'s (2010) job engagement scale. However, they changed the referent to one's co-workers (e.g., *"My co-workers and I really 'throw' ourselves into our work"*). Notice that the items also include oneself (My co-workers and I) which captures the notion of collective organizational engagement being a shared perception among organizational members.

Another good example is research on team work engagement (TWE) which is defined as a "shared, positive and fulfilling, motivational emergent state of work-related well-being" (Costa et al., 2014a, p.35). Like work engagement, TWE is a multidimensional construct that consists of team vigor, team dedication, and team absorption. The UWES has been used to measure TWE by using the team as the referent (a referent-shift composition model) rather than oneself by replacing "I" with "we," "our," and "us" in the items. For example, Costa et al. (2014a) asked individuals to respond to questions about the work engagement of their group (e.g., *"At our work, we feel bursting with energy"*). Notice that by using "we" the respondent is included in the group. According to Costa et al. (2014a), this was done to "reinforce the idea of individual belongingness to the group by using first-person plural pronouns ('we,' 'our,' 'us'). We believe that the use of these pronouns also helps the respondents to focus on the team and not on individual work that may not be relevant for them collectively" (p.38).

Torrente et al. (2012) conducted a study on the mediating effect of team work engagement for the relationship between social resources and team performance. They reworded vigor, dedication, and absorption items by replacing "I" with "My team" and "we" which also includes the respondent in the team. Thus, research on TWE shifts the referent from "I" to "We."

Changing the referent of employee engagement measures is relatively easy. The referent of work engagement scales can be changed from oneself to the desired referent – the team, business unit/department, or organization by simply replacing words such as "I" with "My" to measure the engagement of one's team (My team), department/functional area (My department), or organization (My organization), or just my co-workers for any particular target. One can also decide if the referent should or should not include the individual (e.g., My co-workers versus My co-workers and I).

Table 4.2   Measuring employee engagement referents

General measures based on Saks (2006, 2019)
My team/department/organization is highly engaged in their job.
My team/department/organization is highly engaged in their team.
My team/department/organization is highly engaged in their department.
My team/department/organization is highly engaged in their organization.

Inserting target into items from Rothbard (2001)
My team/department/organization spends a lot of time thinking about their work/team/department/organization.
My team/department/organization focuses a great deal of attention on their work/team/department/organization.

Inserting target into items from Rich et al. (2010)
My team/department/organization exerts their full effort to their job/team/department/organization.
My team/department/organization is interested in their job/team/department/organization.
At work, my team/department/organization devotes a lot of attention to their job/team/department/organization.

Using an opening statement to indicate the target
Indicate the extent to which each item listed below describes your team/department/organization when they are doing tasks and activities for their job/team/department/organization.
Intensity.
Effort.
Interested.
Excited.
Attention.
Absorption.

Using scale items specific to a target (e.g., department)
Indicate the extent to which members of your team/department/organization are fully and completely immersed and engaged when performing each of the following tasks and activities for your department.
Attend department meetings.
Participate in department special events.
Participate in department committees.
Working on department initiatives.
Attend department functions.

4.5.1   Summary

In summary, although most research on employee engagement has used oneself as the referent, it is possible to change the referent in what is known as a referent-shift, by replacing words that pertain to oneself to reflect the desired referent. Table 4.2 shows how the items in Table 4.1 can be converted to various referents.

4.6   Measuring employee engagement

Given the different scales that have been developed to measure employee engagement how is one to decide what measure to use for research or practice? When deciding on a measure of employee engagement it is important to begin with a clear and well-written and understood definition. This is important because it helps to identify the content that should be used to write or choose items to measure employee engagement. It is also a good idea to keep in mind the kind of items that have been used to measure the related constructs that were described in Chapter 2 to make sure that the items used to measure employee engagement do not overlap in any way with the items used to measure these other constructs. To be sure, Table 4.3 presents sample items used to measure each of these related constructs. In addition, it is also important to avoid items that refer to antecedents of engagement (e.g., challenging, interesting work) and consequences of engagement (helping co-workers, intention to stay).

As indicated earlier, there is some content overlap among the items used in the different measures of employee engagement which should be considered when choosing or writing items such as: attention, focus, concentrate, absorbed, effort, energy, intensity, enthusiastic, excited, lost track of time, and immersed. There also tends to be agreement that employee engagement involves a cognitive, emotional, and a physical or behavioral component. Thus, scale items can be written based on these factors. Once the items have been determined it is relatively straightforward to add the desired target (a specific task, job, team, department/function, organization) and to include the desired referent by using terms such as "I," "My," "We," or just referring to "My co-workers" or "My co-workers and I."

Table 4.3   Measures of related constructs

Construct	Sample Item
Job satisfaction	In general, I am satisfied with my job.
Organizational commitment	I feel a strong sense of belonging to my organization.
Job involvement	The most important things that happen to me involve my present job.
Organizational identification	When someone praises this organization, it feels like a personal compliment.
Intrinsic motivation	I feel a great sense of personal satisfaction when I do my job well.
Organizational citizenship behavior	I take action to protect the organization from potential problems.

4.7 Conclusion

The measurement of employee engagement is perhaps the most important issue when it comes to employee engagement as everything else hinges on it. If you don't have a valid measure of employee engagement, it will not be possible to know for sure if employees are engaged and to what extent they are engaged or disengaged, the predictors and outcomes of engagement, what to do to improve engagement, and if engagement interventions are effective for improving employee engagement. Furthermore, as noted by Cole et al. (2012), "unless researchers can clearly define and measure engagement as a unique phenomenon that is conceptually and empirically independent from existing constructs, their work will face continued criticism, scientific progress may lose pace, and knowledge transfer between scientific and practitioner domains will be hampered" (p.1573).

Although there are many measures of employee engagement that have been developed, they are not interchangeable and will likely result in different research findings and implications for practice. That being said, there are some similarities when it comes to the main things to consider when choosing or designing a measure of employee engagement. Besides deciding on the items to measure employee engagement, it is also necessary to identify the target and the referent. Fortunately, existing scales of job and work engagement can be easily revised and adapted for different targets and referents of employee engagement.

5 Antecedents and consequences of employee engagement

In Chapter 2, we noted that it is important to differentiate employee engagement from other, similar work constructs such as job satisfaction, organizational commitment, and job involvement. One way to accomplish this is by exploring the nomological network of a construct. A nomological network helps to make clear "what something is" by examining the system of variables with which the construct is associated, including antecedents and outcomes (Cronbach & Meehl, 1955, p.290).

In this chapter, we describe the nomological network of employee engagement by describing its antecedents and consequences. Given the many antecedents and consequences that have been studied, we have organized the antecedents in terms of Kahn's (1990) psychological conditions of meaningfulness, safety, and availability and classified them as individual-level, group-level, leader-level, and organization-level antecedents. We also discuss antecedents when the referent is not the self. The consequences are described in terms of whether they are individual-level, group-level, and organizational-level outcomes.

5.1 Antecedents of employee engagement

Several meta-analyses and reviews have examined the antecedents of employee engagement (e.g., Bailey et al., 2017; Christian et al., 2011; Crawford et al., 2010; Halbesleben, 2010; Lesener et al., 2019; Lichtenthaler & Fischbach, 2019; Mauno et al., 2010; Young et al., 2018). There are two important things to note about these reviews. First, they focus on employee engagement at the individual level of analysis. Specifically, they focus on job/work engagement. As such, our understanding of the nomo-logical network of employee engagement at the team, unit/department, and organization levels, in addition to task engagement, is particularly underspecified. Second, in line with the JD-R model, they focus on resources as a general category of antecedents. We will therefore begin by considering resources as antecedents of employee engagement.

5.1.1   Resources as antecedents

Building on the distinctions among the different kinds of resources that have been considered within the JD-R model (Bakker & Demerouti, 2007, 2017), Nielsen et al. (2017) distinguished among resources at four different levels: individual (e.g., self-efficacy), group (e.g., social support), leader (e.g., transformational leadership), and organization (e.g., human resource practices). In their systematic review and meta-analysis, they found that resources at all four levels were positively associated with well-being, and there were no significant differences in the strength of the association at different levels.

Lesener et al. (2019) conducted a similar analysis but focused on the drivers of employee engagement and examined longitudinal evidence at three of the four levels explored by Nielsen et al. (2017). They found that job resources at the group, leader, and organizational levels all predicted work engagement over time, but organizational-level resources were the strongest predictors. Thus, the available evidence suggests that resources at multiple levels serve as antecedents of employee engagement, and that organizational-level resources might be especially important.

One way to think about the many resources that have been linked to employee engagement is in relation to Kahn's (1990) three psychological conditions at the individual, group, leader, and organization level.

5.1.2   Psychological conditions as antecedents

As indicated in Chapter 3, the JD-R model classifies variables as job demands or job resources; however, it does not explain which resources are most important or why some resources might be more important than others (Saks & Gruman, 2014). As such, rather than being an *explanatory model* that explains the underlying processes involved in producing employee engagement, the JD-R model is more of a *descriptive model* that serves as a heuristic device and must be supplemented with other theoretical frameworks that can specify causal mechanisms (Schaufeli & Taris, 2013). In contrast, Kahn's (1990) theory serves as an explanatory theoretical framework that indicates that certain resources foster employee engagement because they satisfy the psychological conditions that are important for personal engagement (Saks & Gruman, 2014).

Crawford et al. (2014) note that most of the resources that foster employee engagement can fit within the three psychological conditions described by Kahn (1990). For example, a challenging job can foster psychological meaningfulness, organizational justice perceptions can foster psychological safety, and recovery opportunities can foster psychological availability.

Following the lead of Crawford et al. (2014), we discuss the antecedents of employee engagement in terms of the psychological conditions they satisfy. Additionally, in line with the reviews examining the drivers of employee engagement at different levels, within each antecedent condition we present representative drivers of employee engagement at the individual, group, leader, and organization levels.

5.1.2.1   Psychological meaningfulness

As indicated in Chapter 3, psychological meaningfulness refers to the extent to which people derive meaning from their work and feel that they are receiving a return on their investments for their performance. People experience meaningfulness when they feel worthwhile, useful, and valuable and when they are not taken for granted (Kahn, 1990).

Individual level. At the individual level, one of the drivers of psychological meaningfulness is job crafting, which refers to "the physical and cognitive changes individuals make in the tasks or relational boundaries of their work" (Wrzesniewski & Dutton, 2001, p.179). Tims et al. (2012) found that engagement was positively associated with job crafting in the form of increasing social resources (e.g., asking colleagues for advice), structural resources (e.g., trying to learn new things), and challenging job demands (e.g., voluntarily undertaking new tasks). In their meta-analysis of the effects of job crafting, Lichtenthaler and Fischbach (2019) found that promotion-focused job crafting, which reflects people's needs for growth and development, was positively related to engagement. As noted by Wrzesniewski and Dutton (2001), changing the work environment through job crafting can make the work more meaningful – a proposition that has been empirically confirmed (Tims et al., 2016).

Group level. Another source of meaning derives from the relationships people have at work. Kahn and Fellows (2011) suggest that work relationships foster meaningfulness when employees feel connected to others and are treated with respect and appreciation. Work relationships can validate the tasks employees perform and the roles they occupy, and can enhance meaningful identities (Kahn, 2007). Rosso et al. (2010) suggest that relationships at work foster meaningfulness by creating a sense of belongingness through social identification processes that allow employees to feel part of something special, and interpersonal connections that generate feelings of comfort and support. Relationships also influence meaningfulness via the active, constructive, sense-making processes through which employees interactively come to appraise the worth and meaning of their role, job, and self (Wrzesniewski et al., 2003).

Leader level. The ability to infuse meaning into organizational experience is a core component of leadership (Podolny et al., 2005), and a number of studies have demonstrated that leaders foster employee engagement partly by promoting a sense of meaningfulness at work. For example, in a sample of Australian employees, Ghadi et al. (2013) found that transformational leadership was associated with employees' perceptions of meaning in work, and meaning in work partially mediated the relationship between transformational leadership and engagement. Similar results have been observed in other studies demonstrating that meaningfulness is associated with various forms of leadership (e.g., engaging, empowering, ethical) and at least partially mediates the relationship between leadership and employee engagement (Demirtas et al., 2017; Lee et al., 2017; Rahmadani et al., 2019).

Organization level. As recognized in the job characteristics model (Hackman & Oldham, 1980), meaningfulness can be a product of the way work is designed. Kahn (1990) suggested that rich, complex projects that offer challenge, variety, autonomy, and clarity would foster meaningfulness and generate engagement. In support of these ideas, meta-analytic results demonstrate that a number of job characteristics including job complexity, task significance, variety, autonomy, and feedback are positively related to engagement (Christian et al., 2011; Crawford et al., 2010).

Saks (2019) found that among the five core job characteristics, skill variety is the main job characteristic associated with employee engagement. As suggested by Christian et al. (2011), the job characteristics most strongly related to employee engagement might be those that foster a sense of meaningfulness.

5.1.2.2 Psychological safety

As described in Chapter 3, psychological safety has to do with the extent to which individuals feel safe employing and expressing themselves at work without fear of negative consequences to their self-image, status, or career (Kahn, 1990).

Individual level. At the individual level, psychological safety is promoted by relatively stable dispositional characteristics that influence how comfortable employees feel expressing and employing themselves. For example, Albrecht et al. (2015) suggest that neuroticism might lead employees to view the work environment as threatening and unsafe, and therefore might be negatively associated with engagement. Indeed, empirical evidence reveals a negative relationship between neuroticism and engagement, or, conversely, a positive relationship between emotional stability and engagement (Young et al., 2018).

A meta-analysis of the relationship between employee engagement and various aspects of personality found that personality accounted for 48.1 percent of the variance in employee engagement. All of the Big 5 personality factors demonstrated associations with engagement, but positive affectivity, proactive personality, conscientiousness, and extraversion demonstrated the strongest relationships (Young et al., 2018).

Another dispositional factor that has implications for psychological safety is self-esteem. Individuals with fragile or low self-esteem have a tendency to view situations as less safe and react defensively (Kernis et al., 2008). Compared to people with secure high self-esteem, people with low or fragile self-esteem overgeneralize the negative implications of self-esteem threats and therefore find potential threats more threatening (Kernis et al., 2008). Although they do not assess the specific form of self-esteem, a handful of studies have demonstrated an association between self-esteem and engagement (Judge et al., 2003; Xanthopoulou et al., 2007).

Group level. At the group level, psychological safety is promoted by interpersonal relationships that offer support, trust, and an opportunity to fail without negative consequences (Kahn, 1990). May et al. (2004) found that co-worker relations that involved trusting each other, valuing others' input, and valuing others as individuals were positively related to psychological safety, although the relationship was not particularly strong. However, these results are bolstered by other studies demonstrating an association between co-worker social support and psychological safety (Guchait et al., 2014; Singh et al., 2017), and meta-analytic findings demonstrating that social support is positively associated with engagement (Crawford et al., 2010; Christian et al., 2011; Halbesleben, 2010). Crawford et al. (2014) note that the available evidence suggests that social support is, in fact, a "key factor associated with enhanced levels of employee engagement" (p.63).

Another group-level factor that can impact psychological safety is the organizational climate, which refers to employees' "shared perceptions regarding the policies, practices, and procedures that an organization rewards, supports, and expects" (Kuenzi & Schminke, 2009, p.637; Schneider & Reichers, 1983). One of the ways organizational climates support engagement is by fostering shared perceptions of psychological safety (Brown & Leigh, 1996). For example, Albrecht et al. (2018) found that an organizational engagement climate was positively associated with employee engagement. Meta-analytic results support these studies demonstrating that a positive organizational climate is associated with engagement (Crawford et al., 2010).

Leader level. Leaders are another key determinant of the degree to which employees feel safe employing and expressing themselves at work. To the extent that leaders set a tone that fosters openness and builds high-quality relationships with subordinates, employees are more likely to feel safe and become engaged. As Nembhard and Edmondson (2006) explain, "if a leader is democratic, supportive, and welcomes questions and challenges, team members are likely to feel greater psychological safety in the team and in their interactions with each other" (p.947). A number of empirical studies have found a positive relationship between various forms of leadership (e.g., authentic, ethical, inclusive, transformational) and psychological safety (e.g., Carmeli et al., 2010; Carmeli et al., 2013; Liu et al., 2015; Walumbwa & Schaubroeck, 2009), and psychological safety has been shown to mediate the relationship between humble leadership and employee engagement (Walters & Diab, 2016).

Meta-analytic results have found that employee engagement is consistently associated with leader-level variables that foster psychological safety such as leadership styles, supervisor support, and the quality of leadership-member relationships (Christian et al., 2011; Lesener et al., 2019).

Organization level. The structure and design elements of an organization can also impact psychological safety. As Kahn (1990) noted, psychological safety is promoted by situations that are trustworthy, secure, and predictable. Organizations that have policies that are capricious or poorly enforced will undermine safety whereas those that enact policies that are fair and reliable will promote it. Research has found that both procedural justice, which concerns the fairness of the methods used to make decisions (Colquitt, 2001), and distributive justice, which involves the distribution of outcomes in a manner consistent with allocation norms such as equity (Colquitt, 2001), are associated with psychological safety and engagement (J. Chen et al., 2018; Saks, 2006; Haynie et al., 2016).

Considered from the opposite angle, organizational-level issues that undermine security and predictability, and thus compromise psychological safety, can inhibit employee engagement. Meta-analytic results demonstrate that administrative hassles, role conflict, and role overload are negatively associated with employee engagement (Crawford et al., 2010).

5.1.2.3   Psychological availability

As described in Chapter 3, psychological availability is the belief that one has the physical, emotional, and psychological resources to invest oneself in the performance of a role and to be engaged in a particular moment.

Individual level. At the individual level, psychological availability is promoted by personal resources which are relatively malleable and amenable to development. For example, Chan et al. (2017) found that self-efficacy was associated with work engagement through the mediating effects of family and work demands and work-life balance. The authors concluded that self-efficacy serves as a resource that helps employees manage demands and promote well-being in the form of engagement. Similarly, Ouweneel et al. (2012) found that daily levels of hope assessed before work corresponded with daily levels of employee engagement assessed after work.

The resources of self-efficacy and hope, along with optimism and resilience, have been synthesized into a higher-order construct called psychological capital (PsyCap; Luthans & Youssef-Morgan, 2017). Alessandri et al. (2018) found that not only was PsyCap positively related to employee engagement, but changes in PsyCap paralleled changes in engagement. Personal resources such as optimism, self-efficacy, and resilience can not only act as predictors of engagement but can also help employees mobilize other resources (Bakker & Demerouti, 2008).

Employees will also foster higher levels of engagement if they are able to replenish their depleted personal resources while away from work. Sonnentag (2003) found that employees manifest higher levels of engagement when they report feeling recovered in the morning as a result of participating in replenishing leisure activities the day before.

Group level. Kahn (1990) suggested that availability is compromised by distractions and insecurities that consume people and leave them with fewer resources with which to engage themselves at work. For instance, employees may become distracted by concerns about their compatibility with their work group (i.e., person-group or PG fit) or organization (i.e., person-organization or PO fit; Kristoff-Brown et al., 2005). A high degree of compatibility should therefore reduce distractions and insecurities, promote psychological availability, and increase engagement. Supporting this idea, Cai et al. (2018) found that PG fit was related to engagement in a sample of employees from a Chinese IT company. Saks and Gruman (2011) found that person-job (PJ) fit was positively related to engagement in a sample of organizational newcomers. Similar results were obtained by Alfes et al. (2016) who found a positive relationship between PO fit and engagement in a sample of employees from the waste collection industry in the U.K.

Leader level. Leaders play a significant role in promoting psychological availability by enhancing employee resources and minimizing demands (e.g., work-home conflict). Schaufeli (2015) found that resources mediated the relationship between engaging leadership and engagement and suggested that engaging leaders foster engagement by monitoring demands and increasing organizational, work, developmental, and social resources. Leaders also impact employees' personal resources. Tims et al. (2011) found that transformational leadership was positively associated with self-efficacy and optimism, and optimism mediated the relationship between transformational leadership and engagement. A handful of studies have shown that leadership is associated with employees' PsyCap which, in turn, generates engagement (S. Chen, 2015; Li, 2019; Xu et al., 2017). For example, Park et al. (2017) found that empowering leadership was associated with PsyCap, and PsyCap mediated the relationship between empowering leadership and engagement.

Basic psychological needs (i.e., autonomy, competence, relatedness) can be considered resources in that they are "essential nutriments," like water and food, that are required in order to thrive (Ryan & Deci, 2000, p.75). In two samples, Rahmadani et al. (2019) found that engaging leadership was associated with the satisfaction of basic psychological needs and that the satisfaction of these needs mediated the relationship between engaging leadership and engagement. Similarly, Kovjanic et al. (2013) found that transformational leadership was associated with the satisfaction of all three needs, and the relationship between transformational leadership and engagement was mediated by satisfaction of the needs for competence and relatedness. As suggested by Serrano and Reichard (2011), one of the ways leaders promote engagement is by enhancing employees' resources.

Organization level. At the organization level, human resource management (HRM) practices can influence psychological availability by impacting the resources available to employees. For example, work-life balance practices such as flextime provide employees with greater control over the resource of time. In a review of the empirical literature, Wood et al. (2020) suggested that work-life balance can foster employee engagement because it provides resources that allow employees to engage in their work.

Training and development opportunities can also impact availability by allowing employees to build new resources. In their meta-analysis, Lesener et al. (2019) found that organizational resources including development opportunities were positively related to engagement. Other meta-analytic evidence shows that this relationship holds when the association between development opportunities and engagement is examined in isolation (Crawford et al., 2010). Mentoring is another HRM practice that promotes development and can provide employees with resources in the form of information, feedback, and career advice. A number of studies have found that mentoring is associated with employee engagement (Ghosh et al., 2018; Wang et al., 2018; Whitten, 2016).

HRM architecture includes compensation systems that provide material resources in the form of rewards. Meta-analytic evidence provides tentative support for the idea that rewards and recognition are positively related to employee engagement (Crawford et al., 2010). Considered from a broader perspective, Zhong et al. (2016) found that high performance HR practices were associated with engagement directly and also indirectly through perceived organizational support.

5.1.3   Antecedents of employee engagement with referents other than the self

The vast majority of studies on the antecedents of employee engagement focus on the self as the referent. However, as noted in Chapter 4, some studies have examined other referents of engagement such as one's co-workers or team members. These studies tend to examine antecedents of engagement that are comparable to those investigated with the self as referent and generate similar results.

For example, Tims et al. (2013) modified the UWES to form a team work engagement scale and found that team job crafting was positively related to team work engagement. Using a similar method to assess team work engagement, Torrente et al. (2012) found that team social resources including a supportive team climate were related to team work engagement. Barrick et al. (2015) developed a measure of collective organizational engagement that was based on Kahn's (1990) formulation of the construct but with items assessing the engagement of employees in the organization (e.g., *"Nearly everyone at work feels passionate and enthusiastic about our jobs"*). They found that organizational resources including job characteristics, HRM practices, and transformational leadership were positively related to collective organizational engagement.

Thus, there is evidence that many of the antecedents that have been found to influence employee engagement when the self is the referent also influence engagement with other referents, and these antecedents fit within the psychological conditions of meaningfulness, safety, and availability. However, changing the referent might have some consequences for the antecedents of engagement. For example, different dynamics are involved when the referent of engagement is a collective as opposed to an individual and this might make certain antecedents more salient and important. As Costa et al. (2014b, p.416) suggest:

> Whereas individual work engagement is essentially dependent on job resources and demands, team work engagement, as a collective construct, is dependent on the individual actions and cycles of interaction responsible for creating a shared pattern of behavior (Morgeson & Hoffman, 1999). Therefore, with the same resources and in an equally challenging environment, some teams might develop a higher level of engagement than others, because the affective, cognitive, and motivational outcomes of different patterns of interaction are likely to be different.

Costa et al. (2014b) note that collective engagement depends primarily on the dynamics of the team, not job resources. As such, the antecedent factors that drive collective forms of engagement might be those that most strongly impact group dynamics. When the referent of engagement is not at the individual level, variables such as leadership that fosters a team orientation, team climate, and interdependence (Costa et al., 2014b) take on new relevance because of the ways they impact processes and the psychological conditions which support or hinder group interactions.

A related notion is that one antecedent of the various referents of employee engagement might be other referents. For example, employees might report lower (higher) levels of engagement if they believe that the teams of which they are a part display low (high) levels of team engagement. A handful of studies have shown evidence of crossover effects such that engagement at the group level is associated with engagement at the individual level (Bakker et al., 2006; Tims et al., 2013).

5.1.4   Antecedents of employee engagement: summary

Many variables have been studied as antecedents of employee engagement, and these variables can be classified according to Kahn's (1990) psychological conditions. Table 5.1 presents a list of variables that have been shown to serve as antecedents of employee engagement, sorted by the psychological antecedents they satisfy. Note that some variables can satisfy multiple psychological conditions. For example, opportunity for development can promote psychological availability because it allows

Table 5.1   Antecedents of employee engagement

Psychological meaningfulness	Psychological safety	Psychological availability
Job crafting	Personal dispositions	Role overload
Job enrichment	Co-worker relations	Work-role conflict
Job challenge	Leader-member exchange	Family-work conflict
Job responsibility	Workplace climate	Work resources
Autonomy	Social support	Personal resources
Skill variety	Supervisor support	Need satisfaction
Task significance	Perceived organizational	Time urgency
Task identity	support	Off-work recovery
Job complexity	Distributive justice	Human resource
Leadership	Procedural justice	practices
Feedback from the job	Job security	Job demands
Feedback from others	Role clarity	Administrative
Work role fit	Co-worker norms	hassles
Opportunities for		Physical demands
development		Work conditions
Rewards and recognition		Outside activities
Participation		
Problem solving		

employees to build resources but it can also promote meaningfulness because it permits individuals to invest in themselves and potentially receive a return on that investment. Attesting to the varied impact of antecedents, in a diary study Fletcher et al. (2018) found that the work context variables of task clarity, access to resources, and co-worker support were associated with all three psychological conditions.

The antecedents presented in this chapter represent job and personal resources that can foster employee engagement. We should recall, however, that, as noted in Chapter 3, job demands can also serve as antecedents of employee engagement (Crawford et al., 2010). Hindrance demands (e.g., role conflict) can compromise employee engagement whereas challenge demands (e.g., time urgency) can promote it. In addition, job resources can interact with job demands in generating employee engagement. Bakker and Demerouti (2017) note that job resources are particularly important when job demands are high. In essence, resources serve as a buffer against the strain produced by hindrance demands and boost the motivational impact of challenge demands (Bakker & Demerouti, 2017).

5.2   Consequences of employee engagement

A variety of consequences have been found to be associated with employee engagement (e.g., Bailey et al., 2017; Halbesleben, 2010; Rich et al., 2010). As was the case with antecedents, the vast majority of studies on employee engagement have examined outcomes at the individual level. However, there are some studies that have examined outcomes at other levels, sometimes with referents other than the individual. Therefore, we can categorize the consequences of employee engagement at the individual, group, and organization levels.

5.2.1   Individual-level outcomes

At the individual level, employee engagement has been associated with job attitudes such as job satisfaction, employee well-being, behaviors such as organizational citizenship behavior (OCB), as well as job performance. With respect to job attitudes, many studies have found that employee engagement is positively related to job satisfaction and organizational commitment, and negatively related to turnover intentions (Bailey et al., 2017; Cole et al., 2012; Halbesleben, 2010; Saks, 2006).

With respect to well-being, in a three-phase longitudinal investigation of Finnish dentists, Hakanen and Schaufeli (2012) found that employee engagement consistently predicted lower depressive symptoms and higher life satisfaction. In their review, Bailey et al. (2017) reported that employee engagement is negatively related to stress/burnout, and positively related to life satisfaction and positive affect. Meta-analytic evidence demonstrates that employee engagement is positively related to health and negatively related to health complaints (Cole et al., 2012; Halbesleben, 2010). This might help to explain why Schaufeli et al. (2009) found that engagement predicted a lower frequency of involuntary absenteeism over the course of a year.

With respect to task performance, employee engagement is associated with persistence (Kovjanic et al., 2013) and innovation (Kwon & Kim, 2020). Yalabik et al. (2013) found that engagement was positively related to job performance indexed by supervisors' performance appraisal ratings. Similarly, Alessandri et al. (2018) found that engagement was positively related to employees' supervisor-rated job performance, and engagement mediated the relationship between PsyCap and job performance. In their review, Bailey et al. (2017) reported a positive relationship between employee engagement and task performance in every study they examined.

In their survey of research on the relationship between employee engagement and performance, Kim et al. (2012) concluded that "work engagement has direct and/or indirect positive effects on employees' performance within organizations and plays a mediating role in the relationship between antecedents (efficacy, coaching, and colleague support) and performance" (p.265). Based on their meta-analytic review, Christian et al. (2011) estimated the mean corrected correlation between employee engagement and task performance to be .43 and concluded that engagement partially mediates the relationship between antecedents and task performance.

Employee engagement is also related to extra-role performance and organizational citizenship behavior (Christian et al., 2011; Rich et al., 2010; Saks, 2006). For example, Eldor and Harpaz (2016) found that engagement mediated the relationship between learning climate and extra-role performance. In their meta-analysis, Christian et al. (2011) estimated the mean corrected correlation between engagement and contextual performance to be .34 and concluded that engagement partially mediates the relationship between antecedents and contextual performance. In their review, Bailey et al. (2017) found nine studies that reported a significant relationship between employee engagement and organizational citizenship behavior. Employee engagement has also been found to be related to low levels of deviant work behavior (Shantz et al., 2016).

5.2.2 Group-level outcomes

Group-level outcomes have generally been examined with respect to employee engagement with the group or team as the referent. The majority of these investigations have examined group performance as an outcome variable. For example, Mäkikangas et al. (2016) found that individual and team engagement was positively related to perceived team performance, and Tims et al. (2013) found that team work engagement partially mediated the relationship between team job crafting and self-rated team performance. Costa et al. (2015) found that team work engagement was related to objective team performance, and Torrente et al. (2012) found that team work engagement fully mediated the relationship between team social resources and supervisor ratings of team performance.

In their review of the literature on engagement and higher-level performance outcomes such as organizational or team performance, Bailey et al. (2017) noted that "the majority of reviewed studies showed a positive link between engagement and a variety of performance outcomes, such as team performance ..." (p.40). Team engagement has also been shown to be positively associated with team satisfaction (Guchait, 2016) and team task creativity (Rodríguez-Sánchez et al., 2017).

5.2.3   Organization-level outcomes

As we noted in Chapter 1, one of the reasons that employee engagement matters is because of its potential to impact organization outcomes such as firm performance. In one of the first studies to test relationships between engagement and organization outcomes based on data from 36 companies in diverse industries, Harter et al. (2002) found that engagement was associated with productivity, profitability, and customer satisfaction.

More recently, Xanthopoulou et al. (2009b) found that daily levels of work engagement were positively associated with daily financial performance at three branches of a fast-food restaurant. In a sample of publicly traded organizations, Schneider et al. (2017) found that workforce engagement (the aggregate of the work engagement of individual employees in an organization) predicted subsequent company performance measured in terms of return on assets (ROA), net margin, customer satisfaction, and company reputation. Similarly, Barrick et al. (2015) found that collective organizational engagement (shared perceptions of organizational members that members of the organization are, as a whole, physically, cognitively, and emotionally invested in their work) was positively related to firm performance measured as ROA. They also found that collective organizational engagement mediated the relationship between organizational resources and firm performance.

In summary, several studies have reported positive relationships between employee engagement and organization-level outcomes. However, as noted by Schaufeli (2014), caution is warranted in interpreting many organization-level studies because the research is often industry led, lacks transparency and rigor, and the measures of engagement often overlap with the outcomes or antecedents of engagement.

5.2.4   Consequences of employee engagement: summary

As shown in Table 5.2, employee engagement has been found to be related to a number of outcomes at the individual, group, and organization levels. Most of the research on this topic has investigated outcomes at the individual level, highlighting the opportunity for more research at other levels. However, overall, the available research evidence indicates that employee engagement can promote desirable individual-level outcomes such as job satisfaction, OCB, job performance, and employee health and well-being; group-level outcomes such as team performance and team satisfaction; and organization-level outcomes such as organizational performance. Thus, employee engagement appears to be a significant driver of subjective and objective indicators of success at all levels of an organization.

Table 5.2   Consequences of employee engagement

Individual-level outcomes	Group-level outcomes	Organization-level outcomes
Attitudes	Attitudes	Performance
Intentions	Intentions	Productivity
Behavior	Behavior	Profitability
Performance	Performance	Customer satisfaction
Health and wellness	Health and wellness	

5.3   Conclusion

As shown in Figure 5.1, employee engagement has been found to be related to a number of antecedents and consequences. The antecedents, which are often thought of as resources, can occur at different levels (individual, group, leader, and organization) and can be grouped within Kahn's (1990) three psychological antecedents, which offers a theoretical framework for explaining why certain resources generate employee engagement. Employee engagement has been found to be related to many consequences at the individual, group, and organization levels, and there is some research that has examined antecedents and consequences with different referents.

However, we must be cautious of drawing conclusions about these relationships because most of them are based on studies that used the UWES or a modified version of it and, as discussed in Chapter 4, the UWES has been shown to overlap with other constructs and might not represent the best or purest measure of employee engagement. Additionally, there is little research on antecedents and consequences of employee engagement targets other than employee job and work engagement. We will revisit this topic in Chapter 9.

Figure 5.1   Antecedents and consequences of employee engagement

6 Getting newcomers engaged

Newcomers to organizations are a unique group of employees that deserve special attention when it comes to employee engagement. This is because newcomers are more open and willing to become engaged than more tenured employees who are more set in their ways. In other words, it will be more difficult to engage employees who have been disengaged for many years than newcomers who want to fit into their new job and organization. Thus, newcomers are more likely to respond positively to initiatives and programs to improve engagement. As a result, organizations have a window of opportunity to get newcomers engaged as soon as they enter the organization and to ensure that they stay engaged. The most important and critical time for getting newcomers engaged is during the initial entry and socialization period (Saks & Gruman, 2011).

At the same time, there is ample evidence to suggest that although newcomers enter organizations excited and enthusiastic about their new job and ready, able, and willing to be highly engaged employees (*engagement readiness*), their engagement will fluctuate and likely decline during the entry-socialization process. Thus, a key issue is how to get newcomers engaged as soon as they enter the organization and to maintain and develop high levels of newcomer engagement after the initial entry-socialization period.

In this chapter, we discuss the entry and socialization process and how it can be designed so that newcomers are engaged as soon as they enter the organization and stay engaged throughout the socialization period. This requires an understanding of newcomer engagement maintenance curves and socialization resources theory (SRT) which will be discussed in this chapter. We begin with a consideration of the entry experience and organizational socialization.

6.1   The entry experience and organizational socialization

The organizational entry process has often been described as anxiety-provoking and stressful for newcomers (Saks & Ashforth, 2000). Katz (1985) described the transition into a new organization as one that places the newcomer in a "high anxiety-producing situation" (p.137). *Organizational socialization*, or what is sometimes called *on-boarding*, refers to the "process by which an individual comes to appreciate the values, abilities, expected behaviors, and social knowledge essential for assuming an organizational role and for participating as an organizational member" (Louis, 1980, pp.229–230). Thus, it is primarily a learning process that requires newcomers to acquire information about their job, role, group, and the organization (Klein & Weaver, 2000).

The most often used theory to describe newcomers' entry experiences and the socialization process is *uncertainty reduction theory*. The basic idea is that when newcomers enter organizations, they experience high levels of uncertainty and are motivated to reduce their uncertainty so that the work environment and the organization are more predictable, understandable, and controllable. As newcomers acquire information and reduce their uncertainty, their job performance and job attitudes will improve, and they will be less likely to leave the organization (Saks & Ashforth, 1997). Thus, according to uncertainty reduction theory, the major goal of newcomers is to reduce their uncertainty (Saks & Gruman, 2018).

As a result, the emphasis of socialization research has been on programs and practices that are designed to provide newcomers with information to reduce job demands (e.g., role ambiguity and role conflict) and uncertainty. For example, socialization tactics, which have to do with the ways in which newcomers' entry experiences are structured, have been found to be strong predictors of many socialization outcomes such as job satisfaction, organizational commitment, intentions to quit, and job performance (Saks et al., 2007). Institutionalized socialization tactics which involve a structured and formal socialization process have been found to be associated with positive socialization outcomes in part because they provide newcomers with information that reduces uncertainty (Saks et al., 2007).

However, in a study on socialization tactics and newcomer engagement, Saks and Gruman (2011) did not find a direct relationship between socialization tactics and newcomer engagement. Rather, they found that socialization tactics have an indirect relationship to engagement that operates through person-job (PJ) fit perceptions, positive emotions, and self-efficacy. In other words, socialization tactics (institutionalized tactics) were positively related to PJ fit perceptions, positive emotions, and self-efficacy, which were in turn positively related to newcomer engagement. However, a study on newcomers working in hotels in China did find a significant relationship between institutionalized socialization tactics and work engagement (Song et al., 2015).

Saks and Gruman (2011) speculated on why they did not find that socialization tactics were directly related to newcomer engagement. They suggested that socialization tactics might not lead to Kahn's (1990) three psychological conditions for engagement (meaningfulness, safety, and availability), and socialization tactics might not provide newcomers with the resources that are important and necessary for them to be engaged in their job. They noted the need to identify socialization practices that are particularly important for newcomer engagement.

Research on organizational socialization has also found that entry stressors can have a strong negative effect on newcomers' adjustment and socialization. For example, a study by Saks and Ashforth (2000) found that four entry stressors (role conflict, role ambiguity, role overload, and unmet expectations) were negatively related to job satisfaction, organizational commitment, organizational identification, and job performance and positively related to frustration, intention to quit, and stress symptoms. They also found that the stressors were much more strongly related to newcomer adjustment than newcomer dispositions. Saks and Ashforth (2000) concluded that newcomer adjustment and socialization is largely the result of the situation or the organizational setting that newcomers encounter during the first four months of organizational entry. They suggested that organizations reduce the stressors that newcomers encounter when they enter organizations. Although Saks and Ashforth (2000) did not measure engagement, the stressors they measured are similar to the job demands that have been found to be negatively related to employee engagement (Crawford et al., 2010).

In summary, research on organizational socialization has focused on providing newcomers with information and knowledge to reduce their uncertainty and facilitate their learning of socialization content. However, this does not appear to be an effective means of getting newcomers engaged. Therefore, in the next section we consider how existing models and theories of employee engagement might be useful for understanding how to engage newcomers.

6.2   Kahn's (1990) psychological conditions and newcomer engagement

When considering the engagement of newcomers, Kahn's (1990) theory seems to be especially relevant with respect to the psychological conditions that lead to engagement. As indicated in Chapter 3, Kahn (1990) identified three psychological conditions that are associated with personal engagement: psychological meaningfulness, psychological safety, and psychological availability. Kahn (1990) also noted that individuals ask themselves three questions to determine the extent to which they will choose to be engaged or disengaged: "(1) How meaningful is it for me to bring myself into this performance? (2) How safe is it to do so? and (3) How available am I to do so?" (p.703).

The three psychological conditions seem to be especially important for newcomers who are anxious and uncertain about their new job and role. Thus, based on Kahn's (1990) theory we can expect newcomers to be more engaged when they feel worthwhile, useful, and valuable and not taken for granted (psychological meaningfulness); when they feel they can be themselves and not fear negative consequences to their self-image, status, or career (psychological safety); and when they have the physical, emotional, and psychological resources to invest themselves in their new job and role within the organization and cope with job demands (psychological availability).

According to Kahn's (1990) research, newcomers are most likely to experience psychological meaningfulness when they are assigned tasks that have some variety and autonomy; when they identify with their role and it is attractive and fits with their preferred self-image, and when their role has some status or influence that makes them feel valued, valuable, important, and needed; and when they have rewarding interpersonal work interactions with co-workers and clients as part of their job. Among these factors, enriched work tasks that consist of interesting and challenging work and frequent interactions with others seem to be especially important for newcomers to experience psychological meaningfulness.

Newcomers are most likely to experience psychological safety when they have interpersonal relationships that are open, supportive, trusting, and flexible; when they can safely express themselves; when they can try things and fail without fearing negative consequences; when they have some control over their work; and when they stay within the boundaries of organizational norms and expectations. In addition, supportive and trusting management is also important for newcomers' psychological safety. Interactions and relationship development with organizational members seems to be especially important for newcomers to experience psychological safety.

Newcomers are most likely to experience psychological availability when they have the physical and emotional resources required to invest themselves and engage in their job and role; when they feel secure and confident about their job and status and about their fit with the organization; and when they are not overly preoccupied by issues and events in their lives outside of work. Kahn (1990) found that psychological availability was negatively affected by distractions that deplete an individual's physical and emotional energy as well as individual insecurity and distractions outside of work. Thus, minimizing newcomers' job demands and providing them with the resources to perform their job and cope with job demands seems to be especially important for fostering newcomers' psychological availability.

6.2.1   Summary

In summary, using Kahn's (1990) theory of personal engagement newcomers must experience the three psychological conditions that are important for engagement. Therefore, newcomers should be provided with work tasks and assignments that are interesting and challenging; they should have opportunities to interact and develop relationships with organizational members; and job demands should be minimized and they should be provided with resources so that they will be able cope with job demands and perform their job and work roles effectively.

Although Kahn's (1990) theory provides a good foundation for understanding what is required for newcomer engagement, his study did not focus on newcomers so it is not clear what socialization-specific resources are most important for newcomers or when such resources should be provided to them. Thus, Kahn's theory (1990) provides a good starting point, however, it is not geared specifically to the engagement of newcomers.

6.3   The job demands-resources model and newcomer engagement

The job demands-resources (JD-R) model can also be used to understand the engagement of newcomers. Recall from Chapter 3 that the JD-R model divides the work environment into job demands and job resources. Job resources are motivational and can lead to positive attitudes, behavior, and well-being while high job demands exhaust employees' physical and mental resources and can lead to a depletion of energy and health problems. Job resources are also important because they help individuals cope with job demands and they buffer the negative effects of job demands on work engagement (Bakker & Demerouti, 2007, 2008).

As indicated in the previous chapter, job resources are positively related to work engagement and (hindrance) job demands are negatively related to work engagement. Resources such as social support, skill variety, autonomy, and performance feedback have been found to be positively related to work engagement while job demands such as work pressure have been found to be related to employee burnout and disengagement (Bakker & Demerouti, 2007, 2008). Other job resources that have been found to be positively related to work engagement include opportunities for development, rewards and recognition, a positive workplace climate, and work role fit. Hindrance job demands that are negatively related to work engagement include administrative hassles, emotional conflict, organizational politics, resource inadequacies, role conflict, and role overload (Crawford et al., 2010).

6.3.1   Summary

In summary, the JD-R model also provides a good starting point for understanding how to get newcomers engaged. According to the JD-R model, this involves providing various resources to newcomers and minimizing or eliminating hindrance job demands. However, this is a very general approach for developing the engagement of newcomers. It does not indicate what resources are of particular importance for the engagement of newcomers, and it does not indicate when various resources should be provided to newcomers during the organizational entry-socialization process. A more informative and effective approach is to identify socialization-specific resources and to provide them at certain times during the organizational entry-socialization process. This requires a consideration of newcomer engagement maintenance curves and socialization-specific resources.

6.4 Newcomer engagement maintenance curves

Kahn's (1990) theory and the JD-R model are helpful for understanding how to engage newcomers (e.g., focus on psychological conditions, provide job resources, minimize or eliminate hindrance job demands); however, they are limited because they do not focus on specific socialization resources and they do not consider how newcomers' engagement can change during the organizational entry process.

Many studies have found that soon after organizational entry, there is a decline in newcomers' perceptions of job attractiveness, job satisfaction, organizational commitment, and motivation (Boswell et al., 2005; Boswell et al., 2009; Lawler et al., 1975; Van Maanen, 1975; Vroom & Deci, 1971). For example, Boswell et al. (2009) found that newcomers' job satisfaction declines following organizational entry tapering off over the course of a year. Further, the decline in job satisfaction has been found to be related to higher turnover intentions and newcomer turnover (Wang et al., 2017). Boswell et al. (2005) refer to this decline in newcomers' job satisfaction following organizational entry as a "hangover effect."

The hangover effect occurs when the initial high and positive attitudes associated with starting a new job (the honeymoon effect) wear off as newcomers experience the reality shock of becoming familiar with their job, experiencing its more mundane and unpleasant features, and realizing that the reality of their new job does not live up to what they had expected (Boswell et al., 2005; Wang et al., 2017).

Maia et al. (2016) found that the affective organizational commitment of most newcomers declined during the first year but increased for a minority of newcomers who had greater person-job fit and job challenge. This finding suggests that certain work conditions can reduce the hangover effect and maintain high levels of organizational commitment. Similarly, a study by Wang et al. (2017) found that very high levels of social tactics (social cues and available role models) can reverse the hangover effect and reduce newcomer turnover.

It is also likely that newcomers' engagement declines following organizational entry and during the socialization process. Newcomers enter organizations with high expectations, and they are excited and enthusiastic about starting a new job. Thus, most newcomers will begin their new jobs with a high level of *engagement readiness*. That is, they will be eager, willing, and ready to fully engage themselves in their new job and role. However, just like job attractiveness, job satisfaction, organizational commitment, and motivation, their engagement is also likely to decline during the socialization period. In other words, many newcomers can be expected to experience an *engagement hangover effect*.

However, as indicated earlier, Maia et al. (2016) found that the affective organizational commitment of some newcomers increased, and this was due to greater person-job fit and job challenge. Thus, it is likely that the engagement of newcomers can also be prevented from declining and might even increase during the socialization process and this will likely depend on newcomers' socialization experiences. Therefore, the socialization process needs to be designed specifically to maintain and develop newcomers' engagement.

Before discussing how socialization can prevent a decline in newcomers' engagement it is worth noting the different ways that newcomers' engagement can fluctuate following organizational entry and during the socialization process. We can better understand how newcomers' engagement can change and fluctuate throughout this period by considering *newcomer engagement maintenance curves*.

Newcomer engagement maintenance curves indicate the different patterns and changes in newcomers' engagement during the first year of organizational-entry and socialization. Saks and Gruman (2018) described different engagement maintenance curves that represent the different ways that newcomers' engagement can fluctuate during the first year of organizational entry. Each curve assumes that newcomers enter organizations with a reasonably high level of engagement readiness and that newcomers are highly engaged when they begin their new job. Once newcomers enter the organization their engagement can increase, decrease, or stay the same.

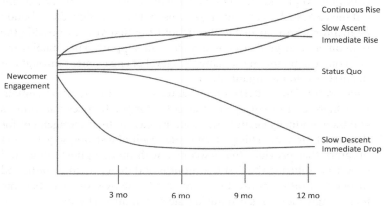

Figure 6.1   Newcomer engagement maintenance curves

As shown in Figure 6.1, there are at least six possible newcomer engagement maintenance curves:

1. *Immediate Drop.* In the worst-case scenario, there is an immediate drop in newcomer engagement following organizational entry. This is likely the result of little to no socialization resources being provided to newcomers which leaves them alone and unable and unwilling to stay engaged. These newcomers become disengaged very soon after entry.
2. *Slow Descent.* This pattern is typical of research on job attitudes and the hangover effect in which there is a slow decline over the course of the first year. Thus, newcomers are initially highly engaged for the first several months following entry. However, after several months their engagement begins to decline and eventually tapers off at a much lower level, at which point the newcomer is no longer engaged. This pattern is typical of short and limited socialization programs that maintain the newcomers' engagement for a few months, but once

formal socialization ends, and the newcomer is left on his or her own, their engagement begins to fall. This pattern is the result of a short and incomplete socialization program that is lacking in resources and attention to newcomers' needs.

3. *Status Quo.* This pattern is representative of newcomers who maintain their relatively high level of entry engagement throughout the first year in the organization. This reflects a socialization program that continues to provide the newcomer with various resources throughout the year, such as training programs and being assigned to a buddy or mentor who is available throughout the first year to provide the newcomer with guidance, assistance, and support. This enables the newcomer to maintain the same high level of engagement throughout the first year in the organization.

4. *Slow Ascent.* This pattern is represented by newcomers who maintain their high level of engagement at entry for the first several months and then gradually begin to show an increase in their engagement for the rest of the year. This pattern is the result of a strong socialization program that provides the newcomer with many opportunities and experiences during the first few months and then provides continued formal and informal practices that enable the newcomer to become increasingly more engaged during the rest of the first year.

5. *Immediate Rise.* This pattern is representative of newcomers whose engagement increases during the first several months and then tapers off at a level that is higher than what it was at entry. This is the result of a very strong socialization program that enables newcomers to become highly engaged early on and to then maintain that high level of engagement throughout the first year.

6. *Continuous Rise.* This pattern represents the most desirable as it depicts newcomers who continue to increase their engagement throughout the first year. This is the result of a very rigorous and comprehensive socialization program that involves many different formal and informal program elements that provide newcomers with many resources throughout the first year. These socialization programs are designed to keep newcomers engaged throughout the first year of organizational entry and beyond.

These six engagement maintenance curves demonstrate the various fluctuations that can occur with respect to the engagement of newcomers during the organizational entry-socialization process. Ideally, organizations want at the very least to have newcomers maintain their high levels of entry engagement. However, the most desirable patterns are those in which newcomers' engagement increases and remains high throughout the first year. Thus, a key issue for organizations is how to prevent a decline in newcomers' engagement and, more importantly, how to increase it throughout the first year.

Kahn's (1990) theory and the JD-R model are too general to provide clear answers to these questions. What is required is a theory that is more focused on the organizational socialization process and is more specific about how to socialize and engage newcomers. A new theory of organizational socialization that describes how to socialize newcomers throughout the first year of organizational entry is *socialization resources theory* (SRT). In the next section, we describe socialization resources theory and newcomer engagement.

6.5 Socialization resources theory and newcomer engagement

Saks and Gruman (2012) developed socialization resources theory (SRT) based on a review of the academic and practitioner literature on organizational socialization. The main premise of SRT theory is that newcomers require a variety of resources throughout the organizational entry-socialization process to manage the transition to a new job and/or organization and for a successful adjustment and socialization. They identified 17 socialization resources that should be provided to newcomers at various time periods throughout the organizational entry-socialization process.

The focus of SRT is socialization-specific resources that are important for newcomers' adjustment and socialization and that can be provided to newcomers by the organization and organizational members. With respect to engagement, job resources have been found to be more important than job demands (Bakker & Demerouti, 2008), although it is important to minimize or remove stressful job demands. Thus, what is most important for maintaining and developing newcomers' engagement is providing socialization resources throughout the entry-socialization process.

SRT describes the resources that should be provided to newcomers at four different times during the entry-socialization process. Thus, it serves as a useful theory to describe the resources that newcomers require to become highly engaged throughout their first year. In total, Saks and Gruman (2012) identified the following 17 socialization resources: (1) Anticipatory socialization; (2) Formal orientation; (3) Proactive encouragement; (4) Formal assistance; (5) Social events; (6) Socialization agents; (7) Supervisor support; (8) Relationship development; (9) Job resources; (10) Personal planning; (11) Training programs; (12) Assignments; (13) Information; (14) Feedback; (15) Recognition and appreciation; (16) Follow-up; and (17) Program evaluation.

The 17 socialization resources are to be provided to newcomers at four time periods: (1) Prior to organizational entry; (2) Immediately after organizational entry; (3) Following formal orientation; and (4) At the end of the socialization period. Thus, the socialization resources can be aligned with the newcomer engagement maintenance curves such that the injection of socialization resources at each period helps to maintain and build newcomers' engagement.

Following are the socialization resources for each of the four time periods:

Socialization resources prior to organizational entry. The first resource that newcomers should receive occurs before they actually enter the organization (*anticipatory socialization*). Prior to the first day of work, newcomers should be contacted by the organization at which time they receive a welcome message and are provided with contact information if they have questions, concerns, or need assistance. They are also invited to attend social events so that they can meet other newcomers and members of the organization and begin to develop relationships and meet organizational members who can provide them with support, guidance, and assistance. This also helps to build newcomers' interest and excitement for their new job and organization and enhances their engagement readiness. Thus, it ensures that newcomers will enter the organization ready, willing, and able to be highly engaged.

Socialization resources immediately after organizational entry. It is important to provide newcomers with a variety of resources as soon as they enter the organization to prevent a decline in their engagement and to begin to build and develop it. These resources include *formal orientation* programs that provide newcomers with information about their job, role, and the organization; encouraging newcomers to be proactive (*proactive encouragement*) by asking co-workers for information, feedback, and assistance, and by developing relationships with members of the organization; and assigning newcomers a buddy or mentor (*formal assistance*) who will be available throughout the entry-socialization process to provide the newcomer with social support and other resources such as feedback, information, and recognition.

With respect to the assignment of mentors and buddies, it would be wise to choose highly engaged members of the organization as there is some evidence for contagion or crossover effects in which the engagement of workers can influence the engagement of their colleagues or team members, especially when they interact and communicate more frequently (Bakker & Demerouti, 2008; Bakker et al., 2006; Bakker & Xanthopoulou, 2009). In other words, the level of engagement of mentors and buddies is likely to transfer to newcomers such that newcomers are likely to become as engaged or disengaged as their mentors and buddies. Therefore, highly engaged employees should be chosen as mentors and buddies, and they should frequently interact and communicate with newcomers.

Socialization resources following formal orientation. Once the formal orientation program ends it is important to continue to provide newcomers with resources. Failure to continue to provide newcomers with resources at the end of the formal orientation program is likely to result in a drop in their engagement (the slow descent maintenance curve). The socialization resources at this time are classified into two dimensions: social capital resources and work-related resources.

Social capital resources are important for providing newcomers with social support throughout the entry-socialization process which is one of the most important predictors of engagement. In fact, social support from the organization, supervisors, and co-workers has been found to be positively related to employee engagement (Crawford et al., 2010).

Social capital resources include *social events* (formal events and activities) that provide newcomers with opportunities to meet and interact with other members of the organization; members of the organization acting as *socialization agents* by going out of their way to get to know, help, and assist newcomers; supervisors who keep track of how their newcomers are adjusting and provide them with continuous and ongoing support, guidance, assistance, and resources (*supervisor support*); and time that is made for newcomers to meet and interact with other members of their department or functional area and the organization (*relationship development*).

Work-related resources are important for newcomers' job performance and for enabling the newcomer to perform their job and work tasks effectively. Work-related resources include *job resources* which refer to any type of material resource that a newcomer requires to perform his/her job (e.g., technology, tools, equipment); *personal planning* refers to the extent to which the newcomers' manager has discussed expectations and set performance goals which is not only motivational but also helps to reduce role conflict and role ambiguity; *training programs* that provide newcomers with the knowledge and skills they require to perform their jobs and strengthen their self-efficacy which is a personal resource that is important for engagement and contributes to newcomers' growth and development; *assignments* that involve work tasks that are interesting and challenging and provide newcomers with task and skill variety and some degree of control or autonomy; *information* about their job, role, group, and the organization that is necessary to perform their job and function effectively in their work group and the organization; *feedback* from members of the organization and their supervisor about their job performance and work behavior; and *recognition and appreciation* received from members of the organization for their efforts, performance, and work behavior.

Socialization resources at the end of the socialization process. At the end of the socialization period, the socialization process should not just end without continued contact with and support for newcomers. It is important to stay in touch with newcomers and make sure that they have the resources and the support they require. To make sure that newcomers are highly engaged and continue to be engaged, there are at least two important resources that should be provided to newcomers at the end of the socialization process.

First, it is important to *follow up* with newcomers to see how they are adjusting and if they require any additional support and resources. This ensures that the socialization process does not just end and leave newcomers without the support and resources that they require to perform their job effectively, cope with job demands, and to stay highly engaged. Thus, there should be several follow-ups after the socialization period has ended.

Second, *program evaluation* involves gathering input and feedback from newcomers about their socialization experiences. This is necessary to evaluate the organization's socialization practices and programs and to attend to any shortcomings that have been identified by newcomers. This should focus on the extent to which newcomers received the resources they needed and to an adequate degree. Any shortcomings identified can then be dealt with by providing those resources that have not been provided or were inadequate. This can help to prevent a decline in newcomers' engagement at the end of the socialization program and it can also help with the socialization of future newcomers. Follow-up and evaluation are both important for maintaining newcomers' engagement at the end of the organizational entry-socialization period.

6.5.1   Summary

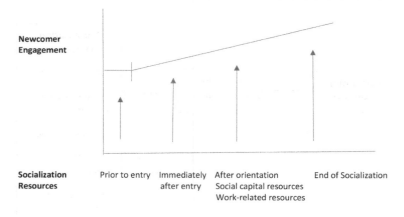

Figure 6.2   Socialization resources and newcomer engagement

As shown in Figure 6.2, socialization resources should be provided to newcomers before, during, and after the formal socialization program to maintain and develop high levels of newcomer engagement. Failure to provide newcomers with socialization resources when they enter an organization is likely to result in a decline in newcomer engagement. Furthermore, if socialization resources are only provided at the beginning of the socialization period, newcomers' initial high levels of engagement are likely to decline and taper off. Socialization resources should be provided throughout the organizational entry-socialization period. Both formal and informal socialization resources from the organization and organizational members should be provided to newcomers throughout the socialization process.

In addition, and as indicated earlier in the chapter, job demands can have a negative effect on newcomers' engagement, so they should be minimized. Socialization resources should, however, help to lessen the negative effects of job demands on newcomer engagement given that job resources buffer the negative effects of job demands on engagement and that resources are most important for engagement when job demands are high (Bakker & Demerouti, 2008). Furthermore, socialization resources will also help to increase personal resources such as self-efficacy, optimism, and resilience which can also have a positive effect on newcomer engagement (Bakker & Demerouti, 2008).

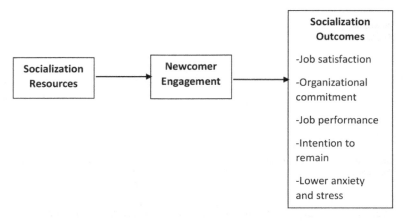

Figure 6.3   Socialization resources, newcomer engagement, and socialization outcomes

Finally, as shown in Figure 6.3, socialization resources will not only result in high levels of newcomer engagement, but they will also result in positive socialization outcomes given that engagement is positively related to job attitudes, behaviors, performance, and health and well-being (Bailey et al., 2017). Thus, socialization resources are important for newcomer engagement as well as the successful adjustment and socialization of newcomers.

6.6 Conclusion

Newcomers are an important group of employees when it comes to employee engagement. When newcomers enter organizations, they have high expectations of their job and the organization, and they are ready and willing to fully engage themselves as a new member of the organization. However, there is a substantial body of research which indicates that soon after entry, newcomers' attitudes and motivation decline.

Similarly, within a relatively short period of time following organizational entry the engagement of newcomers is also likely to decline unless the socialization program is designed to maintain a high level of newcomer engagement. Newcomer engagement maintenance curves indicate the different patterns and changes that can occur in newcomers' engagement during the first year of organizational entry and socialization. They also show when various resources are required to prevent a decline and maintain high levels of engagement.

This requires providing socialization resources to newcomers throughout the organizational entry-socialization process. Failure to provide newcomers with the socialization resources they require to be highly engaged in their job and role will likely result in a decline in their engagement soon after organizational entry. Not only will this be a missed opportunity to keep newcomers highly engaged, but it will also make it much more difficult to improve their engagement once it has fallen and they become disengaged employees.

Furthermore, getting newcomers engaged early on and maintaining their engagement is also likely to result in a successful socialization. Therefore, organizations should monitor the engagement of newcomers and ensure that they are providing newcomers with the resources they require to be highly engaged throughout the organizational entry-socialization process. Socialization resources should be formal and informal, and they should come from the organization, supervisors and managers, and organizational members.

7 Global issues of employee engagement

Employees in all countries and cultures might experience employee engagement, but caution must be exercised when drawing inferences from the available research on the meaning and antecedents of engagement across the globe. Most of the research on employee engagement has been conducted in countries with similar characteristics. These countries tend to have an economic system based on private ownership, a democratic political system, and an emphasis on individualism, which raises questions about whether the research findings and conclusions from employee engagement research apply equally well in countries with different characteristics and cultures (Rothmann, 2014).

One way to understand the source of these differences is to place constructs in cultural context and explore cross-cultural distinctions in the way constructs are considered and experienced, in addition to cross-cultural similarities. Adopting a cross-cultural lens can enhance our understanding of employee engagement by testing the universality of the construct, expanding the range of qualities associated with it, illuminating culture-specific aspects of it, and reducing ethnocentrism (Aycan & Gelfand, 2012).

In this chapter, we consider the importance of cultural differences when it comes to the meaning and measurement of employee engagement, the applicability of employee engagement theories across cultures, and the implications of studying employee engagement across the globe. We begin with a consideration of cultural differences.

7.1 Conceptualizing culture

There are a number of ways to conceptualize culture. Aycan and Gelfand (2012) note that culture can be conceived using classification systems based on values (Schwartz et al, 2012), norms (Gelfand et al., 2006), and beliefs (Bond et al., 2004). However, the most popular method involves the taxonomy of five cultural values developed by Hofstede (1980; Hofstede & Bond, 1988).

In Hofstede's taxonomy, *power distance* refers to "the extent to which a society accepts the fact that power in institutions and organizations is distributed unequally" (Hofstede, 1980, p.45). *Uncertainty avoidance* reflects "the extent to which a society feels threatened by uncertain and ambiguous situations" (Hofstede, 1980, p.45) and therefore prefers "structured over unstructured situations" (Hofstede, 1994, p.5). *Masculinity/ Femininity* represents the extent to which a society is dominated by traditionally masculine values such as "assertiveness, performance, success and competition," as opposed to traditionally feminine values such as "the quality of life, maintaining warm personal relationships, service, care for the weak, and solidarity" (Hofstede, 1994, p.6). *Individualism/ Collectivism* reflects the degree to which people are expected to look after themselves and their immediate family (individualism), versus distinguishing between out-groups and in-groups such as relatives and organizations, which they expect to protect them and to which they feel tremendous loyalty (collectivism; Hofstede, 1980). Confucian dynamism, otherwise referred to as *short-term versus long-term orientation*, reflects the degree to which a culture manifests a long-term orientation directed towards values of persistence and thrift, or a short-term orientation reflecting values oriented towards the past and present such as fulfilling social obligations and respecting tradition (Hofstede & Bond, 1988; Taras et al., 2010).

This taxonomy of cultural values allows us to shed light on cross-cultural differences in the meaning, theories, antecedents, and outcomes associated with employee engagement, and to develop a more robust understanding of the construct. However, we should bear in mind that research on this topic is sparse. Below we present some arguments and evidence for how and why employee engagement might differ around the globe, but the conclusions should be regarded as tentative until further empirical support is obtained.

7.2 The meaning of employee engagement across cultures

Organizational constructs, such as employee engagement, do not necessarily have the same meaning around the globe, and might thus lack conceptual equivalence across cultures (Hui & Triandis, 1985). For example, research has shown that the meaning and/or factor structure of measures of job satisfaction (Liu et al., 2004), organizational commitment (Cheng & Stockdale, 2003), participation in decision making (Sagie & Aycan, 2003), achievement (Niles, 1998), and job performance (Varela et al., 2010) are dissimilar in different parts of the world, thus demonstrating a lack of conceptual or construct equivalence (van de Vijver & Tanzer, 2004).

To facilitate cross-cultural comparisons, a construct should be equally meaningful across the various cultures being studied (Hui & Triandis, 1985). As noted in Chapter 2, Kahn (1990) suggested that engagement involves the harnessing of one's self in the roles one occupies at work. However, perceptions of the self and the nature of one's self-concept vary in different cultures. Therefore, what it means to bring oneself to a role might differ across the globe.

Although it has been considered an overgeneralization (Matsumoto, 1999; Oyserman et al., 2002; Takano & Osaka, 2018), a primary feature of Western notions of the self is that people are separate from others and their social context, whereas Eastern notions of the self emphasize connections among people within significant social relationships (Kitayama et al., 1997).

In their classic treatise on culture and the self, Markus and Kitayama (1991) distinguished between an *independent* self-construal which stresses "attending to the self, the appreciation of one's difference from others, and the importance of asserting the self" (p.224), and an *interdependent* self-construal which emphasizes "attending to and fitting in with others and the importance of harmonious interdependence with them" (p.224). Although individuals might manifest both self-construals, the former should be more prevalent in individualistic cultures and the latter in collectivistic cultures (Cross et al., 2011).

Engagement is a motivational construct that involves agency. Markus and Kitayama (1991) explain that "among those with interdependent selves, agency will be experienced as an effort to be receptive to others, to adjust to their needs and demands, and to restrain one's own inner needs and desires" (p.240). Thus, in collectivistic cultures which tend to foster interdependent self-construals, the harnessing of one's self in one's roles might involve socially oriented attributes, such as solidarity, loyalty, deference, imitation, and nurturance, that are absent in traditional notions of employee engagement that are based on independent self-construals (Markus & Kitayama, 1991; Murray, 1938). These qualities might manifest themselves in ways of being cognitively, emotionally, or physically engaged, or demonstrating vigor, dedication, or absorption that are different from the ways in which they have heretofore been conceived.

Yang (2006) explains that compared to people from individualistic societies, the personality and sense of self that people in collectivistic cultures develop involve more relationship, group, and generalized-other foci that reflect a social orientation. Thus, when individuals in collectivistic cultures invest and employ themselves in their roles they might tend to manifest more socially oriented forms of employee engagement such as employee team engagement, employee business unit or department engagement, and employee organization engagement.

Among individuals in collectivistic cultures, the nature of all forms of engagement might differ from the way they are currently conceptualized in that they might involve more relationally oriented aspects of the self. This highlights the need for both emic and etic forms of research (Berry, 1989). Etic approaches explore culture-general, or universal, features of phenomena. Efforts to examine the potential similarities and comparability of employee engagement across cultures are an example of an etic approach.

Emic, or indigenous, approaches examine features of a phenomenon that are unique to a particular culture. An example might be a study exploring how employee engagement is manifested among those with an interdependent self-construal in a particular collectivistic culture. Importantly, these two forms of research are not mutually exclusive. For example, emic research conducted in an Eastern culture could serve to identify aspects of employee engagement that turn out to be universal (Cheung et al., 2011).

As far as we are aware, there is currently no research exploring the cross-cultural equivalence or culture-specific nature of employee engagement in non-Western cultures. Given that cultural differences might play a role in the specific meaning of employee engagement in different parts of the world, such research is sorely needed to avoid construct bias, which is when constructs differ across cultures (van de Vijver & Tanzer, 2004).

One study that has explored how a self-concept-related issue relates to employee engagement across geographic borders is Garczynski et al.'s (2013) examination of self-concept differentiation. Self-concept differentiation refers to the tendency to manifest different aspects of one's personality in the different social roles one occupies, such as at work and at home (Donahue et al., 1993). Garczynski et al. (2013) found that Indian employees demonstrated less self-concept differentiation than American employees. That is, whereas American employees tended to view themselves as exhibiting different aspects of their self-concepts in their personal lives and work lives, Indian employees tended to view themselves as exhibiting the same aspects of their self-concept in the different contexts. Additionally, high levels of self-concept differentiation were associated with less engagement, but only among Americans. Garczynski et al. (2013) suggested that "possessing a self-concept that ties into the needs and wants of the group may enable employees from collectivist cultures to be more present at work, regardless of self-concept differentiation" (p.419).

7.3 The measurement of employee engagement across cultures

It has been claimed that the most commonly used measure of employee engagement, the UWES, is factorially invariant across countries, and that scores are a reliable indicator of work engagement internationally (Shimazu et al., 2010). However, Goliath-Yarde and Roodt (2011) found that UWES total scale scores and sub-scale scores differed among a sample of employees from different cultural groups in South Africa. Additionally, Klassen et al. (2012) demonstrated variability in the factor structure of the UWES when comparing Western and non-Western groups of teachers. Klassen et al. (2012) suggested that the factor structure of the UWES should be tested in particular contexts because it seems to fluctuate in different cross-cultural settings.

As might be expected based on the preceding discussion, when we measure employee engagement around the globe we find differences in the level of employee engagement that employees exhibit. For instance, Garczynski et al. (2013) found that employees in India displayed higher levels of engagement than American employees. Similarly, Kożusznik et al. (2012) observed that social service employees in Poland had lower levels of engagement than those in Spain. Deci et al. (2001) found that employees in the United States had higher levels of engagement than employees in Bulgaria. In a comparison among 16 nations, Shimazu et al. (2010) found that Japanese employees had much lower levels of employee engagement than employees from any other country.

We must be cautious in interpreting these results because although they seem to indicate that people in different parts of the world display dissimilar levels of employee engagement, they might also reveal that people from different regions and cultures interpret and endorse employee engagement scale items in idiosyncratic ways (Rothmann, 2014). For instance, Goliath-Yarde and Roodt (2011) found that employees from different cultural groups in South Africa responded differently to 14 out of the 17 items on the UWES.

Shimazu et al. (2010) suggested that engagement levels might be low among Japanese employees because in collectivistic cultures, which place great value on social harmony and in which suppressing positive emotions might be a mark of moral distinction, employees might be reluctant to endorse engagement scale items reflecting positive affect. They further suggested that low scores might not reflect low engagement levels per se, but instead might be indicative of reduced measurement accuracy among Japanese participants. In short, variations in employee engagement scores in different cultures might not reflect differences in levels of employee engagement, but differences in the way scale items are interpreted, or what is referred to as item bias (van de Vijver & Tanzer, 2004).

Additionally, instead of reflecting cross-cultural differences, discrepancies in employee engagement scores might reflect differences in the socioeconomic conditions in various parts of the world. At the time of their study, Deci et al. (2001) noted that among Bulgarians, who scored lower on engagement than Americans, "the dominant experiences of the citizens of this former East-bloc country have involved a totalitarian rather than democratic political system, state-owned companies operated by central planning principles rather than private owned companies operated by market-economy principles, and collectivistic rather than individualistic cultural values" (pp.930–931). Without research that controls for the effect of such varied circumstances it is difficult to know if there are inherent cultural differences in the experience of employee engagement or if differences in engagement levels reflect distinct social, organizational, political, and/or economic conditions.

Along these lines, Schaufeli (2018) found that employee engagement scores varied among 35 European countries with Dutch workers scoring the highest and Serbian employees scoring the lowest. With some exceptions, employees in Northern Europe and the Alpine region tended to have high engagement scores and those in Southern and Eastern Europe had low scores. He also found that engagement demonstrated a negative association with average work hours in a country, which was highest in Southern and Eastern Europe, and a positive, curvilinear association with a country's economic activity (GDP) and productivity. In short, in productive countries which demanded fewer working hours, employees were more engaged. Additionally, based on five measures of a country's governance, he found that engagement was negatively correlated with corruption and gender inequality, and positively correlated with integrity and democracy. With respect to national culture, individualism and indulgence were positively associated with engagement, whereas power distance and uncertainty avoidance were negatively associated with engagement. When the culture values were considered simultaneously, only individualism emerged as a significant predictor. Finally, when economic, governance, and culture variables were considered simultaneously, only productivity emerged as a significant predictor.

These results highlight the importance of research on how cultural and non-cultural factors might interact in producing engagement in different settings (Gelfand et al., 2008). Without controlling for non-cultural, cross-national variables, differences in employee engagement levels might be incorrectly attributed to cultural differences.

7.4 Culture and theories of employee engagement

As noted in Chapter 3, there are a number of theories that have been used to explain employee engagement, such as the job demands-resources model (Bakker & Demerouti, 2007), social exchange theory (Saks, 2006), and Kahn's (1990) theory of personal engagement and psychological presence. However, there is reason to believe that the conceptual underpinnings of these theories might not operate similarly in all cultures.

7.4.1 The job demands-resources (JD-R) model

Recall that the JD-R model divides working conditions into job demands and job resources. The JD-R model has been shown to display cross-cultural stability and variability. For example, there is some evidence that the JD-R model generalizes across countries and cultures. Research has found that job crafting increases employees' challenging job demands and job resources and is positively related to employee engagement in the Netherlands (Tims et al., 2012) and Japan (Sakuraya et al., 2017).

There is, however, also evidence of cross-cultural variation. Sanchez and McCauley (2006) found that the resources that are related to employee engagement differ across nations. While growth and development opportunities were important in the U.S., they were not as important in the U.K. or China. Regular performance feedback demonstrated the opposite pattern. Farndale and Murrer (2015) found that financial rewards and team climate were more strongly related to employee engagement in Mexico and the U.S. than in the Netherlands. Brough et al. (2013) found that work hours were positively related to employee engagement in an Australian sample but negatively related to engagement in a Chinese sample (p.260).

Rattrie et al. (2020) conducted a meta-analysis of 120 cross-national studies based on the JD-R to explore cross-cultural differences in the relationships among demands, resources, and engagement (and burnout). They found that, as expected, resources were positively related to engagement while demands were negatively related. After coding the countries for cultural dimensions, they also found that national culture moderated these effects. Specifically, the negative effect of demands on engagement was stronger in masculine cultures compared to feminine cultures, and also in tight cultures in which deviance from social norms is less tolerated (Gelfand et al., 2006).

When control variables were included, it was found that long-term orientation weakened the positive relationship between resources and engagement, and individualism strengthened the relationship. Rattrie et al. (2020) suggested that these effects might stem from challenges associated with psychologically distancing oneself from demands in masculine and tight cultures, and the enhanced motivation to use personally valuable knowledge about resources in individualist and short-term oriented cultures. Thus, national culture has the effect of sometimes intensifying and sometimes muting the effects of demands and resources on engagement. We therefore cannot assume that the resources and demands that comprise the JD-R model operate comparably around the globe in generating employee engagement.

7.4.2 Social exchange theory

As described in Chapter 3, social exchange theory has often been used as a theoretical model to explain the employee engagement process (Bailey et al., 2017). Social exchange theory involves the relationships that form as people engage in interdependent transactions in which resources are exchanged in a reciprocal fashion based on economic and social principles (Cropanzano et al., 2017). However, the nature of these exchanges and the way resources are perceived and used tend to differ across cultures (Kraemer & Chen, 2012).

Kraemer and Chen (2012) compared exchange characteristics in the United States and China. They suggested that in the United States social exchange is characterized by narrow, short-term, market-like transactions that focus on the instrumental needs of participants, whereas in China social exchange involves a broader set of longer-term, symbolic actions focused on hierarchical norms and reciprocal obligation.

The breadth of social exchange also differs in the two countries. In the United States the resources exchanged by supervisors and subordinates are restricted to the work context; in China, resources provided by supervisors extend beyond the job into employees' personal lives. Whereas American employment relations tend to involve resources based on economic exchanges, Chinese employment relations involve resources that also include loyalty and devotion. In such cultures, the way in which certain resources, such as the use of a company car, are interpreted can have more symbolic as opposed to instrumental value. As Kraemer and Chen (2012) note, "the extent to which certain types of social resources (e.g., socio-emotional) are used in workplace exchange as well as the way they are expressed (symbolic/substantive) depends on culture" (p.296).

Thus, the variety of resources, the value of particular resources, and their potency in fostering engagement during social exchange might vary across cultures. Put another way, different cultures have different norms and expectations about social exchange that must be considered to understand the exchange characteristics that will promote, or thwart, employee engagement.

7.4.3 Kahn's theory of personal engagement

As described in Chapter 3, Kahn (1990) identified three psychological conditions that influence the extent to which people experience moments of personal engagement: psychological meaningfulness, psychological safety, and psychological availability. However, the factors that satisfy these three psychological conditions and the relationship between them and engagement might demonstrate cross-cultural variability.

7.4.3.1 Psychological meaningfulness

As noted in Chapter 5, leadership is instrumental in providing employees with meaning at work. However, the nature of the leadership required to accomplish this might fluctuate across cultures because the style of leadership that employees find meaningful is likely to vary according to cultural prescriptions. In support of this idea, Li et al. (2020) found that national culture moderated the relationship between leadership styles and employee engagement.

Out of the 56 possible interactions testing the moderating effects of eight cultural characteristics on the relationship between seven leadership styles and engagement, they observed ten significant effects. For example, the relationship between authentic leadership and engagement is stronger in countries higher in power distance. The relationship between empowering leadership and engagement is stronger in countries higher in future orientation. And the relationship between servant leadership and engagement is stronger in countries with low uncertainty avoidance. They also found that the relationship between engagement and transactional leadership, ethical leadership, and servant leadership was not influenced by national culture, suggesting some cross-cultural stability in the forms of leadership that employees find desirable, meaningful, and that generate engagement (Javidan et al., 2006).

It is also possible that meaningfulness is less important in some cultural contexts than others. Rahmadani et al. (2019) explored the mediating effect of the need for meaningfulness in the relationship between engaging leadership and work engagement. They found that the need for meaningfulness served as a significant mediator for employees in Russia but not for employees in Indonesia. However, they suggested that one reason for this difference is that the jobs occupied by Indonesian employees might have been inherently meaningful.

7.4.3.2   Psychological safety

Psychological safety might not operate as an antecedent of employee engagement in the same fashion across the globe. Psychological safety is promoted partly by having interpersonal relationships that foster trust, but the basis of trust has been shown to differ cross-culturally with individualists favoring dispositional signs of trust such as ability and integrity, and collectivists favoring situational signs such as similarity and benevolence (Branzei et al., 2007). Therefore, the drivers of psychological safety might vary in different cultures. Similarly, psychological safety is promoted by perceptions of fairness and justice. However, the basis of such perceptions differs across cultures.

According to Gelfand et al. (2007), there are cultural differences in perceptions and outcomes of both distributive and procedural justice. For example, the effects of justice perceptions on outcomes such as satisfaction, performance, and absenteeism are stronger among cultures low in power distance. In cultures high in power distance justice perceptions that foster psychological safety might exert less of an effect on employee engagement.

The meaning and importance of psychological safety might also differ around the globe. For example, Rothmann (Oliver & Rothmann, 2007; Rothmann & Rothmann, 2010; Rothmann & Welsh, 2013) conducted three studies exploring the effects of Kahn's (1990) psychological antecedents on the engagement of employees in South Africa, which has been considered high in power distance (Hofstede, 1980), and its neighbor, Namibia. Rothmann found that the measures of psychological safety demonstrated poor reliability in all three studies, and in one study was subsequently abandoned (Rothmann & Welsh, 2013). In the remaining two studies, psychological safety failed to mediate the relationship between the drivers of psychological safety (supervisor relations, co-worker relations, and co-worker norms) and employee engagement. It is unclear whether these results indicate that items reflecting psychological safety are interpreted differently in non-Western cultures, whether psychological safety itself means different things in different cultures, or whether psychological safety is less important as an antecedent of employee engagement in certain cultures.

7.4.3.3 Psychological availability

The resources associated with psychological availability might also differ across the globe. For instance, human resource practices produce different effects internationally. Andreassi et al. (2014) compared the effects of high-performance management practices on job satisfaction in four cultural regions. They found that team work had a stronger effect on job satisfaction in collectivistic cultures, and work-life balance had a stronger effect in individualistic cultures. They also found that both communication from management and training had a stronger effect in cultures characterized by low uncertainty avoidance, and recognition had a stronger effect in feminine cultures. Thus, it appears that the value employees place on various human resource practices is cross-culturally variable. Given that "a job resource is only resourceful if it is valued by the individual employee" (Van Veldhoven et al., 2020, p.13), it would seem that the ability of human resource practices to provide resources that promote psychological availability and employee engagement will vary in different cultural settings.

Kahn (1990) suggested that the psychological antecedents that foster employee engagement are similar to the conditions that characterize contracts. The contract metaphor, which highlights rights and protections as opposed to duties and obligations, might not apply equally well to the antecedents of engagement in cultures characterized by more familial relations (collectivism), solidarity (femininity), or those in which unequal power is expected (high power distance). Conversely, it might be particularly applicable in cultures that dislike ambiguity and prefer a high degree of structure (high uncertainty avoidance).

7.5 Studying employee engagement around the globe

Employee engagement is a motivational construct that was developed in the context of Western culture. Aycan and Gelfand (2012) note that motivational theories developed in the West are limited because they are based on assumptions that "reflect the cultural value orientations of individualism, low power distance, masculinity, uncertainty tolerance, and self-determination. However, such assumptions underlying motivational theories are not as valid in cultures characterized by collectivism, power distance, fatalism, uncertainty avoidance, or femininity" (p.25).

Having been developed in the context of Western culture, the cross-cultural generalizability of employee engagement remains uncertain. In order for research on employee engagement to advance, the various ways in which employee engagement is conceptualized, measured, and promoted across cultures needs to be examined further to explore cross-cultural similarities and differences (see Table 7.1).

Employee engagement in a particular culture might be the same as engagement in all other cultures, some other cultures, and no other cultures (Cheng et al., 2011; Kluckhohn & Murray, 1953). Our understanding of the nature, antecedents, and outcomes of employee engagement will be enhanced by etic research that explores universal aspects of the construct, in addition to emic, indigenous studies that occur outside of Western cultures. For example, based on a sample of nurses in China, Lu et al. (2011) found that one of the drivers of employee engagement was family mastery, which refers to the degree to which employees control their family lives.

Caution must be exercised when attributing differences in future cross-cultural studies on employee engagement. Most cross-cultural research is not cross-cultural, but cross-national (Matsumoto, 1999), and cross-country comparisons do not necessarily reflect cross-cultural comparisons (Byrne, 2015). Also, it is important to recognize that there is often a variety of cultural groups within a particular country, and individuals might not reflect the cultural values of the groups to which they belong.

As Hofstede (1980) noted, a description of a national culture does not equate to a description of the characteristics of any particular individual within that culture. Drawing conclusions about individuals based on country or culture-level findings is to commit the ecological fallacy (Brewer & Venaik, 2014). For example, Schaufeli (2018) notes that his results demonstrating a negative relationship between engagement and work centrality at the national level do not imply a similar association at the individual level, where, in fact, research has demonstrated a relationship in the opposite direction (Dalal et al., 2012). Research on cross-cultural differences in employee engagement should therefore be complemented with research on cultural differences at the individual level, for example on idiocentrism and allocentrism, the individual-level equivalents of individualism and collectivism (Triandis, 1989).

Table 7.1   Cross-cultural research questions about employee engagement

Topic	Sample cross-cultural research questions
Conceptualization of employee engagement	What is the meaning of employee engagement across cultures? How does the meaning of employee engagement differ across cultures? In what ways is the meaning of employee engagement the same across cultures?
Measurement of employee engagement	How should employee engagement be measured across cultures? Does the measurement of employee engagement need to be modified in specific cultures? Is the factor structure of measures of employee engagement scales equivalent across cultures?
Promotion of employee engagement	How do we best promote employee engagement in different cultures? To what extent and in what ways do the theories underlying employee engagement apply in different cultures? Are there practices for promoting employee engagement that might be effective in one culture but ineffective or even counterproductive in another culture?

7.6   Conclusion

Although people around the world might experience employee engagement, these experiences are not necessarily equivalent. Because there are cross-cultural differences in the self-concept, the ways in which people bring themselves to their roles and manifest employee engagement might differ around the globe. Furthermore, employees in different parts of the world might interpret scale items in distinct ways that might result in inconsistencies in the ways these employees respond to employee engagement scale items, complicating cross-cultural comparisons of scores. In addition, the underpinnings of the theories used to explain employee engagement might not operate the same way among different cultures or individuals with particular cultural characteristics. Thus, one has to be cautious when generalizing the results of employee engagement research across cultures. Much more cross-cultural research is needed on the way employee engagement is manifested, measured, and best promoted before valid cross-cultural conclusions can be drawn.

8 Employee engagement in practice

While a great deal of research has been conducted on employee engagement, when it comes to putting engagement research into practice it can be overwhelming. With so many studies and so much information, it is difficult to know where to begin. Therefore, in this chapter we try to make sense of employee engagement research and provide some guidelines on how to put employee engagement research into practice.

From a practical perspective, there are really two key issues or questions that organizations need to be concerned about. First, *how engaged are employees in your organization?* Second, *what can you do to increase the engagement of employees in your organization?* This should be straightforward given all the research on employee engagement described in the previous chapters. However, it is actually very challenging.

For example, recall from Chapter 4 that many different measures have been developed to assess employee engagement. This makes it difficult to know how to measure employee engagement. What measure should be used? When it comes to driving employee engagement, it is easy to get lost in the plethora of variables that have been found to be related to employee engagement. One review identified 42 individual and organizational antecedents of employee engagement (Wollard & Shuck, 2011). With so many variables that have been found to predict employee engagement, which ones should be the focus of programs and practices to improve employee engagement?

Thus, the sheer volume of research on employee engagement makes it difficult to translate it into practice. In this chapter, we will try to make sense of the research on employee engagement and provide a road map for how to develop an employee engagement strategy that is based on the research and the science of employee engagement.

First, we provide an employee engagement practice model that consists of seven steps to follow for developing an employee engagement program. Second, we describe how a strategic HRM employee engagement system that consists of a bundle of HRM practices focused on employee engagement will lead to a climate of engagement and an engaged workforce. Third, we describe an employee engagement management model that converts performance management into engagement management thereby embedding employee engagement into the performance management process.

8.1 Employee engagement practice model

In this section, we discuss how to develop an employee engagement practice model to measure and improve employee engagement in organizations. The development of an employee engagement program should consist of the following seven steps or stages:

1. Define employee engagement.
2. Identify the target of employee engagement.
3. Choose or develop a measure of employee engagement.
4. Develop an employee engagement survey.
5. Examine the employee engagement survey results.
6. Develop and implement an employee engagement strategy.
7. Follow-up and evaluation.

Define employee engagement. The starting point for implementing an employee engagement program is to develop a clear and understandable definition of employee engagement that is meaningful and accepted in the organization. In Chapter 2, we noted that there are many definitions of employee engagement. Thus, a good place to start is to review the definitions in Chapter 2 and then revise and adapt them in a manner that works within an organization.

In general, employee engagement involves a willingness to dedicate physical, cognitive, and emotional resources into the performance of one's job or work role (Kahn, 1990). Some key aspects of employee engagement that might be included in a definition are being attentive, focused, and absorbed in one's job; exerting effort, energy, and intensity when performing one's job; and being enthusiastic, excited, and positive about one's job.

In addition, it is also important to avoid defining employee engagement in a way that overlaps with other constructs. Therefore, one should review the definitions of other constructs in Table 2.1 to make sure that the definition of employee engagement is clearly different and distinct from these related constructs. Thus, the definition of employee engagement should avoid terms that are used in other constructs such as discretionary effort, satisfaction, commitment, involvement, identification, and intent to stay.

Identify the target of employee engagement. As indicated in Chapter 2, employee engagement is a role-specific construct and should be defined and measured in terms of a specific role or target. Therefore, once employee engagement has been defined, the definition and focus can shift to the desired role or target.

In Chapter 2, we described the following targets of employee engagement: employee task engagement, employee job/work engagement, employee team engagement, employee business unit or department engagement, and employee organization engagement. Thus, when defining employee engagement, we can refer to the extent to which an employee is engaged (e.g., absorbed, attentive, focused, enthusiastic, excited, etc.) when performing their job, a particular task, team-related tasks, department or business unit activities and roles, as well as organization-related tasks and duties.

It is important to be clear about the target or targets of employee engagement that one is most interested in as it will determine the measures used to assess employee engagement. Failure to identify the role or target of employee engagement can result in a measure of employee engagement that is inappropriate for an organization's needs and objectives which will then result in information about employee engagement that will be inaccurate and misleading (e.g., measuring job engagement when the concern is organization engagement). Furthermore, the most effective practices for increasing employee engagement will depend on the target of engagement that an organization wants to improve. Therefore, before measuring employee engagement it is critical that the target of greatest interest be identified.

Choose or develop a measure of employee engagement. Once employee engagement has been defined and the target has been identified, a measure of employee engagement can be chosen or developed. In Chapter 4, we described many measures of employee engagement that have been developed in the academic literature. In addition, we also showed how some of these measures can be adapted for different targets (see Table 4.1) as well as different referents (see Table 4.2). Thus, one can choose a measure from these tables or develop a new measure.

When deciding on which measure to use, there are two things that should be kept in mind. First, the choice of a measure of employee engagement should be made with the definition in mind. That is, the measure and the items should very clearly reflect the definition of employee engagement that one has decided on. This will ensure that the measure of employee engagement has both face validity and content validity.

With respect to *face validity*, this means that the employee engagement items actually look and sound like what they are supposed to be measuring. Thus, an item that asks about job satisfaction would not meet the criteria of face validity. Face validity is a judgment that should be based on one's knowledge and understanding of what employee engagement means and what the items should look like given its meaning.

Content validity has to do with the extent to which the items on a scale are representative of the construct. In the case of employee engagement, the items should be representative of all aspects of the construct in terms of its meaning and definition. For example, if the definition of employee engagement includes vigor, dedication, and absorption, then there should be items in the engagement scale that measure vigor, dedication, and absorption. Thus, the content of the items used to measure employee engagement should be highly representative of the definition of employee engagement. It is a good idea to have several experts or people who are knowledgeable about employee engagement review the items to make sure that they have face validity and content validity. This will ensure that the measure of employee engagement is actually measuring employee engagement given its meaning and definition.

Second, once the items have been chosen or developed, the target can be added as shown in Table 4.1. For example, using Saks' (2019) single item measures, one can measure any target by simply including the desired target in the item (*"I am highly engaged in my job/a particular task/team/ department/organization"*). In addition, if the desired referent is other than the individual employee, this too can be incorporated into each item (*"My team/department/organization is highly engaged in their job"*). The main issue is to make sure that the items reflect the desired target and referent.

The result of this step should be an employee engagement measure that has face and content validity. Once this stage is complete, it is possible to begin to develop an employee engagement survey and to measure employee engagement.

Develop an employee engagement survey. Once a measure of employee engagement has been chosen or developed the next step is to design an employee engagement survey and measure employee engagement. This step is critical for three reasons: (1) Determining the level of employee engagement in the organization, (2) Determining the relationship between employee engagement antecedents and employee engagement, and (3) Determining the relationship between employee engagement and its consequences.

The first issue to consider is the level of employee engagement in an organization and/or within certain key areas such as functional areas, departments, or job categories. This is an important step because it will provide a baseline indicator of where an organization stands in terms of employee engagement and it will also enable comparisons within an organization that can identify areas where employee engagement is low or where employees are disengaged and therefore where there is a need for interventions to improve employee engagement.

Second, the engagement survey should include measures of different antecedents or predictors of employee engagement. This should be based on the research on employee engagement as well as factors that are of particular concern or are especially relevant in an organization. Based on the research described in Chapter 5, some important antecedents to include in the survey are job characteristics (e.g., feedback, autonomy), social support, rewards and recognition, opportunities for learning and development, and person-job (PJ) and person-organization (PO) fit perceptions. In addition, it is important to keep in mind that you might want to include certain antecedents that are believed to be important for the target of engagement that you are measuring. Thus, if you are measuring employee team engagement or perhaps employee organization engagement, you need to consider antecedents that are likely to be important for these targets in addition to those that we know are important for job or work engagement.

The survey should also include job demands that can have a negative effect on employee engagement. Since the objective is to identify the factors that are strongly related to employee engagement in an organization, it is advisable to review the antecedents in Chapter 5 and then choose those that are considered to be of most interest, concern, and relevance for the organization and for your target of engagement and include them in the employee engagement survey.

Third, the survey should include measures of the process variables described in Chapter 3 given that they are influenced by the antecedents and they influence employee engagement. Recall that the five process variables described in Chapter 3 include need satisfaction, positive emotions, psychological conditions, responsibility, and social exchange. Including these measures is important because the results will indicate the extent to which employees' basic psychological needs are satisfied, if they have positive emotions, if they are experiencing psychological meaningfulness, availability, and safety, if they feel responsible for what they do, and if they have an exchange ideology and a felt obligation to help the organization reach its goals (social exchange theory; see Eisenberger et al., 2001).

Fourth, the employee engagement survey should include measures of the consequences or work outcomes of employee engagement. Given that employee engagement is related to many work outcomes, these should be included in the survey to identify the extent to which employee engagement is related to outcomes that are important for the organization. Therefore, the survey should include measures of job attitudes such as job satisfaction and organizational commitment; intentions such as intention to remain in the organization; behaviors such as organizational citizenship behavior; and stress and wellness measures. These and other outcomes that are important for employees and the organization should be included in the survey.

This stage should result in an employee engagement survey that includes a measure of employee engagement as well as measures of various antecedents, process variables, and work outcomes (see Table 8.1 for categories of survey variables to include). Once the survey has been designed, employees and other stakeholders in the organization should be informed about it as well as its purpose, importance, and its objectives. It is important to inform employees and members of the organization about the importance of the survey and the support of senior management and any participating unions. Once the purpose and importance of the survey have been communicated to members of the organization it should be distributed to all employees or a sample of employees. It is also important to assure employees of their anonymity and the confidentiality of their responses, and to inform them that the survey results will be aggregated at the unit and/or organization level.

Examine the employee engagement survey results. Once the surveys have been completed the results should be examined for three things: (1) Employee engagement scores, (2) Relationships between the antecedents, process variables, and employee engagement, and (3) Relationships between employee engagement and the consequences.

First, the range and average of the employee engagement scores should be examined to determine the extent to which employees in the organization or in a particular functional area, job category, etc., are engaged or disengaged. This can also involve comparisons across an organization with respect to departments, geographic locations, job levels, etc. This will provide information on the extent to which employee engagement scores differ across an organization and the range of scores across various comparative categories.

Table 8.1   Employee engagement categories of survey variables

Antecedents	Process variables	Consequences
Job characteristics	Psychological conditions	Job satisfaction
Social support	Need satisfaction	Organizational
Justice perceptions	Positive emotions	commitment
Opportunities for	Responsibility	Intention to remain
development	Social exchange	Organizational
Rewards and recognition		citizenship behavior
Role overload		Job performance
Work-role conflict		Stress
Role clarity		Wellness
Supervisor support		Burnout

Second, the relationship between the antecedents and employee engagement should be examined to identify the extent to which each of the antecedents is related to employee engagement and the strength of the relationships. The antecedents that are significantly related to employee engagement should be noted and then the average scores of these antecedent variables should be reviewed with particular attention to those antecedents that are very low in the case of resources (e.g., support) and those that are very high with respect to demands (e.g., role overload). These variables should be tagged for attention in the next stage. In addition, differences in the average scores on these variables across departments, regions, and job categories should also be noted for further attention.

The relationships between the antecedents and the process variables should also be examined to determine the extent to which the antecedents are related to the process variables. Those variables that are most strongly related to each of the process variables should be noted. In addition, the relationships between the process variables and employee engagement should also be examined to identify the extent to which each process variable is related to engagement. Process variables that are most strongly related to engagement should be noted.

Third, the relationship between employee engagement and the consequences should be examined to identify the extent to which employee engagement is related to each consequence and the strength of these relationships. These relationships will help to indicate if employee engagement is having an impact on work outcomes that are important for the organization. Keep in mind that the relationship between employee engagement and the consequences will depend in part on the target of engagement. For example, compared with organization engagement, job engagement is likely to be more strongly related to job performance.

The end result of this stage should be an understanding of the extent to which employees are engaged or disengaged in the organization and where in the organization employees are most and least engaged; what antecedents are most strongly related to the process variables and employee engagement, and to what extent there is too little (in the case of resources) or too much (in the case of demands) of these antecedents; the extent to which each of the process variables are related to employee engagement and which process variables are most strongly related; and what consequences are most affected by employee engagement and deserve special attention because they are important to employees and the organization.

The survey results should be discussed with groups of employees to get their input on the results and their suggestions about potential interventions for improving their engagement. The survey results should also be discussed with management and supervisors who should also provide input on possible changes and interventions. Employee input and participation is especially important given that employees might have some ideas and insights that are important for understanding the results and what is required to improve employee engagement in the organization. Their buy-in to the process is also important for the successful development and implementation of an employee engagement strategy.

Develop and implement an employee engagement strategy. The results and interpretation of the employee engagement survey should be used to develop an employee engagement strategy that focuses on making changes to the antecedents that were tagged for further attention. First, those areas of the organization that have lower levels of employee engagement should be noted for attention. Second, the antecedents that are positively related to the process variables and employee engagement but are not as high as they should be and are also related to work outcomes should be the focus of interventions to improve them. Third, the demands that are negatively related to employee engagement and are higher than they should be (e.g., role overload) should be the focus of interventions to reduce them. Fourth, the process variables that are most strongly related to employee engagement and are in the low-to-mid-range should be improved by increasing those antecedents that are most strongly related to them. Fifth, those consequences that are being strongly impacted by employee engagement should be noted, given that changes in employee engagement will likely result in changes in these consequences.

Once it has been determined what antecedents need special attention, an employee engagement strategy should be developed. The employee engagement strategy should indicate exactly what steps, actions, and interventions will be taken to make changes to the antecedent variables that require attention. For example, if supervisor support needs to be improved, how will this happen? Will supervisors receive training on how to provide more support for employees? If some of the job characteristics require attention such as feedback, how will this happen? How and when will employees be provided with more feedback? If some of the job demands need to be eliminated or reduced such as role overload or role ambiguity, what will be done to lower them and when will this be done?

The end result of this stage should be an employee engagement strategy which describes the antecedent variables that are going to be changed as well as how they will be changed, when the change will take place, and the stakeholders (e.g., employees, supervisors, managers, etc.) who will be involved in the process.

Follow-up and evaluation. After the employee engagement strategy has been implemented there should be a follow-up and evaluation of the strategy. This should involve two components. First, there should be a follow-up and evaluation of the actual engagement strategies that were implemented. This should consider the extent to which they were implemented (e.g., Have supervisors received training on how to be more supportive for employees?), how effectively they were implemented (e.g., Was the training executed as planned?), as well as how effective they have been (e.g., Are supervisors providing more support to employees?).

Second, the employee engagement survey should be conducted again to determine the extent to which there have been changes in employee engagement and the antecedents and process variables that were targeted for change. The employee engagement scores from the previous survey should be compared to the scores from the follow-up survey. It can take some time before there are noticeable changes from the time that the strategies were implemented. Nonetheless, it is important to note if there has been an improvement in engagement scores in those parts of the organization or for those job categories that scored low on the previous survey. There should also be an improvement in the antecedents and process variables that were targeted for change (e.g., Is the score for supervisor support higher than it was on the previous survey? Have employees' scores on the basic psychological needs improved?). It is also worthwhile to continue to examine the relationship between the antecedents and employee engagement, the antecedents and the process variables, the process variables and employee engagement, and employee engagement and the consequences, and look for any changes from the previous survey.

It might take several follow-ups to notice any real change in employee engagement scores and in the antecedents and process variables that were

Table 8.2   Employee engagement practice model

Step	Summary
1. Define employee engagement	Develop a definition of employee engagement that is based on the definitions in the literature (see Chapter 2) and is also meaningful and acceptable in your organization. Consider using terms such as attentive, focused, absorbed, effort, energy, intensity, enthusiastic, excited, and positive.
2. Identify the target of employee engagement	Choose one or more of the following targets to focus on when measuring employee engagement: employee task engagement, employee job/ work engagement, employee team engagement, employee business unit or department engagement, and employee organization engagement.
3. Choose or develop a measure of employee engagement	Make sure the measure and the items are based on the definition of employee engagement and ensure that the measure has face validity and content validity.
4. Develop an employee engagement survey	Develop an employee engagement survey that includes the measure of employee engagement as well as antecedents that are believed to influence employee engagement, process variables, and consequences that are believed to be important outcomes of employee engagement for employees and the organization. Discuss the survey with employees and other stakeholders in the organization and then distribute it to employees for completion.
5. Examine the employee engagement survey results	Review the survey results in terms of levels of employee engagement in and around the organization; the relationships between the antecedents, process variables, and employee engagement; and the relationships between employee engagement and the consequences. Discuss the results with employees and identify antecedents to focus on for improving employee engagement.

Step	Summary
6. Develop and implement an employee engagement strategy	Develop an employee engagement strategy that clearly indicates what antecedents and process variables will be the focus of an intervention, what exactly will be done to improve the antecedent, when it will be done, and the stakeholders who will be involved in the process.
7. Follow-up and evaluation	After the employee engagement strategy has been implemented a follow-up and evaluation should be conducted to determine the extent to which each intervention has been implemented and how effective it has been. A follow-up employee engagement survey should also be conducted, and the results compared to those of the previous survey in terms of the levels of employee engagement as well as the antecedents and process variables.

the focus of the employee engagement strategy. If after six months there does not appear to be a noticeable change in employee engagement scores or in the antecedents and process variables that were the target of an intervention then further investigation will be required to determine why the changes are not working and what further action is required. This might require additional changes to the antecedents, or it might require that other antecedents need to be part of the employee engagement strategy.

8.1.1 Summary

Table 8.2 summarizes the seven steps in the employee engagement practice model. Developing and implementing a strategy to improve employee engagement will require a considerable amount of time and effort. However, following each of the steps of the model will help to ensure that there is a clear path to understanding the extent to which employees in an organization are engaged and what changes are required to improve employee engagement. With an employee engagement strategy in place and the continuous monitoring of employee engagement scores, organizations should be able to create a working environment that will result in a highly engaged workforce and positive work outcomes.

8.2 Strategic human resources management and employee engagement

The employee engagement practice model is useful for monitoring employee engagement levels in an organization and for identifying key antecedents that drive employee engagement and require improvement. However, a more complete and system-wide approach to employee engagement should also include human resource management (HRM) practices that are designed to facilitate and enhance employee engagement. In this way, employee engagement can be strategically embedded and integrated into a system of HRM policies and practices and result in an HRM employee engagement strategy (Albrecht et al., 2015; Saks, 2017).

Strategic HRM involves the use of a bundle or system of interrelated and internally consistent HRM practices (Boon et al., 2019; Jiang et al., 2013; Takeuchi et al., 2009). A bundle of interrelated HRM practices creates synergistic effects that are greater than individual HRM practices and more likely to be similarly interpreted and acted upon by employees (Alfes et al., 2013). Furthermore, a bundle of interrelated HRM practices also helps to produce a strong HRM system in which there is agreement among employees about what the organization considers to be important and what is expected of them (Ostroff & Bowen, 2016).

According to Barrick et al. (2015), HRM practices represent organizational resources that can create collective organizational engagement "by shaping the nature of the employee-firm relationship" (p.116). They also note that HRM practices can facilitate employee engagement by enhancing Kahn's (1990) three psychological conditions of meaningfulness, safety, and availability. They found that HRM practices had a significant positive effect on collective organizational engagement.

There is now considerable evidence that bundles of HRM practices are positively related to employee engagement. For example, Alfes et al. (2013) found that perceptions of HRM practices were positively related to employee engagement, and employee engagement mediated the relationship between perceived HRM practices and organizational citizenship behavior (OCB) and turnover intentions. Boon and Kalshoven (2014) found that employee perceptions of high-commitment HRM practices (creating a long-term relationship with employees) were positively related to employee engagement, and employee engagement mediated the relationship between high-commitment HRM and organizational commitment. Zhong et al. (2016) found that perceived organizational support (POS) partially mediated the relationship between high-performance HRM practices and employee engagement. Cooke et al. (2019) found that resilience mediated the relationship between high-performance work systems (HPWS) and employee engagement. Thus, bundles of HRM practices seem to be especially important for employee engagement.

HRM practices are a key factor in the development of an organizational climate (Jiang et al., 2013). An organizational climate is a "*shared* perception of what the organization is like in terms of practices, policies, procedures, routines, and rewards – what is important and what behaviors are expected and rewarded" (Bowen & Ostroff, 2004, p.205). Organizational climate links HRM practices to employee attitudes and behaviors and mediates the relationship between HRM practices and employee and organizational outcomes (Jiang et al., 2013; Takeuchi et al., 2009).

HRM practices shape employees' climate perceptions by sending signals to employees about what is important and valued by the organization, what is expected, how they should interact with each other, and the appropriate responses (Bowen & Ostroff, 2004; Chuang & Liao, 2010; Han et al., 2020; Ostroff & Bowen, 2016). Thus, a bundle of HRM practices that are designed to facilitate employee engagement will send signals to employees about the importance of employee engagement and result in the formation of a climate for employee engagement (Albrecht et al., 2015). In a climate of employee engagement, employees will have *shared* perceptions that employee engagement is important, expected, and will be rewarded.

Albrecht (2014) described the creation and maintenance of an organizational climate for employee engagement noting that the creation of a high-engagement climate means that engagement is a central focus of an organization's systems, policies, processes, and practices. Albrecht et al. (2018) found that organizational resources such as human resource practices were positively related to an engagement climate, job resources, and employee engagement. In addition, an engagement climate was positively related to job resources and employee engagement and mediated the relationship between organizational resources and employee engagement.

Thus, HRM practices are an important factor in the development of an employee engagement climate.

In summary, when it comes to employee engagement practice one of the most important things an organization can do is to develop a strategic HRM employee engagement system that consists of a bundle of HRM practices that will lead to the development of an employee engagement climate and a highly engaged workforce. The key then is to determine what HRM practices are important for the development of a strategic HRM employee engagement system and an employee engagement climate.

8.2.1 Strategic HRM employee engagement system

Albrecht et al. (2015) described an HRM engagement strategy that consists of selection, socialization, performance management, and training and development. We extend this strategy by including a more complete set of HRM practices that in combination form a strategic HRM employee engagement system.

HRM practices that are important for employee engagement include selection, socialization, job design, training and development, flexible work arrangements, participation in decision making, and performance management.

Selection. Although most of the attention associated with improving employee engagement has focused on job resources and job demands, there is some evidence that individual differences are also related to employee engagement. For example, several studies have found that person-job (PJ) and person-organization (PO) fit perceptions are positively related to employee engagement (Crawford et al., 2010; Saks & Gruman, 2011). Rich et al. (2010) found that value congruence – or the extent to which one's personal values are congruent with those of the organization – was positively related to job engagement.

In addition, as noted in Chapter 5, there is also evidence that personality traits are related to employee engagement. In a meta-analysis of personality and employee engagement, Young et al. (2018) found that personality traits explained almost 50 percent of the variance in employee engagement. The strongest predictors were positive affectivity, proactive personality, conscientiousness, and extraversion.

Based on these findings, it seems that hiring for engagement is a viable approach for creating an engaged workforce. A selection system for employee engagement might include an assessment of job applicants' PJ and PO fit perceptions as well as personality traits such as positive affectivity, proactive personality, conscientiousness, and extraversion. Hiring individuals with a strong PJ and PO fit and who also score high on these personality traits might be an effective means of building a highly engaged workforce (Young et al., 2018).

Socialization. In Chapter 6, we described how socialization resources should be provided throughout the organizational entry and socialization process to develop and maintain high levels of newcomer engagement. In addition, socialization programs should also focus on developing high PJ and PO fit perceptions of newcomers (Chatman, 1991; Saks & Gruman, 2011) given that fit perceptions are positively related to employee engagement (Crawford et al., 2010; Saks & Gruman, 2011).

Job design. As indicated in Chapter 5, job characteristics have consistently been found to be positively related to employee engagement. For example, Christian et al. (2011) found that autonomy, task variety, task significance, problem-solving, feedback, and job complexity were positively related to employee engagement.

Barrick et al. (2015) found that enriching entry-level motivating work design (autonomy, task significance, task identity, variety, and feedback) was positively related to collective organizational engagement. They noted that when organizations implement "job characteristics to enhance motivation at lower levels of the organization, employees collectively sense that their work has value and purpose, which generates a shared perception of psychological meaningfulness throughout the firm" (p.116). Further, some of the job characteristics can also enhance psychological safety and availability. Thus, an important HRM practice for facilitating employee engagement is to design jobs that have the core characteristics of the job characteristics model.

Training and development. Opportunities for learning, training, and development have been found to be an important job resource for facilitating employee engagement. For example, Bakker and Bal (2010) found that opportunities for development were positively related to work engagement, and Eldor and Harpaz (2016) found that a positive learning climate (employee perceptions of the degree to which the atmosphere in the organization encourages learning) was positively related to employee engagement. Sarti (2014) found that learning opportunities were the strongest predictor of work engagement among six job resources in a study on caregivers in long-term care facilities.

Training and development and opportunities for learning can provide employees with the knowledge, skills, and personal resources (e.g., self-efficacy) required to perform their jobs, thereby enhancing their psychological availability and engagement (Albrecht et al., 2015).

Flexible work arrangements. Flexibility in the workplace provides employees with the opportunity to "make choices influencing when, where, and for how long they engage in work-related tasks" (Bal & De Lange, 2015, p.127). Bal and De Lange (2015) found that the availability of flexibility was positively related to employee engagement. Masuda et al. (2017) found that the availability of telecommuting was directly and indirectly related to employee engagement through perceived supervisor goal support and goal progress. Flexible work arrangements are likely to make employees more psychologically available and improve their psychological safety.

Participation in decision making. Participation in decision making and employee voice have been found to be positively related to employee engagement (Conway et al., 2016). For example, Yoerger et al. (2015) found that participation in decision making during meetings (the degree to which employees are allowed or encouraged to share their thoughts, feelings, and ideas in the meeting) was positively related to employee engagement. Rees et al. (2013) found that employee perceptions of voice behavior about improving the functioning of the work group had a direct and indirect effect on employee engagement. Holland et al. (2017) found that direct voice was positively related to work engagement and this relationship was mediated by senior management trust. Thus, providing employees with opportunities to participate in decision making and allowing them voice in matters that affect them will enhance their psychological meaningfulness and safety and enhance employee engagement.

Performance management. Performance management is an ongoing process that involves a variety of activities aimed at evaluating and promoting individual and team performance. While the focus is usually performance, Gruman and Saks (2011) argued that the performance management process should be designed so that employee engagement is integrated and embedded into the performance management process (what they call engagement management). Performance management activities such as setting performance and development goals and providing ongoing feedback and recognition have been shown to influence employee engagement, and employee engagement influences performance (Gruman & Saks, 2011; Mone et al., 2011).

Including employee engagement in the performance management process helps to focus on the needs of individual employees given that the drivers of employee engagement are likely to vary from employee to employee. Thus, employee engagement should be managed the same way that job performance is managed, especially given that employee engagement precedes and predicts job performance (Gruman & Saks, 2011). This not only allows for a more individualized approach to employee engagement, but by embedding employee engagement into the performance management process it ensures that employee engagement receives continuous and ongoing attention. An employee engagement management model that describes this process in more detail is described at the end of this chapter.

8.2.2   Summary

While each of the HRM practices described in this section can have a positive effect on employee engagement, the strongest effect is most likely to result when there is a bundle of HRM practices that are strategically focused on employee engagement. Furthermore, a system of interrelated HRM practices that focus on employee engagement is expected to result in an employee engagement climate in which employees have shared perceptions about the importance of being engaged in their job and work roles. Individual HRM practices are not likely to result in a strong engagement climate. Finally, a strong climate of employee engagement is expected to result in a highly engaged workforce.

Figure 8.1 shows a model of a strategic employee engagement HRM system. The model shows the main HRM practices which make up a strategic employee engagement HRM system and how this will facilitate the development of an employee engagement climate that will mediate the effect of the strategic employee engagement HRM system on employee engagement.

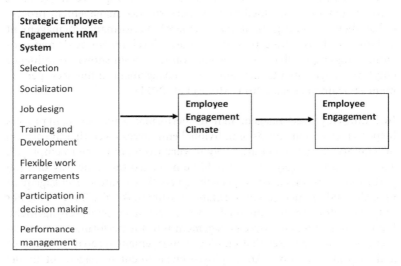

Figure 8.1   Strategic employee engagement HRM system and employee engagement climate

8.3   The employee engagement management process

Once the employee engagement practice model has been implemented to diagnose and potentially increase levels of engagement, and HRM systems have been developed to create a climate for employee engagement, the organization can then try to promote and maintain desirable levels of employee engagement by implementing the employee engagement management process. The employee engagement management process (Gruman & Saks, 2011) builds on models of performance management and involves facilitating employee engagement and performance by managing the operational context in which work is performed. The process was originally conceived as a way to promote employee engagement as a precursor to high performance, but our focus here is on the promotion and maintenance of employee engagement itself.

The first step in the employee engagement management process involves a *performance agreement* during which performance goals are established. When developing a performance agreement goals should be established that not only reflect the needs of the organization but also the needs, goals, and desires of individual employees. This promotes psychological meaningfulness and subsequently employee engagement. The performance agreement should also consider psychological contracts by discussing and agreeing upon the reciprocal obligations between employee and employer. If employees believe that the conditions necessary for employee engagement are absent, a contract violation might be perceived which could undermine their level of employee engagement. The performance agreement establishes the criteria and standards upon which employee engagement can be built.

The second step of the employee engagement management process is *engagement facilitation*, which involves ensuring that employees have the resources they need to engage themselves in their roles. Many of the issues involved in engagement facilitation have already been discussed as antecedents of engagement (see Chapter 5) and the development of HRM systems. The different and crucial issue during engagement facilitation is that managers should perform frequent, regular assessments to confirm that employees have the resources they need to become engaged, much the same way that performance management is an ongoing activity. These assessments then allow for continual adjustments to be made to the level and type of resources provided.

To facilitate employee engagement organizations should not only design jobs as outlined in Chapter 5 but ensure that employees fit well with the changing nature of the jobs they perform and have a say in the design of their work and the roles they occupy. Regular coaching should also be provided to offer advice and support when needed. Coaching can help to build psychological capital in employees through goal setting training, positive feedback, cognitive-behavioral techniques, and assistance in recovering from mistakes. Leadership can also facilitate employee engagement in this step by providing challenging assignments, allowing employees to have adequate autonomy, and participating in decisions that affect them. Finally, formal training can be provided to help employees develop skills and personal resources that allow them to cope with shifting job demands. Engagement facilitation ensures that employees have the resources they need to engage themselves on an ongoing basis.

The final step in the employee engagement management process is *performance and engagement appraisal and feedback*, which involves an assessment of employees' engagement behavior, such as persistence and proactivity, in addition to their performance. To promote employee engagement, it is important that employees regard this step as predictable, fair, and just, because unpredictable, unfair, unjust processes undermine psychological safety and employee engagement. In this stage, managers and employees discuss the extent to which employees have demonstrated behavioral engagement, achieved their goals, and have been provided with the resources necessary to accomplish their tasks. This stage is also an opportunity for managers to provide feedback, which must be done carefully so as not to undermine psychological safety.

Table 8.3 presents an overview of the employee engagement management process. Together, the three steps of the employee engagement management process help to foster a work context in which employee engagement can be enhanced and maintained. They are also likely to generate

Table 8.3   The employee engagement management process

Step	Content
Step 1: Performance agreement	Establish organizational goals considering the needs, goals, and desires of individual employees. Discuss psychological contracts and agree upon reciprocal obligations.
Step 2: Engagement facilitation	Provide ongoing assessment and adjustment of resources focusing on: • Job design • Coaching and support • Leadership • Training
Step 3: Performance and engagement appraisal and feedback	Assess employees' behavioral engagement and performance. Provide feedback.

high performance by creating a context in which employees are more cognitively, affectively, and behaviorally engaged.

8.4 Conclusion

In this chapter, we have tried to make sense of the many studies on employee engagement and to describe how to translate employee engagement research and science into practice. While this might seem like a daunting task, we have described three approaches that make use of the research and science of employee engagement.

First, we described an employee engagement practice model which consists of seven steps that include the development of an employee engagement survey in order to produce meaningful results that can be used to develop an employee engagement strategy that involves making changes to important antecedents of employee engagement. Second, we described how to design an HRM system composed of a bundle of HRM practices which is strategically focused on developing a climate of employee engagement and an engaged workforce. When these HRM practices are used together as an HRM engagement system, they will result in an employee engagement climate that will then produce a more engaged workforce. Finally, we described how the performance management process can be refocused into an employee engagement management process that focuses on improving employee engagement and enhancing job performance.

While these three approaches can be used as stand-alone strategies for driving employee engagement in organizations, the most successful approach is to use all three of them together. Thus, organizations should frequently use surveys to measure and monitor employee engagement; design HRM practices to focus on employee engagement and develop an employee engagement climate; and monitor, evaluate, and improve the engagement of individual employees on an ongoing basis through the engagement management process.

9 Employee engagement: problems and prospects

Although much has been learned about employee engagement, there remain many issues that have received little or no research attention. In this chapter, we present some suggestions for future research. A full appreciation of employee engagement requires that we consider both the pros and potential cons of the construct. To structure this discussion, we apply the balance framework (Gruman et al., 2018) to employee engagement to provide a nuanced perspective of the construct and highlight a variety of important, but largely unexplored, research questions. We then discuss several issues that must be addressed for research on employee engagement to advance, including research on the antecedents and consequences of different targets of employee engagement, longitudinal research, and intervention studies.

9.1   A balanced view of employee engagement

Employee engagement is generally considered to be a positive, desirable construct representing a form of workplace well-being (e.g., Nielsen et al., 2017). Bakker et al. (2008) explicitly refer to employee engagement as a *"positive,* fulfilling, affective-motivational state" (emphasis added, p.187), and Halbesleben et al. (2009) note that "the engagement literature seems to suggest that engagement is a good thing from the perspective of both employers and employees alike" (p.1452). However, the positivity of employee engagement might be somewhat more equivocal.

Gruman et al. (2018) developed *the balance framework* to underscore the nuanced nature of ostensibly positive constructs, highlighting that their positivity might be ambiguous and contingent. The balance framework consists of five forms of balance: balance as tempered view of constructs, balance as mid-range, balance as complementarity, balance as contextual sensitivity, and balance between conscious and unconscious phenomena. Applying the balance framework to employee engagement highlights issues that have received little empirical attention and presents new avenues for research (see Table 9.1). We will consider each form of balance in turn, focusing on employee job/work engagement because it has received the most attention conceptually and empirically.

9.1.1 Balance as tempered view of constructs

Balance as tempered view of constructs highlights the fact that ostensibly positive phenomena might not be unambiguously balanced. Constructs that seem positive might have negative qualities, and vice versa. This suggests that there might be a "dark side" to employee engagement that warrants conceptual and empirical consideration. Indeed, there is research suggesting that there might be undesirable qualities associated with the experience of employee engagement.

Engagement has been shown to be associated with negative outcomes at work. Wang et al. (2019) found that employee engagement was positively related to knowledge hiding, territorial behavior, and pro-job unethical behavior through the indirect effect of job-based psychological ownership. Wang et al. (2019) suggest that this occurs because engagement leads employees to view their work as an extended sense of themselves which generates efforts to protect their ownership of the work and prevent others from interfering with it.

Engagement has also been found to be associated with negative outcomes in employees' personal lives. In three samples, Halbesleben et al. (2009) found that engagement compromised employees' family time by generating time-based, strain-based, and behavior-based work interference with family. The authors suggested that this happens because when employees are engaged and expend resources at work it leaves fewer resources available to them to devote to their family lives. Similarly, Rothbard (2001) found a depletion effect from work engagement to family engagement for women.

Scholars have suggested a variety of other potential negative aspects of engagement. For example, Sonnentag (2011) suggests that engagement might lead to compromised health and well-being over time. George

(2011) suggests that losing one's job might be particularly distressing for those who are more, as opposed to less, engaged. Engaged employees might also be inclined to proactively alter their jobs so that they can spend

Table 9.1 Applying the balance framework to employee engagement research

Form of balance	Issue	Sample research questions
Balance as tempered view of constructs	There might be a "dark side" to employee engagement.	Are there negative outcomes associated with employee engagement? Is there a "dark form" of employee engagement?
Balance as mid-range	Employee engagement might be best experienced at moderate levels.	What happens when employees are too engaged? What is the optimal range of employee engagement?
Balance as complementarity	Antecedents might interact in generating employee engagement and employee engagement might interact with other variables in producing outcomes.	How do antecedents interact in generating employee engagement? How does employee engagement interact with other variables in producing positive and negative outcomes?
Balance as contextual sensitivity	Employee engagement may be more or less positive in particular contexts.	What contexts are most conducive to employee engagement? Are there particular situations in which employee engagement leads to undesirable outcomes?
Balance between conscious and unconscious phenomena	Producing desirable outcomes involves both conscious and unconscious processes.	How do conscious and unconscious processes operate in generating employee engagement? How do conscious and unconscious processes operate in generating outcomes associated with employee engagement?

more time on enjoyable tasks and less time on disliked tasks. Although this might benefit the employee it might be a disadvantage for the employer (George, 2011). Bakker et al. (2011) question whether engagement might potentially foster high arousal that can distract employees and compromise performance, or whether the positive affect that characterizes engagement might lead to heuristic cognitive processing and a failure to consider details when required.

There might also be a dark *form* of engagement. It will be recalled that Schaufeli et al. (2002) portray engagement as a *"positive*, fulfilling, work-related state of mind that is characterized by vigor, dedication, and absorption" (emphasis added, p.74). But certainly, one could feel vigorous, dedicated, and absorbed as part of a negative state of engagement, for example, while angrily pursuing a lawsuit against one's unjust employer, frustratingly trying to convince an obstinate colleague about the merits of one's business proposal, or jealously strategizing how to undermine a competitor at work. Aside from the obvious difference in valence, is "negative" engagement qualitatively different from "positive" engagement? Is it fostered by different antecedents? Does it lead to different consequences? For instance, might negative engagement produce deleterious health and well-being outcomes that exceed those Sonnentag (2011) suggests might occur with "positive" engagement? A more balanced view of employee engagement recognizes that it is not unambiguously positive. More research is needed on the "dark side" and "dark form" of employee engagement.

9.1.2 Balance as mid-range

The second component of the balance framework, balance as mid-range, suggests that positive phenomena might be best experienced at moderate, as opposed to high levels. This idea has classic roots. In his famous "doctrine of the mean," the ancient Greek philosopher Aristotle (2004), argued that virtue lies between the vices of excess and deficiency, suggesting, for example, that at high levels the virtues of courage, patience, and wittiness become the vices of rashness, irascibility, and buffoonery respectively. In more recent times this phenomenon has been referred to as the "too-much-of-a-good-thing" effect (Pierce & Aguinis, 2013), reflecting the idea that "all positive traits, states, and experiences have costs that at high levels may begin to outweigh their benefits, creating the non-monotonicity of an inverted U" (Grant & Schwartz, 2011, p.62).

As noted by George (2010), the employee engagement literature implicitly assumes that more engagement is always better. However, it might be that engagement can be overdone. Bakker et al. (2011) suggested that "'overengagement' can ... have negative consequences. For example, although engaged employees are not workaholics, they may become so engaged in their work that they take work home" (p.18) which can lead to overwork, ineffective recovery, damage to relationships, and burnout (Bakker et al., 2008; Schaufeli & Salanova, 2011).

Similarly, Sonnentag (2011) wonders whether employee engagement might demonstrate a curvilinear association with desirable outcomes. In line with the too-much-of-a-good-thing effect, she suggests that "up to a certain level, work engagement might be positively related to these outcomes but at extremely high levels, it might become detrimental" (p.35). Bakker et al. (2011) propose that research should examine the potential deleterious effects of high levels of engagement.

A number of authors have suggested that high levels of engagement can be taxing. Building on Kahn's (1990) observation that engagement requires energetic resources, Macey and Schneider (2008) note that engagement can be draining because it requires the expenditure of personal resources and that, at least to some extent, there is a limited pool of resources available to an employee. Similarly, Halbesleben et al. (2009) suggest that it is possible for employees to be overinvested in work and that over time an excess of engagement might deplete the very resources on which it depends. More research is needed on the ideal range of engagement.

Importantly, some of the resources that serve as antecedents of engagement might themselves demonstrate a non-monotonic association with employee engagement. In his "Vitamin Model," Warr (2007) argued that certain resources, such as opportunities for skill use and variety, have toxic effects at high levels. More recently, Van Veldhoven et al. (2020) similarly noted that "having more of a job resource is not always beneficial" (p.14), and that whether variables should be considered resources or demands can be ambiguous. There is some preliminary research supporting these ideas with respect to employee engagement. Although time urgency can foster employee engagement (Crawford et al., 2010), employee engagement has been shown to be compromised when employees have too much time pressure (Sheng et al., 2019). Employee engagement is also diminished when employees perceive too much meaning at work (Vogel et al., 2020). However, very little empirical attention has been paid to the curvilinear effects of employee engagement or its antecedents (cf., Caesens et al., 2016). More research is needed on this important topic.

9.1.3 Balance as complementarity

Balance as complementarity concerns the fact that to understand positive phenomena it might be necessary to consider how multiple variables operate in tandem. With respect to employee engagement this concerns how multiple variables might function jointly to generate it and how it might operate in combination with other variables in promoting or inhibiting desirable outcomes.

Multiple variables might operate conjointly in generating employee engagement. For example, Sheng at al. (2019) found that the curvilinear association between time pressure and engagement was moderated by psychological capital (PsyCap). Specifically, when PsyCap was high Sheng et al. (2019) observed a generally linear association between time pressure and employee engagement. However, when PsyCap was low they observed a curvilinear relationship, with employee engagement being compromised at high levels of time pressure. Thus, time pressure interacted with PsyCap in generating employee engagement.

PsyCap is a personal resource that might operate similarly among all employees, but some of the resources that drive employee engagement might operate differently across employees. Vogel et al. (2020) found that the degree to which meaning fostered employee engagement depended on whether the amount of meaning provided by employees' jobs matched how much meaning they needed. In short, the resource was effective in generating engagement to the extent that it complemented individual employees' needs, highlighting that resources are impactful only when they are valued by employees (Van Veldhoven et al., 2020). More research is needed on how various antecedents function synergistically in generating employee engagement.

Employee engagement might also interact with individual differences in producing desirable outcomes. For instance, Halbesleben et al. (2009) found that although engagement was associated with work interference with family, this association was less pronounced among engaged employees who were high in conscientiousness. Thus, it was not the main effect of engagement that was of concern but the interaction between engagement and conscientiousness, with the latter allowing employees to regulate their investment of self and avoid role conflict. Similarly, Wang et al. (2019) found that the effects of engagement on knowledge hiding, territorial behavior, and pro-job unethical behavior only occurred among employees high in avoidance motivation.

Positive outcomes might also be fostered by balancing engagement with disengagement. For instance, it might be beneficial to engage while performing desirable aspects of one's role, but to disengage when handling disagreeable aspects, such as when terminating an employee (Margolis & Molinsky, 2008). Similarly, desirable long-term outcomes might require balancing engagement at work with disengagement when away from work in order to allow for effective recovery. Not only are recovery experiences associated with engagement (ten Brummelhuis & Bakker, 2012), but recovery experiences, such as psychological detachment from work, have been shown to be particularly restorative and produce positive affect for employees with high levels of employee engagement (Sonnentag et al., 2008). As Sonnentag et al. (2008) suggest, "a balance between high engagement at work and high disengagement from work during non-work time is highly relevant for protecting employees' well-being" (p.270).

An inability to effectively regulate the engagement/disengagement dynamic might be one factor that eventually produces burnout, which some have suggested might be a long-term consequence of employee engagement (Bakker et al., 2008; Schaufeli & Salanova, 2011). To fully understand the drivers and outcomes of employee engagement it appears advisable to examine the complementary effects of antecedents on employee engagement and the interactive effects of employee engagement and other variables.

9.1.4 Balance as contextual sensitivity

Balance as contextual sensitivity concerns the fact that variables might be considered relatively positive or negative depending on the contexts in which they occur. For example, the negative effects of employee engagement on work interference with family might be mitigated by organizational contexts that offer flextime (Halbesleben et al., 2009). This is an area that is ripe for further investigation because there is very little employee engagement research that explores issues related to context.

Purcell (2014) "bemoans the almost total lack of context in most studies of employee engagement" (p.242), suggesting that contextual and systemic issues must be taken into account to understand the applicability of engagement in work settings.

Similarly, Bakker et al. (2011) suggest that more attention needs to be paid to "the broader contextual organizational factors that impact on engagement" (p.23). Speaking to the importance of context, Jenkins and Delbridge (2013) suggest that "management's ability to deliver engagement is influenced by a number of contingent factors: the wider economy and particular industry sector, specific market conditions, ownership and governance arrangements as well as organizational size and internal structures" (p.2671). Such contextual factors also play a role in whether employee engagement might be more or less desirable for employees.

Jenkins and Delbridge (2013) studied engagement in two organizations operating within different contexts: a small, family-owned business operating in a moderately competitive, growing market, and a division of a large multinational company operating in a highly competitive, declining market. Jenkins and Delbridge (2013) explained how the different contexts facilitated and obstructed managements' efforts to promote engagement by influencing organizational attributes such as values, job features, organizational support, and social relations. They concluded that research on employee engagement should acknowledge "the importance of external and internal organizational contexts and the opportunities and constraints management face when seeking to deliver employee engagement" (p.2687).

Jenkins and Delbridge (2013) noted that the largely failed effort to generate employee engagement in the larger organizations was driven by the goal of achieving competitive advantage as opposed to promoting engagement as an end in itself. In that type of organization, employee engagement was regarded as a tool management could use to manipulate employees for productive ends. Is that positive? Some authors criticize ostensibly positive organizational constructs such as employee engagement on the grounds that they privilege management interests at the expense of employees (e.g., Warren, 2010).

Research on contextual issues would help to reveal circumstances in which engagement might be regarded as negative because it is exploitative. For instance, research could examine an organization's formal policies and enacted management practices in an effort to determine if engagement is being promoted as a form of employee well-being or weaponized as a means of control. Similarly, research could explore employee perceptions of the reasons their organizations promote engagement to determine if they attribute it to issues related to control over – versus the commitment of – employees (Nishii et al., 2008). Such research would shed light on the contexts in which engagement might be regarded as relatively positive or negative and potentially inform our understanding of the antecedents and consequences of employee engagement in different organizational settings.

Research on contexts for employee engagement might benefit from studies incorporating taxonomies of situations. Recent theorizing has suggested a number of typologies of situational characteristics analogous to the typologies developed to characterize individual personalities. For example, Rauthmann et al. (2014) developed the Situational Eight DIAMONDS model which includes situational dimensions such as adversity, positivity, and deception. Similarly, Parrigon et al. (2017) developed the CAPTION model which includes situational dimensions such as positive valence, adversity, and complexity. Such models might be of value in helping researchers identify situational contexts that are more or less supportive of employee engagement and in which employee engagement might be more or less likely to result in positive outcomes.

A final contextual issue concerns the social context. What are the repercussions of being engaged when one's colleagues are not? What are the implications of being engaged in a politically charged environment? Might employing and expressing one's "preferred self" sometimes be reckless and career limiting? Beyond the antecedent condition of psychological safety, are there conditions in which being engaged might be misguided? We refer to the competency of discerning when it is prudent or ill-advised to be engaged and then appropriately moderating one's engagement level as "tactical engagement." Building on the notion of regulating one's engagement level, might employees' ability to diagnose the social context and regulate their engagement level accordingly predict positive and negative outcomes of employee engagement? More research is needed on these topics.

9.1.5 Balance between conscious and unconscious phenomena

The final aspect of the balance framework highlights that much of what underlies human behavior occurs outside of conscious awareness (Bargh & Morsella, 2008) and that effectively understanding positive phenomena requires attention to both conscious and unconscious processes.

Employee engagement is a motivational construct that has both affective and cognitive components. Given that unconscious processes have been implicated in motivational (Dijksterhuis & Aarts, 2010), affective (Winkelman & Berridge, 2004), and cognitive (Dijksterhuis & Nordgren, 2006) processes, more research on unconscious processes and the interplay of conscious and unconscious processes in generating employee engagement is warranted. For example, how do unconscious goals influence the perceived value of resources in generating employee engagement?

Unconscious processes were explicitly detailed in Kahn's (1990) original formulation of psychological presence and personal engagement at work. He noted that the process of determining whether the work environment satisfies the three psychological conditions that lead to engagement is unconscious. Specifically, he indicated that his research participants "seemed to unconsciously ask themselves three questions in each situation and to personally engage or disengage depending on the answers" (p.703). He also suggested that psychological safety is influenced by the "unconscious roles" employees assumed at work (p.709) and argued that getting to the core of understanding psychological presence at work requires studying both conscious and unconscious phenomena. However, as far as we are aware there is no research examining unconscious phenomena in the experience or etiology of employee engagement, factors that influence these unconscious phenomena, or how they may interact with conscious processes in fostering or hindering employee engagement at work.

George (2010) notes that the literature on employee engagement implicitly assumes that conscious engagement is what leads to desirable outcomes at work. She outlines, however, that an extensive body of research demonstrates that desirable outcomes are often produced by unconscious processes that operate when one is not directly engaged with a task. For example, creative solutions to problems often emerge spontaneously when one is distracted or otherwise not fully engaged with a problem (Sio & Ormerod, 2009). This happens because much cognitive processing, if not most of it, occurs unconsciously (Wilson, 2002). George (2010) therefore suggests that "high and sustained conscious engagement [may be] beneficial for certain kinds of activities such as learning new skills or acquiring new knowledge and information (Ouellette & Wood, 1998; Wegner & Bargh, 1998), [but] may be less beneficial for other activities characterized by high uncertainty, ambiguity, the need for creative responses, the processing of large amounts of information, and the use of existing knowledge" (pp.255–256). Importantly, in line with balance as complementarity, conscious and unconscious processes might operate in tandem. For example, creative solutions might be most likely when a period of disengagement follows a period of active engagement with a problem. Research is needed in exploring the outcomes that are best promoted by conscious engagement and those that might be better promoted by alternating between engagement and disengagement, which allows unconscious processes to operate. Such research requires within-person, longitudinal designs (George, 2010).

9.2   Advancing research on employee engagement

In order to advance research on employee engagement there are several key issues that should be addressed. These include conducting more research on different targets of employee engagement, longitudinal research that can better elucidate issues of causality and temporality, and designing high-quality intervention studies.

9.2.1   Targets of employee engagement

In Chapter 2, we described the need to define employee engagement in terms of a specific role or target, and that employees can be engaged to different degrees in various roles that they occupy. However, most research on employee engagement has been on job or work engagement rather than these other roles and targets of engagement. Therefore, one area in particular need of research is the antecedents and consequences of different targets of employee engagement.

9.2.1.1   *Antecedents of targets of employee engagement*

As noted in Chapter 5, the vast majority of research on the antecedents of employee engagement has focused on employee job or work engagement as the target. Very little research has been done on the antecedents of other targets of engagement. There is a literature on task engagement (e.g., Smallwood et al., 2004), but this form of task engagement is largely restricted to motivation and cognitive vigilance and does not involve the investment of the full self which characterizes the employee task engagement construct.

There are two exceptions to this general theme. First, using the vigor and dedication sub-scales of the UWES, Llorens et al. (2007) observed that having control over one's time and work methods was associated with task engagement and this relationship was mediated by self-efficacy. Second, using a measure of task engagement that reflects Kahn's (1990) conceptualization, Newton et al. (2020) demonstrated that engagement on an initial task generated high performance on a subsequent task by fostering a spillover of engagement onto the second task; however, when participants continued to ruminate about the initial task because it was incomplete, engagement on the initial task compromised engagement and performance on the subsequent task. In effect, Newton et al. (2020) demonstrated that task engagement can serve as an antecedent to successive episodes of task engagement. Because there is so little research in this area, research on the antecedents of task engagement represents a fruitful area of future research. Some possible antecedents to consider include task characteristics such as autonomy, task significance, and feedback, as well as task demands such as task complexity and time urgency.

There is also a virtual absence of literature devoted to the antecedents of team engagement and business unit/department engagement, making these topics ripe for future research. Possible antecedents for team engagement might be team-level factors such as team characteristics, a supportive team climate, relational conflict, and identification with the team (Costa et al. 2014a; Torrente et al., 2012). Antecedents to consider for business unit/department engagement include business unit support, leadership, and business unit climate.

By contrast, a number of studies have investigated the antecedents of organization engagement. In the first study, Saks (2006) found that perceived organizational support (POS) and procedural justice predicted organization engagement. Fletcher and Schofield (2019) found that a workplace intervention designed to enhance the meaningfulness employees experienced at work was successful at enhancing organization engagement. Qi et al. (2018) found that work design factors including staffing, standardization, and empowerment were associated with organization engagement through the mediating effect of organizational support and customer focus. In a sample of Indian employees, Farndale (2017) found that the fairness of a specific HR practice – performance appraisal – and POS were associated with organization engagement, and supervisor support mediated the relationship between the fairness of performance appraisals and organization engagement. Finally, Ünal and Turgut (2015) found a positive relationship between person-organization (PO) fit and organization engagement.

Thus, an increasing number of studies have found that factors associated with all of Kahn's (1990) psychological conditions (meaningfulness, safety, availability) are positively associated with organization engagement, but the number of investigations of this topic is limited and the quality of the studies and empirical evidence is generally low. Interestingly, these studies have typically considered antecedents that are similar to those investigated in research on employee job/work engagement, but a handful have also examined organization-level variables such as corporate social responsibility (CSR) and employer branding (e.g., Abdelmotaleb, 2020; Azim, 2016; Bhasin et al., 2019). These variables are most likely to impact psychological meaningfulness. More research is needed on the factors that foster organization engagement, whether organization engagement is promoted by the same psychological antecedents that drive employee job/work engagement, and whether there are differences in the resources, and relative importance of the resources, that predict the different targets of employee engagement.

9.2.1.2   Consequences of targets of employee engagement

The consequences of employee engagement are likely to depend on the target of engagement. For example, task engagement is likely to be a strong predictor of task satisfaction and task performance; team engagement is likely to be a strong predictor of team satisfaction and team performance; business unit/department engagement should predict commitment to one's business unit/department and performance of business unit/department tasks; and organization engagement should be a strong predictor of organizational commitment and organizational citizenship behavior.

However, except for one study demonstrating that task engagement might foster the personal resource of self-efficacy beliefs (Llorens et al., 2007), there is no research on the consequences associated with different targets of employee engagement other than employee job/work engagement. The exception involves the consequences associated with organization engagement, for which there is a growing amount of empirical evidence.

Saks (2006) found that organization engagement was negatively related to intention to quit and positively related to job satisfaction, organizational commitment, and organizational citizenship behavior. He also found that job engagement and organization engagement partially mediated the relationship between a variety of antecedents and consequences. Akingbola and van den Berg (2019) replicated the association between organization engagement and the consequences examined by Saks (2006), and found that organization engagement mediated most of the relationships between the antecedents of value congruence, job characteristics, and rewards and recognition, and the consequences. Based on data from two multinational companies, Farndale et al. (2014) found that organization engagement was positively related to job satisfaction, affective commitment, active learning, initiative, OCBO, and perceived organizational performance. Kim and Koo (2017) found that organization engagement was positively related to self-rated job performance among hotel employees.

The paucity of research on the consequences of the various targets of employee engagement makes this an important avenue for future research. Truss et al. (2014) "question whether the focus of engagement, rather than being on the job itself, would perhaps be better conceived as relating to the organization as a whole" (p.10). We suggest that research on the consequences of the various targets of employee engagement will help to identify where the focus of engagement should be best conceived to generate diverse desired outcomes.

9.2.2 Longitudinal research

Most of the research on employee engagement is cross-sectional (Bailey et al., 2017). As noted by Bailey et al. (2017), cross-sectional studies of employee engagement are limited because the effect of one variable on another (e.g., antecedents impacting employee engagement) might take time to occur, time intervals are not specified even though the magnitude of effects might differ over time, they fail to account for initial levels of variables, and they preclude inferences of causality. As a result, although there is research on the antecedents and consequences of employee engagement, our ability to draw conclusions about causal relationships is limited. Also, with respect to antecedents, most of the longitudinal studies that do exist are based on self-report data, raising questions about common method bias (Lesener et al., 2019). More longitudinal research using multi-source data is needed in order to establish the causal relationships among antecedents and employee engagement, and among employee engagement and outcomes.

Longitudinal research can also explore changes in employee engagement over time. Saks and Gruman (2018) introduced employee engagement maintenance curves (see Chapter 6) which outline different patterns of increasing, decreasing, and stable employee engagement patterns over the course of a year. However, apart from the purported importance of resources, little is known about how employee engagement changes over time and why. Research is needed on the factors that promote increases or decreases in employee engagement, in addition to when and how to intervene to promote an increase in employee engagement and prevent a decrease.

Research is also needed on exploring changes in employee task engagement, employee team engagement, employee business unit or departmental engagement, and employee organization engagement. Additionally, for each target of employee engagement, longitudinal research should examine the reciprocal effects of antecedents, employee engagement, and outcomes to explore gain and loss spirals in which variables mutually reinforce each other producing upward or downward trajectories (Hobfoll, 2001). Knowledge of factors affecting gain and loss spirals would facilitate the development of interventions to promote employee engagement in all its forms.

9.2.3 Intervention studies

More research is needed on interventions that foster employee engagement. Existing evidence suggests that interventions can be effective for increasing employee engagement, but additional research is needed to know what type of interventions are most successful, why they are successful, and under what conditions (Bailey et al., 2017).

In a meta-analysis of 20 employee engagement intervention studies, Knight et al. (2017) found a small but reliable overall effect of interventions, with group interventions showing the largest effect. In a subsequent systematic review based on 40 studies, Knight et al. (2019) found that half of the interventions had a significant positive effect on work engagement or one of its components (e.g., vigor), two had a negative effect, and 18 had no effect. Initial evidence was found for the idea that changes in job and personal resources, job demands, and need satisfaction mediate these effects.

Knight et al. (2019) also explored seven potential moderators and found that job crafting and health promotion interventions (e.g., mindfulness) were most effective in addition to those that were implemented well, driven by individuals themselves, and included employee participation, manager support, and both individual and group components. However, their results were highly variable, underscoring the need for more research.

Research is also needed in exploring the effects of interventions on other targets of employee engagement. The only study that has examined an intervention designed to impact a target of engagement other than employee job/work engagement is the study noted earlier by Fletcher and Schofield (2019) in which a meaningfulness intervention succeeded at enhancing organization engagement.

Future research should explore how interventions at the different levels discussed in Chapter 5 (individual, group, leader, organization) impact the various targets of employee engagement and, in line with balance as contextual sensitivity, the circumstances that promote and hinder their success. This research should also explain the mechanisms that mediate the effects.

A better understanding of context and process is key to advancing employee engagement intervention research. Knight et al. (2019) note that context might impact the effectiveness of employee engagement interventions with, for example, offices, hospitals, and factories possibly requiring different design elements. Thorough research on employee engagement interventions should not only explore whether interventions are effective or not, but should examine "what works for whom in which circumstances" by studying the mechanisms of successful interventions, the contexts that trigger them, and how they generate outcomes (Nielsen & Miraglia, 2017, p.41).

Furthermore, intervention research on employee engagement should discuss routinely whether the interventions were implemented successfully (Knight et al., 2019) and consider the boundary conditions that limit their generalizability (Busse et al., 2017). For instance, job crafting interventions might be particularly effective for employees who lack important job resources and health promotion interventions might be more effective for employees who experience high levels of stress (Knight et al., 2019).

9.3   Conclusion

Employee engagement is still a relatively new construct in management and has generated a considerable amount of attention from academics and practitioners. However, there remain many unanswered research questions about the construct that warrant attention. Issues associated with the potential "dark side" of employee engagement have been considered conceptually by a few authors but, except for a few papers, the topic has been virtually unexplored empirically. Future research on these topics is warranted, along with research applying the balance framework to different targets of employee engagement other than employee job/work engagement. The antecedents and consequences of employee task, team, and business unit/department engagement are virtually unexplored, and those associated with employee organization engagement have only received a modicum of attention. Also, more longitudinal research and high-quality intervention studies are needed. Research along these lines will shed more light on the nature, antecedents, and consequences of employee engagement, along with the ways in which employee engagement can be best promoted.

10 Strategic employee engagement

In this book we have covered the main issues and topics about employee engagement. Therefore, in this final chapter we will take stock of what we have covered and provide an updated model of employee engagement. This chapter also covers three additional topics that we feel will become increasingly important for employee engagement research and practice. First, we discuss what it means to take a more strategic approach to employee engagement or what we call *strategic employee engagement*. Second, we discuss the importance of care in fostering employee engagement and the potential effects of caring organizations on employee engagement. And third, we compare job engagement to organization engagement and note some important differences that might make organization engagement more important than job engagement.

10.1 What do we know about employee engagement?

At this point in the employee engagement journey it is worth taking stock of where we have been and what has been learned. We began the journey stating that employee engagement matters because it has implications for employees and organizations, and that organizations with highly engaged employees will outperform their competitors and have a competitive advantage.

In Chapter 2, we described how employee engagement is different from other constructs such as job satisfaction and organizational commitment, and that it is a multidimensional motivational construct. Compared to other constructs such as job satisfaction, employee engagement involves the investment of an individual's full and complete self in the performance of a task, job, or any work-related role. Thus, employee engagement is a role-specific construct that refers to different roles or targets.

In Chapter 3, we described several theories such as job characteristics theory and social exchange theory that have been used to explain the employee engagement process. We also discussed the JD-R model and Kahn's (1990) theory of personal engagement and psychological presence, which are the main theories that have been used to study employee engagement. These theories suggest that a number of process variables such as Kahn's (1990) three psychological conditions (meaningfulness, safety, availability), needs satisfaction, positive emotions, responsibility, and social exchange relationships explain why antecedents (job resources, demands, personal resources) will result in higher levels of employee engagement.

In Chapter 4, we reviewed the measures of employee engagement that have been developed in the academic literature and noted that while there are some similarities among them, they are not interchangeable and are likely to produce different research results. When deciding on how to measure employee engagement, we noted that it is important to first decide on the items to include in the measure and then identify the target and the referent.

The focus of Chapter 5 was on the antecedents and consequences of employee engagement. We described the antecedents in terms of four levels (individual, group, leader, and organization) and categorized them in relation to Kahn's (1990) three psychological conditions of meaningfulness, safety, and availability. The consequences of employee engagement were described in terms of individual, group, and organization outcomes.

In Chapter 6, we noted that newcomers to organizations represent a unique and special group of employees to focus on for the purpose of employee engagement. Newcomer engagement maintenance curves were presented to indicate the different patterns and trends of newcomer engagement during the organizational entry-socialization period. We also described socialization resources theory (SRT) and the importance of resources for developing and maintaining newcomer engagement throughout the socialization process.

In Chapter 7, we noted the important role that cultural differences play when it comes to the meaning, measurement, and antecedents and consequences of employee engagement. As a result, we have to be cautious when generalizing the results of employee engagement research across cultures.

In Chapter 8, we described several approaches for translating employee engagement research into practice. First, we described the employee engagement practice model which consists of seven steps for developing and implementing an employee engagement survey and then using the data to determine the practices and interventions that should be implemented to improve employee engagement. Second, we described a strategic HRM employee engagement system that consists of HRM practices that should be used to develop an employee engagement climate that will result in a highly engaged workforce. Finally, we described how the employee engagement management process can be used to promote and facilitate employee engagement on an ongoing basis.

In Chapter 9, we described a number of issues that require more research attention. We presented the balance framework which consists of five forms of balance and indicates that there can be negative consequences associated with employee engagement and that more engagement is not always better as there can be a dark side to employee engagement.

Although we have learned a great deal about employee engagement, we still have much to learn when it comes to the antecedents and consequences of different targets of engagement, the extent to which antecedents cause employee engagement and employee engagement causes various consequences, and interventions that are most effective for developing employee engagement.

Now that we have covered the main issues and topics of employee engagement we can return to the employee engagement model that we first presented in Chapter 1 and update and revise it. The employee engagement model shows the sequence of variables that are associated with employee engagement. The model shows that antecedents are related to employee engagement through process variables, and employee engagement leads to employee outcomes which then lead to organization outcomes. We can now provide a more detailed model about the employee engagement process based on what we have learned since Chapter 1.

As shown in Figure 10.1, the antecedent variables (job resources, job demands, and personal resources) can be individual-, group-, leader-, and organizational-level antecedents. The process variables include need satisfaction, positive emotions, psychological conditions (meaningfulness, safety, and availability), responsibility, and social exchange. Employee engagement can refer to one or more targets (employee task engagement, employee job/work engagement, employee team engagement, employee business unit or department engagement, and employee organization engagement). Employee engagement will lead to consequences for individuals and groups (attitudes, intentions, behaviors, performance, and health and wellness outcomes), which will then lead to organization outcomes such as performance, productivity, profitability, and customer satisfaction.

10.1.1 Summary

In summary, Figure 10.1 presents a revised model of the current state of what we know about employee engagement. It remains for future research to identify the extent to which particular antecedents are related to the different targets of employee engagement, and the process variables that are most important for explaining these relationships. Future research is also required to learn more about the extent to which each target of employee engagement is related to employee, group, and organization outcomes.

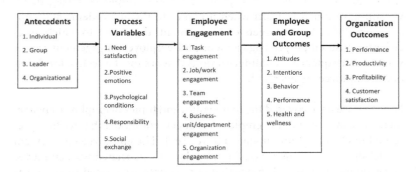

Figure 10.1   Revised model of employee engagement

10.2 Strategic employee engagement

When people think about employee engagement, they generally believe that it is a good thing for all employees to be highly engaged in their jobs all the time. A one-size-fits-all approach assumes that all employees should always be highly engaged. However, this is not a very strategic approach. So, what is a more strategic approach to employee engagement? There are several ways to be more strategic about employee engagement.

First, one might begin with an organization's strategy. This is especially important when an organization is making changes to its goals and objectives. The strategy should be a key factor that determines what is most important when it comes to employee engagement. For example, if the strategy involves being innovative and competing on innovation, then the focus should be employee engagement in innovative tasks and behaviors. In fact, a study by Vinarski-Peretz and Carmeli (2011) (described in more detail in the next section on care and employee engagement) found that Kahn's (1990) psychological conditions were positively related to employee motivation to engage in innovative behavior and engagement in innovative behaviors. Thus, the strategy should dictate what should be emphasized when it comes to employee engagement. What are the most important tasks, activities, and behaviors that employees need to be highly engaged in when they are performing them?

Second, there is a belief that all employees should be or need to be engaged to the same extent all the time. This also implies that the same resources should be given to all employees to increase their employee engagement. However, there might be times when it is particularly important for employees to be highly engaged, such as when performing a task that has major consequences for the organization and its members or when the organization is involved in an activity that is especially important to its strategy. Thus, to be strategic involves knowing when it is most important to intervene to improve employee engagement.

In addition, the resources that are required to engage employees are also likely to vary depending on the situation and the task that employees are performing. For example, if employees are performing a difficult and stressful task, then social support might be especially important for their engagement. If employees are performing a task that is frustrating and very challenging, then opportunities for learning and feedback might be the most important resources for enhancing employee engagement. The point is that the resources that are required to improve employee engagement will vary and depend on the task, situation, and employees.

A final approach to strategic employee engagement involves a consideration of the relevance and importance of different targets of engagement. We have discussed different targets of employee engagement throughout this book and suggested that when measuring employee engagement, the desired target should be indicated. However, an important issue is what target of engagement should an organization be most concerned about? At any given time, some targets might be more important than others. For example, if an organization is about to engage in a change program, then organization engagement will be very important. If an organization is implementing a team approach to perform certain tasks or jobs, then team engagement will be important. Furthermore, there might be differences in the importance of engagement targets throughout an organization. For example, job engagement might be more important for some positions or departments, while organization engagement might be more important for other positions or areas of an organization. Therefore, a strategic approach to employee engagement requires the identification of the target or targets that are most important and require more attention when it comes to resources and interventions for improving employee engagement.

10.2.1 Summary

In summary, while it might seem that all employees should always be highly engaged when they perform their jobs, this represents a one-size-fits-all approach to employee engagement and it is a more general than strategic approach. A strategic approach to employee engagement involves linking an organization's strategy to engagement, identifying tasks and situations in which it is especially important for employees to be highly engaged, and knowing what target or targets to focus on for improving employee engagement. In addition, regardless of an organization's strategy, employees should have a clear understanding of how their job fits with the overall objectives and strategic priorities of their organization, or what is known as strategic alignment which has been found to be positively related to employee engagement (Biggs et al., 2014).

10.3   Care and employee engagement

One area which has not received very much attention but which we believe is a potentially important factor for employee engagement is care or caring. Care and concern for employees has been found to be important for both individual and organization outcomes. For example, Borucki and Burke (1999) found that a concern for employee climate (employees' beliefs and shared perceptions about the extent to which the organization values and cares about employees' well-being) was positively related to sales personnel service performance, which was positively related to store financial performance in a sample of 594 stores of a large retail company.

Chuang and Liao (2010) found that a climate of concern for employees was positively related to employees' helping behavior and subsequent business unit market performance, and Takeuchi et al. (2009) found that a climate of concern for employees was positively related to employee job satisfaction and affective organizational commitment. Weziak-Bialowolska et al. (2020) found that a psychological climate for caring (a climate that "focuses on employees' perceptions of management care about the workforce, and management priorities regarding trust, respect, fairness, caring atmosphere, and safety in the workplace," p.1) was positively related to self-reported productivity, work quality, and work engagement in a sample of apparel workers in Mexico.

There is some evidence that caring is important for employee engagement. For example, social support and in particular perceived organizational support (POS) has been found to be a strong predictor of employee engagement (Rich et al., 2010; Saks, 2006). As indicated in Chapter 3, perceived organizational support refers to employees' beliefs about how much the organization values their contributions and cares about their well-being. When employees experience a high degree of POS it creates a feeling of obligation to care about the organization's welfare and help the organization reach its objectives (Rhoades et al., 2001).

It is noteworthy that several of the items included in the measure of POS refer specifically to care from the organization such as, *"The organization really cares about my well-being,"* and *"The organization cares about my opinions"* (Eisenberger et al., 1986). This provides some indirect evidence that the positive relationship between POS and employee engagement is due at least in part to the belief that the organization cares about its employees.

Organizational care has been defined as "perceptions regarding the broad provision of care by the organization to all employees. It captures beliefs about the extent to which the organization cares for employees in general" (McAllister & Bigley, 2002, p.895).

According to McAllister and Bigley (2002), organizational care involves "a 'deep structure' of values and organizing principles centred on fulfilling employees' needs, promoting employees' best interests, and valuing employees' contributions" (p.895). Caring organizations are those in which employees perceive the organization as caring, supportive, and nurturing (Vinarski-Peretz & Carmeli, 2011). Thus, organizations that care about their employees are responsive to their employees' needs, interests, concerns, and well-being.

Several studies have provided some indirect evidence that caring is important for employee engagement. For example, Cooper-Thomas et al. (2018) investigated the importance of different resources for predicting employee engagement. They categorized seven resources in terms of the six different resources based on resource theory of social exchange (money, goods, services, love, status, information) (Foa & Foa, 2012). They categorized engagement as a love resource because it represents warmth and caring, and when employees are engaged they invest their wholehearted full selves into the performance of their job.

According to resource theory, people are most likely to exchange a resource that is similar to the one they received (Foa & Foa, 2012). Therefore, Cooper-Thomas et al. (2018) predicted that employees will exchange their engagement (a love resource) for love resources that they receive from the organization that demonstrate warmth and caring.

As expected, and in support of resource theory, Cooper-Thomas et al. (2018) found that two of the three "love" resources (learning and development and vision and purpose) were the strongest predictors of employee engagement. Thus, the resources that were most associated with love, care, and warmth were the most strongly related to employee engagement. These results suggest that employees are most likely to be engaged when they receive resources from their organization that demonstrate caring for employees.

Vinarski-Peretz and Carmeli (2011) examined the relationship between care felt and employee engagement in innovative work behaviors. They defined care felt as the extent to which an employee feels that organizational members care for them, and employees feel that their co-workers care about and take care of them, value their contributions, and show concern for their needs. They predicted that care felt leads to engagement in innovative behaviors through Kahn's (1990) three psychological conditions for engagement (i.e., meaningfulness, safety, and availability) and employees' motivation to engage in innovative behaviors. As predicted, care felt was positively related to the psychological conditions and employee motivation to engage in innovative behaviors. In addition, the three psychological conditions mediated the relationship between care felt and employee motivation to engage in innovative behaviors, and motivation to engage in innovative behaviors mediated the relationship between the psychological conditions and engagement in innovative behaviors. Thus, caring was an important predictor of employee engagement in innovative work tasks.

The results of these studies suggest that caring has the potential to be an important predictor of employee engagement. To provide a preliminary test of this, we re-examined the data from Saks (2006) in terms of the care-related items from the POS scale as well as the perceived supervisor support (PSS) scale in relation to job engagement and organization engagement. From the POS scale, we found that the item that was most strongly related to job engagement ($r=.43$) and organization engagement ($r=.51$) was, *"My organization cares about my opinions."* When the engagement measures were regressed on all of the POS scale items, this item emerged as the strongest predictor. When we looked at the correlations for the PSS scale, a similar item (*"My supervisor cares about my opinions"*) was again the most strongly correlated with job engagement ($r=.31$) and organization engagement ($r=.39$) and was also the strongest predictor in the regression analyses. It is noteworthy that the correlations are higher for POS than PSS, and that for both variables the correlations are higher for organization engagement than job engagement. Thus, caring seems to be important for both job engagement and organization engagement but more important for organization engagement.

10.3.1 Summary

In summary, based on the few studies we have reviewed and the correlation and regression analysis of the scale items of the POS and PSS scales, caring appears to be an important factor for employee engagement. We suspect that employees will be more highly engaged in their job and organization when they believe that their organization, management, supervisors, and co-workers care about them. Our main premise is that in accordance with social exchange theory, when employees believe that their organization cares about them, they will return that care to the organization by being more highly engaged in their job and in the organization. Therefore, organizations should implement programs and practices that provide care for employees in terms of their needs and well-being if they want to improve employee engagement.

10.4 Job engagement versus organization engagement

Although the focus and emphasis of research on employee engagement has been job or work engagement, there has been an increasing number of studies on organization engagement in the last five years. In fact, we identified 40 studies that measured organization engagement and most of them also measured job or work engagement. Therefore, we can refer to the results of these studies to get some idea of how job engagement compares to organization engagement.

As first noted by Saks (2006), there is a moderate correlation between job engagement and organization engagement and most studies found support for this relationship. In addition, most studies found that job engagement scores were higher than organization engagement scores. In other words, employees appear to be more highly engaged in their job than in their organization or perhaps more disengaged in their organization than in their job.

There is also evidence that there are differences in the antecedents and consequences of job engagement and organization engagement. With respect to the consequences, Saks (2006) found that while both job engagement and organization engagement were positively related to job satisfaction, organizational commitment, and organizational citizenship behavior, and negatively related to intention to quit, organization engagement was more strongly related to all of these consequences than job engagement. Many other studies have also found that organization engagement is positively related to job satisfaction, organizational commitment, and OCB, and negatively related to turnover intentions, and some studies found organization engagement to be more strongly related to consequences such as organizational commitment and OCB than job engagement. In addition, organization engagement has also been found to mediate the relationships between antecedents and consequences.

Although there are similarities in terms of the antecedents (e.g., POS, justice perceptions), organization-related antecedents such as corporate social responsibility, organizational climate, organizational structural factors, and HRM practices seem to be especially important for organization engagement. Antecedents more specific to the job, such as job characteristics, seem to be more important for job engagement. According to Schneider et al. (2018), "the larger context in which work exists has a stronger impact than the work itself on workforce engagement in work" (p.476), and the primary driver of workforce engagement "is a work context where people experience the organization as being goal directed and demonstrating concern for people" (p.476). We suspect that factors in the work context are especially important for organization engagement.

Given that organization engagement tends to be lower than job engagement (employees appear to be more disengaged in their organization) and that several studies have found organization engagement to be more strongly related to some consequences, we believe that it is perhaps time for employee engagement research to shift its attention away from job and work engagement and instead focus more on the antecedents and consequences of organization engagement. In fact, there are many situations – such as organizational change programs, crises situations, and changes in organization strategy, culture, and structure – where organization engagement will be more important than job engagement. Organizations will increasingly need employees to be highly engaged in the organization not just in their job.

10.4.1 Summary

In summary, the research evidence has consistently found that job engagement and organization engagement are related but differ in several ways. In particular, job engagement tends to be higher than organization engagement even though organization engagement has been found to be more strongly related to work outcomes in several studies. Therefore, much more attention needs to be devoted to learning more about the antecedents and consequences of organization engagement, which has the potential to be more important than job engagement in many situations.

10.5 Conclusion

Employee engagement has and continues to be an area of great interest to academics and practitioners. In this book, we have described what employee engagement means, employee engagement theories, how to measure employee engagement, its antecedents and consequences, how to engage newcomers, how employee engagement differs around the globe, some of the challenges and opportunities associated with employee engagement, and how to translate employee engagement research into practice. Our model of employee engagement demonstrates how different antecedents lead to employee engagement through several process variables, and how employee engagement leads to employee, group, and organization outcomes.

Finally, we concluded this book by describing what makes employee engagement strategic, the importance of care for employee engagement, and how job engagement compares to organization engagement. We hope that you now know and understand why employee engagement matters for employees, organizations, and society, and that you are now more able and prepared to engage yourself in employee engagement research and practice.

References

Abdelmotaleb, M. (2020). The moderating and mediating role of public service motivation and between organization's social responsibility and employee engagement: Evidence from Egyptian public hospitals. *International Review of Public Administration, 25*, 207–223.

Akingbola, K., & van den Berg, H. A. (2019). Antecedents, consequences, and context of employee engagement in nonprofit organizations. *Review of Public Personnel Administration, 39*, 46–74.

Albrecht, S. L. (2014). A climate for engagement: Some theory, models, measures, research, and practical applications. In B. Schneider, & K. Barbera (Eds.), *The Oxford handbook of organizational climate and culture* (pp.400–413). Oxford: Oxford University Press.

Albrecht, S., Breidahl, E., & Marty, A. (2018). Organizational resources, organizational engagement climate, and employee engagement. *Career Development International, 23*, 67–85.

Albrecht, S. L., Bakker, A. B., Gruman, J. A., Macey, W. H., & Saks, A. M. (2015). Employee engagement, human resource management practices and competitive advantage: An integrated approach. *Journal of Organizational Effectiveness: People and Performance, 2*(1), 7–35.

Alessandri, G., Consiglio, C., Luthans, F., & Borgogni, L. (2018). Testing a dynamic model of the impact of psychological capital on work engagement and job performance. *Career Development International, 23*, 33–47.

Alfes, K., Shantz, A., & Alahakone, R. (2016). Testing additive versus interactive effects of person-organization fit and organizational trust on engagement and performance. *Personnel Review, 45*, 1323–1339.

Alfes, K., Shantz, A. D., Truss, C., and Soane, E. C. (2013). The link between perceived human resource management practices, engagement and employee behaviour: A moderated mediation model. *The International Journal of Human Resource Management, 24*, 330–351.

Allen, N. J., & Meyer, J. P. (1990). The measurement and antecedents of affective, continuance, and normative commitment to the organization. *Journal of Occupational Psychology, 63*, 1–18.

Andreassi, J. K., Lawter, L., Brockerhoff, M., & Rutigliano, P. J. (2014). Cultural impact of human resource practices on job satisfaction: A global study across 48 countries. *Cross Cultural Management, 21*, 55–77.

Anthony-McMann, P. E., Ellinger, A. D., Astakhova, M., & Halbesleben, J. R. B. (2016). Exploring different operationalizations of employee engagement and their relationships with workplace stress and burnout. *Human Resource Development Quarterly, 28*(2), 163–195.

Aristotle (2004). *The Nicomachean Ethics.* New York: Penguin Books.

Aycan, Z., & Gelfand, M. J. (2012). Cross-cultural organizational psychology. In S. W. J. Kozlowski (Ed.), *The Oxford handbook of organizational psychology* (Vol. 2, pp. 1103–1160). New York: Oxford University Press.

Azim, M. T. (2016). Corporate social responsibility and employee behavior: Mediating role of organizational commitment. *Review of Business Management, 18*, 207–225.

Bailey, C., Madden, A., Alfes, K., & Fletcher, L. (2017). The meaning, antecedents and outcomes of employee engagement: A narrative synthesis. *International Journal of Management Reviews, 19*, 31–53.

Bakker, A. B., & Bal, P. M. (2010). Weekly work engagement and performance: A study among starting teachers. *Journal of Occupational and Organizational Psychology, 83*, 189–206.

Bakker, A. B., & Demerouti, E. (2007). The job demands-resources model: State of the art. *Journal of Managerial Psychology, 22*, 309–328.

Bakker, A. B., & Demerouti, E. (2008). Towards a model of work engagement. *Career Development International, 13*, 209–223.

Bakker, A. B., & Demerouti, E. (2017). Job demands-resources theory: Taking stock and looking forward. *Journal of Occupational Health Psychology, 22*, 273–285.

Bakker, A. B., & Xanthopoulou, D. (2009). The crossover of daily work engagement: Test of an actor-partner interdependence model. *Journal of Applied Psychology, 94*, 1562–1571.

Bakker, A. B., Albrecht, S. L., & Leiter, M. P. (2011). Key questions regarding work engagement. *European Journal of Work and Organizational Psychology, 20*, 4–28.

Bakker, A. B., van Emmerik, H., & Euwema, M. C. (2006). Crossover of burnout and engagement in work teams. *Work and Occupations, 33*, 464–489.

Bakker, A. B., Hakanen, J. J., Demerouti, E., & Xanthopoulou, D. (2007). Job resources boost work engagement, particularly when job demands are high. *Journal of Educational Psychology, 99*, 274–284.

Bakker, A. B., Schaufeli, W. B., Leither, M. P., & Taris, T. W. (2008). Work engagement: An emerging concept in occupational health psychology. *Work & Stress, 22*, 187–200.

Bal, P. M., & De Lange, A. H. (2015). From flexibility human resource management to employee engagement and perceived job performance across the lifespan: A multisample study. *Journal of Occupational and Organizational Psychology, 88*, 126–154.

Bargh, J. A., & Morsella, E. (2008). The unconscious mind. *Perspectives on Psychological Science, 3*, 73–79.

Barrick, M. R., Thurgood, G. R., Smith, T. A., & Courtright, S. H. (2015). Collective organizational engagement: Linking motivational antecedents, strategic implementation, and firm performance. *Academy of Management Journal, 58*, 111–135.

Berry, J. W. (1989). Imposed etics – emics – derived etics: The operationalization of a compelling idea. *International Journal of Psychology, 24*, 721–735.

Bhasin, J., Mushtaq, S., & Gupta, S. (2019). Engaging employees through employer brand: An empirical evidence. *Management and Labour Studies, 44*, 417–432.

Biggs, A., Brough, P., & Barbour, J. P. (2014). Strategic alignment with organizational priorities and work engagement: A multi-wave analysis. *Journal of Organizational Behavior, 35*(3), 301–317.

Bond, M. H., Leung, K., Au, A., Tong, K., & Chemonges-Nielson, Z. (2004). Combining social axioms with values in predicting social behaviours. *European Journal of Personality, 18*, 177–191.

Boon, C., & Kalshoven, K. (2014). How high-commitment HRM relates to engagement and commitment: The moderating role of task proficiency. *Human Resource Management, 53*, 403–420.

Boon, C., den Hartog, D. N., & Lepak, D. P. (2019). A systematic review of human resource management systems and their measurement. *Journal of Management, 45*, 2498–2537.

Borucki, C. C., & Burke, M. J. (1999). An examination of service-related antecedents to retail store performance. *Journal of Organizational Behavior, 20*, 943–962.

Boswell, W. R., Boudreau, J. W., & Tichy, J. (2005). The relationship between employee job change and job satisfaction: The honeymoon-hangover effect. *Journal of Applied Psychology, 90*, 882–892.

Boswell, W. R., Shipp, A. J., Payne, S. C., & Culbertson, S. S. (2009). Changes in newcomer job satisfaction over time: Examining the pattern of honeymoons and hangovers. *Journal of Applied Psychology, 94*, 844–858.

Bowen, D. E., & Ostroff, C. (2004). Understanding the HRM-firm performance linkages: The role of the "strength" of the HRM system. *Academy of Management Review, 29*, 203–221.

Branzei, O., Vertinsky, I., & Camp, R. D., II. (2007). Culture-contingent signs of trust in emergent relationships. *Organizational Behavior and Human Decision Processes, 104*, 61–82.

Brewer, P., & Venaik, S. (2014). The ecological fallacy in national culture research. *Organization Studies, 35*, 1063–1086.

Britt, T. W. (1999). Engaging the self in the field: Testing the triangle model of responsibility. *Personality and Social Psychology Bulletin, 25*, 696–706.

Britt, T. W. (2003). Motivational and emotional consequences of self-engagement: Voting in the 2000 U.S. presidential election. *Motivation and Emotion, 27*, 339–358.

Britt, T. W., & Bliese, P. D. (2003). Testing the stress-buffering effects of self engagement among soldiers on a military operation. *Journal of Personality, 71*(2), 245–265.

Britt, T. W., Adler, A. B., & Bartone, P. T. (2001). Deriving benefits from stressful events: The role of engagement in meaningful work and hardiness. *Journal of Occupational and Health Psychology, 6*(1), 53–63.

Britt, T. W., Castro, C. A., & Adler, A. B. (2005). Self-engagement, stressors, and health: A longitudinal study. *Personality and Social Psychology Bulletin, 31*(11), 1475–1486.

Britt, T. W., Thomas, J. L., & Dawson, C. R. (2006). Self-engagement magnifies the relationship between qualitative overload and performance in a training setting. *Journal of Applied Social Psychology, 36*, 2100–2114.

Brough, P., Timms, C., Siu, O., Kalliath, T., O'Driscoll, M. P., & Sit, C. H. P. (2013). Validation of the Job Demands-Resources model in cross-national samples: Cross-sectional and longitudinal predictions of psychological strain and work engagement. *Human Relations, 66*, 1311–1335.

Brown, S. P. (1996). A meta-analysis and review of organizational research on job involvement. *Psychological Bulletin, 120*, 235–255.

Brown, S. P., & Leigh, T. W. (1996). A new look at psychological climate and its relationship to job involvement, effort, and performance. *Journal of Applied Psychology, 81*, 358–368.

Busse, C., Kach, A. P., & Wagner, S. M. (2017). Boundary conditions: What they are, how to explore them, why we need them, and when to consider them. *Organizational Research Methods, 20*, 574–609.

Byrne, Z. S. (2015). *Understanding employee engagement: Theory, research, and practice*. New York: Routledge.

Byrne, Z. S., Peters, J. M., & Weston, J. W. (2016). The struggle with employee engagement: Measures and construct clarification using five samples. *Journal of Applied Psychology, 101*, 1201–1227.

Caesens, G., Stinglhamber, F., & Marmier, V. (2016). The curvilinear effect of work engagement on employees' turnover intentions. *International Journal of Psychology, 51*, 150–155.

Cai, D., Sun, Y., & Ma, J. (2018). Linking empowering leadership and employee work engagement: The effects of person-job fit, person-group fit, and proactive personality. *Frontiers in Psychology, 9*, 1304. http://doi: 10.3389/fpsyg.2018.01304

Carmeli, A., Reiter-Palmon, R., & Ziv, E. (2010). Inclusive leadership and employee involvement in creative tasks in the workplace: The mediating role of psychological safety. *Creativity Research Journal, 22*, 250–260.

Carmeli, A., Sheaffer, Z., Binyamin, G., Reiter-Palmon, R., & Shimoni, T. (2013). Transformational leadership and creative problem-solving: The mediating role of psychological safety and reflexivity. *The Journal of Creative Behavior, 48*, 115–135.

Cerasoli, C. P., Nicklin, J. M., & Ford, M. T. (2014). Intrinsic motivation and extrinsic incentives jointly predict performance: A 40-year meta-analysis. *Psychological Bulletin, 140*, 980–1008.

Chan, X. W., Kalliath, T., Brough, P., O'Driscoll, M., Siu, O., & Timms, C. (2017). Self-efficacy and work engagement: Test of a chain model. *International Journal of Manpower, 38*, 819–834.

Chatman, J. A. (1991). Matching people and organizations: Selection and socialization in public accounting firms. *Administrative Science Quarterly, 36*, 459–484.

Chen, J., May, D. R. Schwoerer, C. E., & Augelli, B. (2018). Exploring the boundaries of career calling: The moderating roles of procedural justice and psychological safety. *Journal of Career Development, 45*, 103–116.

Chen, S. (2015). The relationship of leader psychological capital and follower psychological capital, job engagement, and job performance: A multilevel mediating perspective. *The International Journal of Human Resource Management, 26*, 2349–2365.

Cheng, F. M., van de Vijver, F. J. R., & Leong, F. T. L. (2011). Toward a new approach to the study of personality in culture. *American Psychologist, 66*, 593–603.

Cheng, Y., & Stockdale, M. S. (2003). The validity of the three-component model of organizational commitment in a Chinese context. *Journal of Vocational Behavior, 62*, 465–489.

Cheung, F. M., van de Vijver, F. J. R., & Leong, F. T. L. (2011). Toward a new approach to the study of personality in culture. *American Psychologist, 66*, 593–603.

Christian, M. S., Garza, A. S., & Slaughter, J. E. (2011). Work engagement: A quantiative review and test of its relations with task and contextual performance. *Personnel Psychology, 64*, 89–136.

Chuang, C-H., & Liao, H. (2010). Strategic human resource management in service context: Taking care of business by taking care of employees and customers. *Personnel Psychology, 63*, 153–196.

Cole, M. S., Walter, F., Bedeian, A. G., & O'Boyle, E. H. (2012). Job burnout and employee engagement: A meta-analytic examination of construct proliferation. *Journal of Management, 38*, 1550–1581.

Colquitt, J. A. (2001). On the dimensionality of organizational justice: A construct validation of a measure. *Journal of Applied Psychology, 86*, 386–400.

Conway, E., Fu, N., Monks, K., Alfes, K., & Bailey, C. (2016). Demands or resources? The relationship between HR practices, employee engagement, and emotional exhaustion within a hybrid model of employment relations. *Human Resource Management, 55*, 901–917.

Cooke, F. L., Cooper, B., Bartram, T., Wang, J., & Mei, H. (2019). Mapping the relationships between high-performance work systems, employee resilience and engagement: A study of the banking industry in China. *The International Journal of Human Resource Management, 30*, 1239–1260.

Cooper-Thomas, H. D., Xu, J., & Saks, A. M. (2018). The differential value of resources in predicting employee engagement. *Journal of Managerial Psychology, 33*, 326–344.

Costa, P., Passos, A. M., & Bakker, A. (2014a). Empirical validation of the team work engagement construct. *Journal of Personnel Psychology, 13*, 34–45.

Costa, P., Passos, A. M., & Bakker, A. B. (2014b). Team work engagement: A model of emergence. *Journal of Occupational and Organizational Psychology, 87*, 414–436.

Costa, P., Passos, A. M., & Bakker, A. B. (2015). Direct and contextual influence of team conflict on team resources, team work engagement, and team performance. *Negotiation and Conflict Management Research, 8*, 211–227.

Crawford, E. R., LePine, J. A., & Rich, B. L. (2010). Linking job demands and resources to employee engagement and burnout: A theoretical extension and meta-analytic test. *Journal of Applied Psychology, 95*, 834–848.

Crawford, E. R., Rich, B. L., Buckman, B., & Bergeron, J. (2014). The antecedents and drivers of employee engagement. In C. Truss, R. Delbridge, K. Alfes, A. Shantz, & E. Soane (Eds.), *Employee engagement in theory and practice* (pp.57–81). New York: Routledge.

Cronbach, L. J., & Meehl, P. E. (1955). Construct validity in psychological tests. *Psychological Bulletin, 52*, 281–302.

Cropanzano, R., & Mitchell, M. S. (2005). Social exchange theory: An interdisciplinary review. *Journal of Management, 31*(6), 874–900.

Cropanzano, R., Anthony, E. L., Daniels, S. R., & Hall, A. V. (2017). Social exchange theory: A critical review with theoretical remedies. *Academy of Management Annals, 11*, 479–516.

Cross, S. E., Hardin, E. E., & Gercek-Swing, B. (2011). The *what, how, why,* and *where* of self-construal. *Personality and Social Psychology Review, 15*, 142–179.

Cummings, T. G., & Bigelow, J. (1976). Satisfaction, job involvement, and intrinsic motivation: An extension of Lawler and Hall's factor analysis. *Journal of Applied Psychology, 61*, 523–525.

Dalal, R. S., Baysinger, M., Brummel, B. J., & LeBreton, J. M. (2012). The relative importance of employee engagement, other job attitudes, and trait affect as predictors of job performance. *Journal of Applied Social Psychology, 42*, E295–E325.

Dalal, R. S., Brummel, B. J., Wee, S., & Thomas, L. L. (2008). Defining employee engagement for productive research and practice. *Industrial and Organizational Psychology, 1*, 52–55.

Deci, E. L., Ryan, R. M., Gagné, M., Leone, D. R., Usunov, J., & Kornazheva, B. P. (2001). Need satisfaction, motivation, and well-being in the work organizations of a former Eastern bloc country: A cross-cultural study of self-determination. *Personality and Social Psychology Bulletin, 27*, 930–942.

Demerouti, E., Bakker, A. B., Nachreiner, F., & Schaufeli, W. B. (2001). The job demands-resources model of burnout. *Journal of Applied Psychology, 86*, 499–512.

Demerouti, E., Bakker, A. B., Vardakou, I., & Kantas, A. (2003). The convergent validity of two burnout instruments: A multitrait-multimethod analysis. *European Journal of Psychological Assessment, 19*, 12–23.

Demirtas, O., Hannah, S. T., Gok, K., Arslan, A., & Capar, N. (2017). The moderated influence of ethical leadership, via meaningful work, on followers, engagement, organizational identification, and envy. *Journal of Business Ethics, 145*, 183–199.

Dijksterhuis, A., & Aarts, H. (2010). Goals, attention, and (un)consciousness. *Annual Review of Psychology, 61*, 467–490.

Dijksterhuis, A., & Nordgren, L. F. (2006). A theory of unconscious thought. *Perspectives on Psychological Science, 1*, 95–109.

Donahue, E. M., Robins, R. W., Roberts, B. W., & John, O. P. (1993). The divided self: Concurrent and longitudinal effects of psychological adjustment and social roles on self-concept differentiation. *Journal of Personality and Social Psychology, 64*, 834–846.

Eisenberger, R., Huntington, R., Hutchison, S., & Sowa, D. (1986). Perceived organizational support. *Journal of Applied Psychology, 71*, 500–507.

Eisenberger, R., Armeli, S., Rexwinkel, B., Lynch, P. D., & Rhoades, L. (2001). Reciprocation of perceived organizational support. *Journal of Applied Psychology, 86*(1), 42–51.

Eldor, L., & Harpaz, I. (2016). A process model of employee engagement: The learning climate and its relationship with extra-role performance behaviors. *Journal of Organizational Behavior, 37*, 213–235.

Farndale, E. (2017). Two-country study of engagement, supervisors and performance appraisal. *Journal of Asia Business Studies, 11*, 342–362.

Farndale, E., & Murrer, I. (2015). Job resources and employee engagement: A cross-national study. *Journal of Managerial Psychology, 30*, 610–626.

Farndale, E., Beijer, S. E., Vam Veldhoven, M. J. P. M., Kelliher, C., & Hope-Hailey, V. (2014). Work and organisation engagement: Aligning research and practice. *Journal of Organizational Effectiveness: People and Performance, 1*, 157–176.

Fletcher, L., & Schofield, K. (2019). Facilitating meaningfulness in the workplace: A field intervention study. *The International Journal of Human Resource Management.* Advance Online Publication. http://doi.org/10.1080/09585192.2019.1624590

Fletcher, L., Bailey, C., & Gilman, M. W. (2018). Fluctuating levels of personal role engagement within the working day: A multilevel study. *Human Resource Management Journal, 28*, 128–147.

Foa, E. B., & Foa, U. G. (2012). Resource theory of social exchange. In K. Tornblom, & A. Kazemi (Eds.), *Handbook of social resource theory: Theoretical extension, empirical insights, and social applications* (pp.15–32). New York: Plenum Press.

Fredrickson, B. L. (2001). The role of positive emotions in positive psychology: The broaden-and-build theory of positive emotions. *American Psychologist, 56*(3), 218–226.

Gagné, M., & Deci, E. L. (2005). Self-determination theory and work motivation. *Journal of Organizational Behavior, 26*, 331–362.

Garczynski, A. M., Waldrop, J. S., Rupprecht E. A., & Grawitch, M. J. (2013). Differentiation between work and nonwork self-aspects as a predictor of presenteeism and engagement: Cross-cultural differences. *Journal of Occupational Health Psychology, 18*, 417–429.

Gelfand, M. J., Erez, M., & Aycan, Z. (2007). Cross-cultural organizational behavior. *Annual Review of Psychology, 58*, 479–514.

Gelfand, M. J., Leslie, L. L., & Fehr, R. (2008). To prosper, organizational psychology should ... adopt a global perspective. *Journal of Organizational Behavior, 29*, 493–517.

Gelfand, M. J., Nishii, L. H., & Raver, J. L. (2006). On the nature and importance of cultural tightness-looseness. *Journal of Applied Psychology, 91*, 1225–1244.

George, J. M. (2010). More engagement is not necessarily better: The benefits of fluctuating levels of engagement. In S. Albrecht (Ed.), *Handbook of employee engagement: Perspectives, issues, research, and practice* (pp.253–263). Cheltenham, UK and Northampton, MA, USA: Edward Elgar Publishing.

George, J. M. (2011). The wider context, costs, and benefits of work engagement. *European Journal of Work and Organizational Psychology, 20*, 53–59.

Ghadi, M. Y., Fernando, M., & Caputi, P. (2013). Transformational leadership and work engagement: The mediating effect of meaning in work. *Leadership & Organization Development Journal, 34*, 532–550.

Ghosh, R., Shuck, B., Cumberland, D., & D'Mello, J. (2018). Building psychological capital and employee engagement: Is formal mentoring a useful strategic human resource development intervention? *Performance Improvement Quarterly, 32*, 37–54.

Gillet, N., Gagné, M., Sauvagere, S., & Fouquereau, E. (2013). The role of supervisor autonomy support, organizational support, and autonomous and controlled motivation in predicting employees' satisfaction and turnover intentions. *European Journal of Work and Organizational Psychology, 22,* 450–460.

Goliath-Yarde, L., & Roodt, G. (2011). Differential item functioning of the UWES-17 in South Africa. *SA Journal of Industrial Psychology, 37.* doi:10.4102.http://www.sajip.co.za sajip.v37i1.897

Grant, A. M., & Schwartz, B. (2011). Too much of a good thing: The challenge and opportunity of the inverted U. *Perspectives on Psychological Science, 6,* 61–76.

Gruman, J. A., & Saks, A. M (2011). Performance management and employee engagement. *Human Resource Management Review, 21,* 123–136.

Gruman, J. A., Lumley, M. N., & González-Morales, M. (2018). Incorporating balance: Challenges and opportunities for positive psychology. *Canadian Psychology, 59,* 54–64.

Guchait, P. (2016). The mediating effect of team engagement between team cognitions and team outcomes in service-management teams. *Journal of Hospitality & Tourism Research, 40,* 139–161.

Guchait, P., Paşamehmetoğlu, A., & Dawson, M. (2014). Perceived supervisor and co-worker support for error management: Impact on perceived psychological safety and service recovery performance. *International Journal of Hospitality Management, 41,* 28–37.

Hackman, J. R., & Oldham, G. R. (1980). *Work redesign.* Reading, MA: Addison-Wesley.

Hakanen, J. J., & Schaufeli, W. B. (2012). Do burnout and work engagement predict depressive symptoms and life satisfaction? A three-wave seven-year prospective study. *Journal of Affective Disorders, 141,* 415–424.

Halbesleben, J. R. B. (2010). A meta-analysis of work engagement: Relationships with burnout, demands, resources, and consequences. In A. B. Bakker, & M. P. Leiter (Eds.), *Work engagement: A handbook of essential theory and research* (pp.102–117). Hove, East Sussex: Psychology Press.

Halbesleben, J. R. B. (2011). The consequences of engagement: The good, the bad, and the ugly. *European Journal of Work and Organizational Psychology, 21*(1), 68–73.

Halbesleben, J. R. B., Harvey, J., & Bolino, M. C. (2009). Too engaged? A conservation of resources view of the relationship between work engagement and work interference with family. *Journal of Applied Psychology, 94,* 1452–1465.

Halbesleben, J. R. B., Neveu, J. P., Paustian-Underdahl, S. C., & Westman, M. (2014). Getting to the "COR": Understanding the role of resources in conservation of resources theory. *Journal of Management, 40,* 1334–1364.

Han, J., Sun, J.-M., & Wang, H.-L. (2020). Do high performance work systems generate negative effects? How and when? *Human Resource Management Review, 30*(2). Article 100699.

Harter, J. K., Schmidt, F. L., & Hayes, T. L. (2002). Business-unit level relationship between employee satisfaction, employee engagement, and business outcomes: A meta-analysis. *Journal of Applied Psychology, 87,* 268–279.

Haynie, J. J., Mossholder, K. W., & Harris, S. G. (2016). Justice and job engagement: The role of senior management trust. *Journal of Organizational Behavior, 37,* 889–910.

Hobfoll, S. E. (2001). The influence of culture, community, and the nested-self in the stress process: Advancing conservation of resources theory. *Applied Psychology: An International Review, 50*, 337–421.

Hobfoll, S. E. (2002). Social and psychological resources and adaptation. *Review of General Psychology, 6*(4), 307–324.

Hobfoll, S. E., Halbesleben, J., Neveu, J-P., & Westman, M. (2018). Conservation of resources in the organizational context: The reality of resources and their consequences. *Annual Review of Organizational Psychology and Organizational Behavior, 5*, 103–128.

Hofstede, G. (1980). Motivation, leadership and organization: Do American theories apply abroad? *Organization Dynamics, 9*, 42–63.

Hofstede, G. (1994). Management scientists are human. *Management Science, 40*, 4–13.

Hofstede, G., & Bond, M. H. (1988). The Confucius connection: From cultural roots to economic growth. *Organizational Dynamics, 16*, 5–21.

Holland, P., Cooper, B., & Sheehan, C. (2017). Employee voice, supervisor support, and engagement: The mediating role of trust. *Human Resource Management, 56*, 915–929.

Hui, C. H., & Triandis, H. C. (1985). Measurement in cross-cultural psychology: A review and comparison of strategies. *Journal of Cross-Cultural Psychology, 16*, 131–152.

Humphrey, S. E., Nahrgang, J. D., & Morgeson, F. P. (2007). Integrating motivational, social, and contextual work design features: A meta-analytic summary and theoretical extension of the work design literature. *Journal of Applied Psychology, 92*(5), 1332–1356.

Javidan, M., Dorfman, P. W., de Luque, M. S., & House, R. J. (2006). In the eye of the beholder: Cross cultural lessons in leadership from Project GLOBE. *Academy of Management Perspectives, 20*, 67–90.

Jenkins, S., & Delbridge, R. (2013). Context matters: Examining "soft" and "hard" approaches to employee engagement in two workplaces. *The International Journal of Human Resource Management, 24*, 2670–2691.

Jiang, K., Takeuchi, R., & Lepak, D. P. (2013). Where do we go from here? New perspectives on the black box in strategic human resource management research. *Journal of Management Studies, 50*, 1448–1480.

Johnson, G. (2004). Otherwise engaged. *Training, 41*(10), 4.

Judge, T. A., & Bono, J. E. (2001). Relationship of core self-evaluations traits – self-esteem, generalized self-efficacy, locus of control, and emotional stability – with job satisfaction and job performance: A meta-analysis. *Journal of Applied Psychology, 86*, 80–92.

Judge, T. A., Bono, J. E., Locke, E. A. (2000). Personality and job satisfaction: The mediating role of job characteristics. *Journal of Applied Psychology, 85*, 237–249.

Judge, T. A., Heller, D., & Mount, M. K. (2002). Five-factor model of personality and job satisfaction: A meta-analysis. *Journal of Applied Psychology, 87*, 530–541.

Judge, T. A., Hulin, C. L., & Dalal, R. S. (2012). Job satisfaction and job affect. In S. W. J. Kozlowski (Ed.), *The Oxford handbook of organizational psychology* (Vol. 1, pp.496–525). New York: Oxford University Press.

Judge, T. A., Erez, A., Bono, J. E., & Thoresen, C. J. (2003). The core self-evaluations scale: Development of a measure. *Personnel Psychology, 56*, 303–331.

Kahn, W. A. (1990). Psychological conditions of personal engagement and disengagement at work. *Academy of Management Journal, 33*, 692–724.

Kahn, W. A. (1992). To be fully there: Psychological presence at work. *Human Relations, 45*, 321–349.

Kahn, W. A. (2007). Meaningful connections: Positive relationships and attachments at work. In J. E. Dutton, & B. R. Ragins (Eds.), *Exploring positive relationships at work* (pp.189–206). New York: Lawrence Erlbaum Associates.

Kahn, W. A., & Fellows, S. (2011). Employee engagement and meaningful work. In B. Dik, Z. Byrne, & M. Steger (Eds.), *Purpose and meaning in the workplace* (pp.105–126). Washington, DC: American Psychological Association.

Kanfer, R., Frese, M., & Johnson, R. E. (2017). Motivation related to work: A century of progress. *Journal of Applied Psychology, 102*, 338–355.

Kanungo, R. N. (1982). Measurement of job and work involvement. *Journal of Applied Psychology, 67*, 341–349.

Katz, R. (1985). Organizational stress and early socialization experiences. In T. A. Beehr, & R. S. Bhagat (Eds.), *Human stress and cognition in organizations* (pp.117–139). New York: Wiley.

Kernis, M. H., Lakey, C. E., & Heppner, W. L. (2008). Secure versus fragile high self-esteem as a predictor of verbal defensiveness: Converging findings across three different markers. *Journal of Personality, 76*, 477–512.

Kim, M., & Koo, D. (2017). Linking LMX, engagement, innovative behavior, and job performance in hotel employees. *International Journal of Contemporary Hospitality Management, 29*, 3044–3062.

Kim, W., Kolb, J. A., & Kim, T. (2012). The relationship between work engagement and performance: A review of empirical literature and a proposed research agenda. *Human Resource Development Review, 12*, 248–276.

Kitayama, S., Markus, H. R., Matsumoto, H., & Norasakkunkit, V. (1997). Individual and collective processes in the construction of the self: Self-enhancement in the United States and self-criticism in Japan. *Journal of Personality and Social Psychology, 72*, 1245–1267.

Klassen, R. M., Aldhafri. S., Mansfield, C. F., Purwanto, E., Siu, A. F. Y., Wong, M. W., & Woods-McConney, A. (2012). Teachers' engagement at work: An international validation study. *The Journal of Experimental Education, 80*, 317–337.

Klein, H. J., & Weaver, N. A. (2000). The effectiveness of an organizational-level orientation training program in the socialization of new hires. *Personnel Psychology, 53*, 47–66.

Klie, S. (2009). Lower employee engagement tied to declining manager effectiveness. *Canadian HR Reporter, 22*, 14, 18.

Kluckhohn, C., & Murray, H. A. (1953). *Personality in nature, society, and culture.* New York: Knopf.

Knight, C., Patterson, M., & Dawson, J. (2017). Building work engagement: A systematic review and meta-analysis investigating the effectiveness of work engagement interventions. *Journal of Organizational Behavior, 38*, 792–812.

Knight, C., Patterson, M., & Dawson, J. (2019). Work engagement interventions can be effective: A systematic review. *European Journal of Work and Organizational Psychology, 28*, 348–372.

Kovjanic, S., Schuh, S. C., & Jonas, K. (2013). Transformational leadership and performance: An experimental investigation of the mediating effects of basic needs satisfaction and work engagement. *Journal of Occupational and Organizational Psychology, 86*, 543–555.

Kowalski, B. (2003). The engagement gap. *Training, 40*(4), 62.

Kożusznik, M., Rodríguez, I., & Peiró, J. M. (2012). Cross-national outcomes of stress appraisal. *Cross Cultural Management, 19*, 507–525.

Kraemer, J., & Chen, C. C. (2012). Cultural differences in resource exchange at the workplace: A Sino-US comparison. In K. Törnblom, & A. Kazemi (Eds.), *Handbook of social resource theory: Theoretical extensions, empirical insights, and social applications* (pp.283–300). New York: Springer Science + Business Media.

Kristoff-Brown, A. L., Zimmerman, R. D., & Johnson, E. C. (2005). Consequences of individuals' fit at work: A meta-analysis of person-job, person-organization, person-group, and person-supervisor fit. *Personnel Psychology, 58*, 281–342.

Kuenzi, M., & Schminke, M. (2009). Assembling fragments into a lens: A review, critique, and proposed research agenda for the organizational work climate literature. *Journal of Management, 35*, 634–717.

Kwon, K., & Kim, T. (2020). An integrative review of employee engagement and innovative behavior: Revisiting the JD-R model. *Human Resource Management Review*. Advance online publication. https://doi.org/10.1016/j.hrmr.2019.100704

Lawler, E. E. III, Kuleck, W. J. Jr., Rhode, J. G., & Sorensen, J. E. (1975). Job choice and post decision dissonance. *Organizational Behavior and Human Performance, 13*, 133–145.

Lee, K., & Allen, N. J. (2002). Organizational citizenship behavior and workplace deviance: The role of affect and cognition. *Journal of Applied Psychology, 87*, 131–142.

Lee, M. C. C., Adris, M. A., & Delfabbro, P. H. (2017). The linkages between hierarchical culture and empowering leadership and their effects on employees' work engagement: Work meaningfulness as a mediator. *International Journal of Stress Management, 24*, 392–415.

LePine, J. A., Erez, A., & Johnson, D. E. (2002). The nature and dimensionality of organizational citizenship behavior: A critical review and meta-analysis. *Journal of Applied Psychology, 87*, 52–65.

Lesener, T., Gusy, B., Jochmann, A., & Wolter, C. (2019). The drivers of work engagement: A meta-analytic review of longitudinal evidence. *Work & Stress, 34*, 259–278.

Li, P., Sun, J., Taris, T. W., Xing, L., & Peeters, M. C. W. (2020). Country differences in the relationship between leadership and employee engagement: A meta-analysis. *The Leadership Quarterly*. Advance online publication. https://doi.org/10.1016/j.leaqua.2020.101458

Li, Y. (2019). Leadership styles and knowledge workers' work engagement: Psychological capital as a mediator. *Current Psychology, 38*, 1152–1161.

Lichtenthaler, P. W., & Fischbach, A. (2019). A meta-analysis on promotion- and prevention-focused job crafting. *European Journal of Work and Organizational Psychology, 28*, 30–50.

Liu, C., Borg, I., & Spector, P. E. (2004). Measurement equivalence of the German job satisfaction survey used in a multinational organization: Implications of Schwartz's culture model. *Journal of Applied Psychology, 89*, 1070–1082.

Liu, S., Liao, J., & Wei, H. (2015). Authentic leadership and whistleblowing: Mediating roles of psychological safety and personal identification. *Journal of Business Ethics, 131*, 107–119.

Llorens, S., Schaufeli, W., Bakker, A., & Salanova, M. (2007). Does a positive gain spiral of resources, efficacy beliefs, and engagement exist? *Computers in Human Behavior, 23*, 825–841.

Louis, M. R. (1980). Surprise and sense making: What newcomers experience in entering unfamiliar organizational settings. *Administrative Science Quarterly, 64*, 226–251.

Lu, C., Siu, O., Chen, W., & Wang, H. (2011). Family mastery enhances engagement in Chinese nurses: A cross-lagged analysis. *Journal of Vocational Behavior, 78*, 100–109.

Luthans, F. (2002). Positive organizational behavior: Developing and managing psychological strengths. *Academy of Management Executive, 16*, 57–72.

Luthans, F., & Youssef-Morgan, C. M. (2017). Psychological capital: An evidence-based positive approach. *Annual Review of Organizational Psychology and Organizational Behavior, 4*, 339–366.

Macey, W. H., & Schneider, B. (2008). The meaning of employee engagement. *Industrial and Organizational Psychology, 1*, 3–30.

Mael, F. A., & Tetrick, L. E. (1992). Identifying organizational identification. *Educational and Psychological Measurement, 52*, 813–824.

Maia, L. G., Bastos, A. V. B., & Solinger, O. N. (2016). Which factors make the difference for explaining growth in newcomer organizational commitment? A latent growth modeling approach. *Journal of Organizational Behavior, 37*, 537–557.

Mäkikangas, A., Aunola, K., Seppälä, P., & Hakanen, J. (2016). Work engagement – team performance relationship: Shared job crafting as a moderator. *Journal of Occupational and Organizational Psychology, 89*, 772–790.

Margolis, J. D., & Molinsky, A. (2008). Navigating the bind of necessary evils: Psychological engagement and the production of interpersonally sensitive behavior. *Academy of Management Journal, 51*, 847–872.

Markus, H. R., & Kitayama, S. (1991). Culture and the self: Implications for cognition, emotion, and motivation. *Psychological Review, 98*, 224–253.

Maslach, C., & Leiter, M. P. (2008). Early predictors of job burnout and engagement. *Journal of Applied Psychology, 93*, 498–512.

Maslach, C., Schaufeli, W. B., & Leiter, M. P. (2001). Job Burnout. *Annual Review of Psychology, 52*, 397–422.

Masuda, A. D., Holtschlag, C., & Nicklin, J. M. (2017). Why the availability of telecommuting matters: The effects of telecommuting on engagement via goal pursuit. *Career Development International, 22*, 200–219.

Mathieu, J. E., & Zajac, D. M. (1990). A review and meta-analysis of the antecedents, correlates, and consequences of organizational commitment. *Psychological Bulletin, 108*, 171–194.

Matsumoto, D. (1999). Culture and self: An empirical assessment of Markus and Kitayama's theory of independent and interdependent self-construals. *Asian Journal of Social Psychology, 2,* 289–310.

Mauno, S., Kinnunen, U., Mäkikangas, A., & Feldt, T. (2010). Job demands and resources as antecedents of work engagement: A qualitative review and directions for future research. In S. Albrecht (Ed.), *Handbook of employee engagement: Perspectives, issues, research and practice* (pp.111–128). Cheltenham, UK and Northampton, MA, USA: Edward Elgar Publishing.

May, D. R., Gilson, R. L., & Harter, L. M. (2004). The psychological conditions of meaningfulness, safety and availability and the engagement of the human spirit at work. *Journal of Occupational and Organizational Psychology, 77,* 11–37.

McAllister, D. J., & Bigley, G. A. (2002). Work context and the definition of self: How organizational care influences organization-based self-esteem. *Academy of Management Journal, 45,* 894–904.

Meyer, J. P., & Gagné, M. (2008). Employee engagement from a self-determination theory perspective. *Industrial and Organizational Psychology, 1,* 60–82.

Meyer, J. P., Stanley, D. J., Herscovitch, L., & Topolnytsky, L. (2002). Affective, continuance, and normative commitment to the organization: A meta-analysis of antecedents, correlates, and consequences. *Journal of Vocational Behavior, 61,* 20–52.

Mone, E., Eisinger, C., Guggenheim, K., Price, B., & Stine, C. (2011). Performance management at the wheel: Driving employee engagement in organizations. *Journal of Business and Psychology, 26,* 205–212.

Morgeson, F. P., & Hofmann, D. A. (1999). The structure and function of collective constructs: Implications for multilevel research and theory development. *Academy of Management Review, 24,* 249–265.

Murray, H. A. (1938). *Explorations in personality.* New York: Oxford University Press.

Nembhard, I. M., & Edmondson, A. C. (2006). Making it safe: The effects of leader inclusiveness and professional status on psychological safety and improvement efforts in health care teams. *Journal of Organizational Behavior, 27,* 941–966.

Newman, D. A., & Harrison, D. A. (2008). Been there, bottled that: Are state and behavioral work engagement new and useful construct "wine"? *Industrial and Organizational Psychology, 1,* 31–35.

Newman, D. A., Harrison, D. A., Carpenter, N. C., & Rariden, S. M. (2016). Construct mixology: Forming new management constructs by combining old ones. *The Academy of Management Annals, 10*(1), 943–995.

Newton, D. W., LePine, J. A., Kim, J. K., Wellman, N., & Bush, J. T. (2020). Taking engagement to task: The nature and functioning of task engagement across transitions. *Journal of Applied Psychology, 105,* 1–18.

Nielsen, K., & Miraglia, M. (2017). What works for whom in which circumstances? On the need to move beyond the "what works?" question in organizational research. *Human Relations, 70,* 40–62.

Nielsen, K., Nielsen, M., Ogbonnaya, C., Känsälä, M., Saari, E., & Isaksson, K. (2017). Workplace resources to improve both employee well-being and performance: A systematic review and meta-analysis. *Work & Stress, 31,* 101–120.

Niles, S. (1998). Achievement goals and means: A cultural comparison. *Journal of Cross-Cultural Psychology, 29,* 656–667.

Nishii, L. H., Lepak, D. P., & Schneider, B. (2008). Employee attributions of the "why" of HR practices: Their effects on employee attitudes and behaviors, and customer satisfaction. *Personnel Psychology, 61,* 503–545.

Oliver, A., & Rothmann, S. (2007). Antecedents of work engagement in a multinational oil company. *SA Journal of Industrial Psychology, 33,* 49–56.

Organ, D. W., & Ryan, K. (1995). A meta-analytic review of attitudinal and dispositional predictors of organizational citizenship behavior. *Personnel Psychology, 48,* 775–802.

Ostroff, C., & Bowen, D. E. (2016). Reflections on the 2014 decade award: Is there strength in the construct of HR system strength? *Academy of Management Review, 41,* 196–214.

Ouellette, J. A., & Wood, W. (1998). Habit and intention in everyday life: The multiple processes by which past behavior predicts future behavior. *Psychological Bulletin, 124,* 54–74.

Ouweneel, E., Le Blanc, P. M., Schaufeli, W. B., & van Wijhe, C. (2012). Good morning, good day: A diary study on positive emotions, hope, and work engagement. *Human Relations, 65,* 1129–1154.

Oyserman, D., Coon, H. M., & Kemmelmeier, M. (2002). Rethinking individualism and collectivism: Evaluation of theoretical assumptions and meta-analysis. *Psychological Bulletin, 128,* 3–72.

Park, J. G., Kim, J. S., Yoon, S. W., & Joo, B. (2017). The effects of empowering leadership on psychological well-being and job engagement: The mediating role of psychological capital. *Leadership & Organization Development Journal, 38,* 350–367.

Parrigon, S., Woo, S. E., Tay, L., & Wang, T. (2017). CAPTION-ing the situation. A lexically derived taxonomy of psychological situation characteristics. *Journal of Personality and Social Psychology, 112,* 642–681.

Pierce, J. R., & Aguinis, H. (2013). The too-much-of-a-good-thing effect in management. *Journal of Management, 39,* 313–338.

Podolny, J. M., Khurana, R., & Hill-Popper, M. (2005). Revisiting the meaning of leadership. *Research in Organizational Behavior, 26,* 1–36.

Purcell, J. (2014). Disengaging from engagement. *Human Resource Management Journal, 24,* 241–254.

Qi, J., Ellinger, A. E., & Franke, G. R. (2018). Work design and frontline employee engagement. *Journal of Service Theory and Practice, 28,* 636–660.

Rahmadani, V. G., Schaufeli, W. B., Ivanova, T. Y., & Osin, E. N. (2019). Basic psychological needs satisfaction mediates the relationship between engaging leadership and work engagement: A cross-national study. *Human Resource Development Quarterly, 30,* 453–471.

Rattrie, L. T. B., Kittler, M. G., & Paul, K. I. (2020). Culture, burnout, and engagement: A meta-analysis on national cultural values as moderators in JD-R theory. *Applied Psychology: An International Review, 69,* 176–220.

Rauthmann, J. F., Gallardo-Pujol, D., Guillaume, E. M., Todd, E., Nave, C., Sherman, R. A., Ziegler, M., Jones, A. B., & Funder, D. C. (2014). The Situational Eight DIAMONDS: A taxonomy of major dimensions of situation characteristics. *Journal of Personality and Social Psychology, 107,* 677–718.

Rees, C., Alfes, K., & Gatenby, M. (2013). Employee voice and engagement: Connections and consequences. *The International Journal of Human Resource Management, 24*, 2780–2798.

Reis, D., Xanthopoulou, D., & Tsaousis, I. (2015). Measuring job and academic burnout with the Oldenburg Burnout Inventory (OLBI): Factorial invariance across samples and countries. *Burnout Research, 2*, 8–18.

Rhoades, L., Eisenberger, R., & Armeli, S. (2001). Affective commitment to the organization: The contribution of perceived organizational support. *Journal of Applied Psychology, 86*, 825–836.

Rich, B. L., Lepine, J. A., & Crawford, E. R. (2010). Job engagement: Antecedents and effects of job performance. *Academy of Management Journal, 53*, 617–635.

Riketta, M. (2005). Organizational identification: A meta-analysis. *Journal of Vocational Behavior, 66*, 358–384.

Rodríguez-Sánchez, A. M., Devloo, T., Rico, R., Salanova, M., & Anseel, F. (2017). What makes creative teams tick? Cohesion, engagement, and performance across creativity tasks: A three-wave study. *Group & Organization Management, 42*, 521–547.

Rosso, B. D., Dekas, K. H., & Wrzesniewski, A (2010). On the meaning of work: A theoretical integration and review. *Research in Organizational Behavior, 30*, 91–127.

Rothbard, N. P. (2001). Enriching or depleting? The dynamics of engagement in work and family roles. *Administrative Science Quarterly, 46*, 655–684.

Rothmann, S. (2014). Employee engagement in a cultural context. In C. Truss, R. Delbridge, K. Alfes, A. Shantz, & E. Soane (Eds.), *Employee engagement in theory and practice* (pp.163–179). New York: Routledge.

Rothmann, S., & Rothmann, S., Jr. (2010). Factors associated with employee engagement in South Africa. *SA Journal of Industrial Psychology, 36*. doi:10 .4102/sajip.v36i2.925

Rothmann, S., & Welsh, C. (2013). Employee engagement: The role of psychological conditions. *Management Dynamics, 22*, 14–25.

Ryan, R. M., & Deci, E. L. (2000). Self-determination theory and the facilitation of intrinsic motivation, social development, and well-being. *American Psychologist, 55*, 68–78.

Sagie, A., & Aycan, Z. (2003). A cross-cultural analysis of participative decision-making in organizations. *Human Relations, 56*, 453–473.

Saks, A. M. (2006). Antecedents and consequences of employee engagement. *Journal of Managerial Psychology, 21*, 600–619.

Saks, A. M. (2017). Translating employee engagement research into practice. *Organizational Dynamics, 46*, 76–86.

Saks, A. M. (2019). Antecedents and consequences of employee engagement revisited. *Journal of Organizational Effectiveness: People and Performance, 6*, 19–38.

Saks, A. M., & Ashforth, B. E. (1997). Organizational socialization: Making sense of the past and present as a prologue for the future. *Journal of Vocational Behavior, 51*, 234–279.

Saks, A. M., & Ashforth, B. E. (2000). The role of dispositions, entry stressors, and behavioral plasticity theory in predicting newcomers' adjustment to work. *Journal of Organizational Behavior, 21*, 43–62.

Saks, A. M., & Gruman, J. A. (2011). Getting newcomers engaged: The role of socialization tactics. *Journal of Managerial Psychology, 26,* 383–402.

Saks, A. M., & Gruman, J. A. (2012). Getting newcomers on-board: A review of socialization practices and introduction to socialization resources theory. In C. Wanberg (Ed.), *The Oxford handbook of organizational socialization* (pp.27–55). New York: Oxford University Press.

Saks, A. M., & Gruman, J. A. (2014). What do we really know about employee engagement? *Human Resource Development Quarterly, 25,* 155–182.

Saks, A. M., & Gruman, J. A. (2018). Socialization resources theory and newcomers' work engagement: A new pathway to newcomer socialization. *Career Development International, 23,* 12–32.

Saks, A. M., Uggerslev, K. L., & Fassina, N. E. (2007). Socialization tactics and newcomer adjustment: A meta-analytic review and test of a model. *Journal of Vocational Behavior, 70,* 413–446.

Sakuraya, A., Shimazu, A., Eguchi, H., Kamiyama, K., Hara, Y., Namba, K., & Kawakami, N. (2017). Job crafting, work engagement, and psychological distress among Japanese employees: A cross-sectional study. *BioPsychoSocial Medicine, 11.* https://doi.org/10.1186/s13030-017-0091-y

Sanchez, P., & McCauley, D. (2006). Measuring and managing engagement in a cross-cultural workforce: New insights for global companies. *Global Business and Organizational Excellence, 26,* 41–50.

Sarti, C. (2014). Job resources as antecedents of engagement at work: Evidence from a long-term care setting. *Human Resource Development, 25*(2), 213–237.

Schaufeli, W. B. (2014). What is engagement? In C. Truss, R. Delbridge, K. Alfes, A. Shantz, & E. Soane (Eds.), *Employee engagement in theory and practice* (pp.15–35). New York: Routledge.

Schaufeli, W. B. (2015). Engaging leadership in the job demands-resources model. *Career Development International, 20,* 446–463.

Schaufeli, W. B. (2018). Work engagement in Europe: Relations with national economy, governance, and culture. *Organizational Dynamics, 47,* 99–106.

Schaufeli, W. B., & Salanova, M. (2011). Work engagement: On how to better catch a slippery concept. *European Journal of Work and Organizational Psychology, 20,* 39–46.

Schaufeli, W. B., & Taris, T. W. (2013). A critical review of the job demands-resources model: Implications for improving work and health. In G. F. Bauer, & O. Hämmig (Eds.), *Bridging occupational, organizational, and public health: A transdisciplinary approach* (pp.43–68). New York: Springer.

Schaufeli, W. B., Bakker, A. B., & Salanova, M. (2006). The measurement of work engagement with a short questionnaire: A cross-national study. *Educational and Psychological Measurement, 66,* 701–716.

Schaufeli, W. B., Bakker, A. B., & Van Rhenen, W. (2009). How changes in job demands and resources predict burnout, work engagement, and sickness absenteeism. *Journal of Organizational Behavior, 30,* 893–917.

Schaufeli, W. B., Salanova, M., Gonzalez-Roma, V., & Bakker, A. B. (2002). The measurement of engagement and burnout: A two sample confirmatory factor analytic approach, *Journal of Happiness Studies, 3,* 71–92.

Schaufeli, W. B., Shimazu, A., Hakanen, J., Salanova, M., & De Witte, H. (2019). An ultra-short measure for work engagement: The UWES-3 validation across five countries. *European Journal of Psychological Assessment, 35*(4), 577–591.

Schlenker, B. R. (1997). Personal responsibility: Applications of the Triangle Model. In B. M. Staw, & L. L. Cummings (Eds.), *Research in organizational behavior* (Vol. 19, pp.241–301). Greenwich, CT: JAI Press.

Schlenker, B. R., Britt, T. W., Pennington, J., Murphy, R., & Doherty, K. (1994). The triangle model of responsibility. *Psychological Review, 101,* 632–652.

Schneider, B., & Reichers, A. E. (1983). On the etiology of climates. *Personnel Psychology, 36,* 19–39.

Schneider, B., Yost, A. B., Kropp, A., Kind, C., & Lam, H. (2018). Workforce engagement: What it is, what drives it, and why it matters for organizational performance. *Journal of Organizational Behavior, 39,* 462–480.

Schwartz, S. H., Cieciuch, J., Veccione, M., Davidov, E., Fischer, R., Beierlein, C., Ramos, A., Verkasolo, M., Lönnqvist, J., Demirutku, K., Dirilen-Gumus, O., & Konty, M. (2012). Refining the theory of basic individual values. *Journal of Personality and Social Psychology, 103,* 663–688.

Serrano, S. A., & Reichard, R. J. (2011). Leadership strategies for an engaged workforce. *Consulting Psychology, Journal: Practice and Research, 63,* 176–189.

Shantz, A., Alfes, K., & Latham, G. (2016). The buffering effect of perceived organizational support on the relationship between work engagement and behavioral outcomes. *Human Resource Management, 55,* 25–38.

Sheng, X., Wang, Y., Hong, W., Zhu, Z., & Zhang, X. (2019). The curvilinear relationship between daily time pressure and work engagement: The role of psychological capital and sleep. *International Journal of Stress Management, 26,* 25–35.

Shimazu, A., Miyanaka, D., & Schaufeli, W. B., (2010). Work engagement from a cultural perspective. In S. Albrecht (Ed.), *Handbook of employee engagement: Perspectives, issues, research and practice* (pp.364–372). Cheltenham, UK and Northampton, MA, USA: Edward Elgar Publishing.

Shuck, B., Adelson, J. L., & Reio, T. G., Jr. (2017). The employee engagement scale: Initial evidence for construct validity and implications for theory and practice. *Human Resource Management, 56,* 953–977.

Silliker, A. (2010). Engagement falling fast: Study. *Canadian HR Reporter, 23,* 1, 14.

Singh, B., Shaffer, M. A., & Selvarajan, T. T. (2017). Antecedents of organizational and community embeddedness: The roles of support, psychological safety, and need to belong. *Journal of Organizational Behavior, 39,* 339–354.

Sio, U. N., & Ormerod, T. C. (2009). Does incubation enhance problem solving? A meta-analytic review. *Psychological Bulletin, 135,* 94–120.

Smallwood, J. Davies, J. B., Heim, D., Finnigan, F., Sudberry, M., O'Connor, R., & Obonsawin, M. (2004). Subjective experience and the attentional lapse: Task engagement and disengagement during sustained attention. *Consciousness and Cognition, 13,* 657–690.

Soane, E., Truss, C., Alfes, K., Shantz, A., Rees, C., & Gatenby, M. (2012). Development and application of a new measure of employee engagement: The ISA Engagement Scale. *Human Resource Development International, 15,* 529–547.

Song, Z., Chon, K., Ding, G., & Gu, C. (2015). Impact of organizational socialization tactics on newcomer job satisfaction and engagement: Core self-evaluations as moderators. *International Journal of Hospitality Management, 46,* 180–189.

Sonnentag, S. (2003). Recovery, work engagement, and proactive behavior: A new look at the interface between nonwork and work. *Journal of Applied Psychology, 88,* 518–528.

Sonnentag, S. (2011). Research on work engagement is well and alive. *European Journal of Work and Organizational Psychology, 20,* 29–38.

Sonnentag, S., Mojza, E. J., Binnewies, C., & Scholl, A. (2008). Being engaged at work and detached at home: A week-level study on work engagement, psychological detachment, and affect. *Work & Stress, 22,* 257–276.

Stumpf, S. A., Tymon, W. G. Jr., & van Dam, N. H. M. (2013). Felt and behavioral engagement in workgroups of professionals. *Journal of Vocational Behavior, 83,* 255–264.

Takano, Y., & Osaka, E. (2018). Comparing Japan and the United States on individualism/collectivism: A follow-up review. *Asian Journal of Social Psychology, 21,* 301–316.

Takeuchi, R., Chen, G., & Lepak, D. P. (2009). Through the looking glass of a social system: Cross-level effects of high-performance work systems on employees' attitudes. *Personnel Psychology, 62,* 1–29.

Taras, V., Kirkman, B. L., & Steel, P. (2010). Examining the impact of *Culture's Consequences*: A three-decade, multilevel, meta-analytic review of Hofstede's cultural value dimensions. *Journal of Applied Psychology, 95,* 405–439.

ten Brummelhuis, L. L., & Bakker, A. B. (2012). Staying engaged during the week: The effect of off-job activities on next day work engagement. *Journal of Occupational Health Psychology, 17,* 445–455.

Tims, M., Bakker, A. B., & Derks, D. (2012). Development and validation of the job crafting scale. *Journal of Vocational Behavior, 80,* 173–186.

Tims, M., Bakker, A. B., & Xanthopoulou, D. (2011). Do transformational leaders enhance their followers' daily work engagement? *The Leadership Quarterly, 22,* 121–131.

Tims, M., Derks, D., & Bakker, A. B. (2016). Job crafting and its relationship with person-job fit and meaningfulness: A three-wave study. *Journal of Vocational Behavior, 92,* 44–53.

Tims, M., Bakker, A. B., Derks, D., & van Rhenen, W. (2013). Job crafting at the team and individual level: Implications for work engagement and performance. *Group & Organization Management, 38,* 427–454.

Torrente, P., Salanova, M., Llorens, S., & Schaufeli, W. B. (2012). Teams make it work: How team work engagement mediates between social resources and performance in teams. *Psicothema, 24,* 106–112.

Triandis, H. C. (1989). The self and social behavior in differing cultural contexts. *Psychological Review, 96,* 506–520.

Truss, C., Delbridge, R., Alfes, K., Shantz, A., & Soane, E. (2014). Introduction. In C. Truss, R. Delbridge, K. Alfes, A. Shantz, & E. Soane (Eds.), *Employee engagement in theory and practice* (pp.1–11). New York: Routledge.

Ünal, Z. M., & Turgut, T. (2015). The buzzword: Employee engagement. Does person-organization fit contribute to employee engagement? *Iranian Journal of Management Studies, 8,* 157–179.

van de Vijver, F., & Tanzer, N. K. (2004). Bias and equivalence in cross-cultural assessment: An overview. *European Review of Applied Psychology, 47*, 119–135.

Van den Broeck, A., Vansteenkiste, M., De Witte, H., Soenens, B., & Lens, W. (2010). Capturing autonomy, competence, and relatedness at work: Construction and initial validation of the Work-related Basic Need Satisfaction Scale. *Journal of Occupational and Organizational Psychology, 83*, 981–1002.

Van Maanen, J. (1975). Police socialization: A longitudinal examination of job attitudes in an urban police department. *Administrative Science Quarterly, 20*, 207–228.

Van Veldhoven, M., Van de Broeck, A., Daniels, K., Bakker, A. B., Tavares, S. M., & Ogbonnaya, C. (2020). Challenging the universality of job resources: Why, when, and for whom are they beneficial? *Applied Psychology: An International Review, 69*, 5–29.

Varela, O. E., Sagado, E. I., & Lasio, M. V. (2010). The meaning of job performance in collectivistic and high-power distance cultures. *Cross-cultural Management: An International Journal, 17*, 407–426.

Viljevac, A., Cooper-Thomas, H. D., & Saks, A. M. (2012). An investigation into the validity of two measures of work engagement. *The International Journal of Human Resource Management, 23*, 3692–3709.

Vinarski-Peretz, H., & Carmeli, A. (2011). Linking care felt to engagement in innovative behaviors in the workplace: The mediating role of psychological conditions. *Psychology of Aesthetics, Creativity, and the Arts, 5*, 43–53.

Vogel, R. M., Rodell, J. B., & Sabey, T. B. (2020). Meaningfulness misfit: Consequences of daily meaningful work needs-supplies incongruence for daily engagement. *Journal of Applied Psychology, 105*, 760–770.

Vroom, V. H., & Deci, E. L. (1971). The stability of post-decision dissonance: A follow-up study of the job attitudes of business school graduates. *Organizational Behavior and Human Performance, 6*, 36–49.

Walters, K. N., & Diab, D. L. (2016). Humble leadership: Implications for psychological safety and follower engagement. *Journal of Leadership Studies, 10*, 7–18.

Walumbwa, F. O., & Schaubroeck, J. (2009). Leader personality traits and employee voice behavior: Mediating roles of ethical leadership and work group psychological safety. *Journal of Applied Psychology, 94*, 1275–1286.

Wang, D., Hom, P. W., & Allen, D. G. (2017). Coping with newcomer "hangover": How socialization tactics affect declining job satisfaction during early employement. *Journal of Vocational Behavior, 100*, 196–210.

Wang, L., Law, K. S., Zhang, M. J., Li, Y. N., & Liang, Y. (2019). It's mine! Psychological ownership of one's job explains positive and negative workplace outcomes of job engagement. *Journal of Applied Psychology, 104*, 229–246.

Wang, Z., Chen, L., Duan, Y., & Du, J. (2018). Supervisory mentoring and newcomers' work engagement: The mediating role of basic psychological need satisfaction. *Social Behavior and Personality, 46*, 1745–1760.

Warr, P. (2007). *Work, happiness, and unhappiness.* New York: Lawrence Erlbaum Associates.

Warren, S. (2010). What's wrong with being positive? In P. A. Linley, S. Harrington, & N. Garcia (Eds.), *Oxford handbook of positive psychology and work* (pp.313–322). New York: Oxford University Press.

Wefald, A. J., Mills, M. J., Smith, M. R., & Downey, R. G. (2012). A comparison of three engagement measures: Examining their factorial and criterion-related validity. *Applied Psychology: Health and Well-Being, 4,* 67–90.

Wegner, D. M., & Bargh, J. A. (1998). Control and automaticity in everyday life. In D. Gilbert, S. T. Fiske, & G. Lindzey (Eds.), *Handbook of social psychology* (4th ed., pp.446–496). New York: McGraw Hill.

Weziak-Bialowolska, D., Bialowolski, P., Leon, C., Koosed, T., & McNeely, E. (2020). Psychological climate for caring and work outcomes: A virtuous cycle. *International Journal of Environmental Research and Public Health, 17*(7035). doi:10.3390/ijerph17197035

Whitten, D. L. (2016). Mentoring and work engagement for female accounting faculty members in higher education. *Mentoring & Tutoring: Partnerships in Learning, 24,* 365–382.

Wilson, T. D. (2002). *Strangers to ourselves: Discovering the adaptive unconscious.* London: The Belknap Press.

Winkelman, P., & Berridge, K. (2004). Unconscious emotion. *Current Directions in Psychological Science, 13,* 120–123.

Wollard, K. K., & Shuck, B. (2011). Antecedents to employee engagement: A structured review of the literature. *Advances in Developing Human Resources, 13,* 429–446.

Wood, J., Oh, J., Park, J., & Kim, W. (2020). The relationship between work engagement and work-life balance in organizations: A review of the empirical research. *Human Resource Development Review, 19,* 240–262.

Wrzesniewski, A., & Dutton, J. E. (2001). Crafting a job: Revisioning employees as active crafters of their work. *Academy of Management Review, 26,* 179–201.

Wrzesniewski, A., Dutton, J. E., & Debebe, G. (2003). Interpersonal sensemaking and the meaning of work. In R. Kramer, & B. Staw (Eds.), *Research in organizational behavior* (Vol. 25, pp.93–135). Greenwich, CT: JAI Press.

Xanthopoulou, D., Bakker, A. B., Demerouti, E., & Schaufeli, W. B. (2007). The role of personal resources in the job demands-resources model. *International Journal of Stress Management, 14,* 121–141.

Xanthopoulou, D., Bakker, A. B., Demerouti, E., & Schaufeli, W. B. (2009a). Reciprocal relationships between job resources, personal resources, and work engagement. *Journal of Vocational Behavior, 74,* 235–244.

Xanthopoulou, D., Bakker, A. B., Demerouti, E., & Schaufeli, W. B. (2009b). Work engagement and financial returns: A diary study on the role of job and personal resources. *Journal of Occupational and Organizational Psychology, 82,* 183–200.

Xu, J., Liu, Y., & Chung, B. (2017). Leader psychological capital and employee work engagement: The roles of employee psychological capital and team collectivism. *Leadership & Organization Development Journal, 38,* 969–985.

Yalabik, Z. Y., Poaitoon, P., Chowe, J. A., & Rayton, B. A. (2013). Work engagement as a mediator between employee attitudes and outcomes. *The International Journal of Human Resource Management, 24,* 2799–2823.

Yang, K. (2006). Indigenous personality research: The Chinese case. In U. Kim, K. Yang, & K. Hwang (Eds.), *Indigenous and cultural psychology: Understanding people in context* (pp.285–314). New York: Springer.

Yoerger, M., Crowe, J., & Allen, J. A. (2015). Participate or else!: The effect of participation in decision making in meetings on employee engagement. *Consulting Psychology Journal: Practice and Research, 67,* 65–80.

Young, H. R., Glerum, D. R., Wang, W., & Joseph, D. L. (2018). Who are the most engaged at work? A meta-analysis of personality and employee engagement. *Journal of Organizational Behavior, 39,* 1330–1346.

Zhong, L., Wayne, S. J., & Liden, R. C. (2016). Job engagement, perceived organizational support, high-performance human resource practices, and cultural value orientations: A cross-level investigation. *Journal of Organizational Behavior, 37,* 823–844.

Zinger, D. (2010). Avoiding employee engagement pitfalls. *Canadian HR Reporter, 23,* 20, 24.

Index

Titles in the Elgar Advanced Introductions series include:

International Political Economy
Benjamin J. Cohen

The Austrian School of Economics
Randall G. Holcombe

Cultural Economics
Ruth Towse

Law and Development
Michael J. Trebilcock and Mariana Mota Prado

International Humanitarian Law
Robert Kolb

International Trade Law
Michael J. Trebilcock

Post Keynesian Economics
J.E. King

International Intellectual Property
Susy Frankel and Daniel J. Gervais

Public Management and Administration
Christopher Pollitt

Organised Crime
Leslie Holmes

Nationalism
Liah Greenfeld

Social Policy
Daniel Béland and Rianne Mahon

Globalisation
Jonathan Michie

Entrepreneurial Finance
Hans Landström

International Conflict and Security Law
Nigel D. White

Comparative Constitutional Law
Mark Tushnet

International Human Rights Law
Dinah L. Shelton

Entrepreneurship
Robert D. Hisrich

International Tax Law
Reuven S. Avi-Yonah

Public Policy
B. Guy Peters

The Law of International Organizations
Jan Klabbers

International Environmental Law
Ellen Hey

International Sales Law
Clayton P. Gillette

Corporate Venturing
Robert D. Hisrich

Public Choice
Randall G. Holcombe

Private Law
Jan M. Smits

Consumer Behavior Analysis
Gordon Foxall

Behavioral Economics
John F. Tomer

American Foreign Policy
Loch K. Johnson

Water Politics
Ken Conca

Business Ethics
John Hooker

Employee Engagement
Alan M. Saks and Jamie A. Gruman